T0205562

Leveraging Emotional and Artificial Intelligence for Organisational Performance

Catherine Prentice

Leveraging Emotional and Artificial Intelligence for Organisational Performance

 Springer

Catherine Prentice
University of Southern Queensland
Springfield Central, QLD, Australia

ISBN 978-981-99-1867-6   ISBN 978-981-99-1865-2 (eBook)
https://doi.org/10.1007/978-981-99-1865-2

This Springer imprint is published by the registered company Springer Nature Singapore Pte Ltd.
The registered company address is: 152 Beach Road, #21-01/04 Gateway East, Singapore 189721,
Singapore

Contents

Chapter 1
Introduction to Artificial and Emotional Intelligences

The development of full artificial intelligence could spell the end of the human race....It would take off on its own, and re-design itself at an ever-increasing rate. Humans, who are limited by slow biological evolution, couldn't compete, and would be superseded. Stephen Hawking, BBC.
As more and more artificial intelligence is entering into the world, more and more emotional intelligence must enter into leadership. Amit Ray, Author of Compassionate Artificial Intelligence.

1.1 The Rise of Emotional and Artificial Intelligences

Since the concept of human intelligence was induced nearly two centuries ago as cognitive abilities to learn, understand and apply and reason, intelligence has been viewed as a key factor of humanised evolutions manifested in micro, meso and macro levels. Not until 1990s, had cognitive or intellectual intelligence in the intelligence domain been a sole prominent determinant of individual performance and success and an important factor of organisational performance. Daniel Goleman's books on *Emotional Intelligence* in mid 1990s popularised a different domain of human intelligence—emotional intelligence. This intelligence is claimed to trump traditional intelligence in predicting individual or group performance and success at both personal and work domains. Last three decades, emotional intelligence (hereafter interchangeable with EI for rhetorical purpose) has been overwhelmingly discussed, compared, and debated in the business and academic arenas. While EI as a human intelligence is holding its foot in the wide communities, artificial intelligence (hereafter interchangeable with AI) as a machine intelligence has been permeating in personal lives, the business world and academic literature.

© The Author(s), under exclusive license to Springer Nature Singapore Pte Ltd. 2023
C. Prentice, *Leveraging Emotional and Artificial Intelligence for Organisational Performance*, https://doi.org/10.1007/978-981-99-1865-2_1

1.2   What is Emotional Intelligence

Emotional intelligence (EI) is defined as the ability to perceive, respond, and manipulate emotional information without necessarily understanding it and the ability to understand and manage emotions without necessarily perceiving or experiencing them (Mayer et al., 1997). EI consists of four hierarchies of emotional abilities: emotional perception, emotional assimilation, and emotional understanding and management (see Mayer et al., 1997). At the bottom of the hierarchy is emotional perception, indicating the ability to identify, express, and discriminate emotions accurately. Emotional assimilation represents emotion-prioritised thinking by directing attention to important information. Emotional understanding refers to the ability to label and recognise the emotions within words. On the top of the hierarchy is emotion management, broadly including the ability to monitor and manage emotions of oneself and others (Mayer et al., 2001).

1.3   The Power of Emotional Intelligence

EI was introduced into the literature as a valid predictor of individual wellbeing, performance, and success that cannot be accounted for by traditional cognitive intelligence (Austin et al., 2005; Poon, 2004; Schutte et al., 2001, 2007). In general, people with a high level of emotional intelligence build stronger personal relationships (e.g., Schutte et al., 2001), enjoy better health than those with a low level of emotional intelligence (e.g., Austin et al., 2005; Schutte et al., 2007), perform better, experience more career success, and lead more effectively (e.g., George, 2000; Gupta & Bajaj, 2017; Prentice & King, 2011). Emotional intelligence can affect a wide variety of job attitudes and behaviours including employee satisfaction and loyalty. Emotionally intelligence employees are better suited to the occupational environment (Goleman, 1998; Nikolaou & Tsaousis, 2002; Rozell et al., 2004), and more likely to succeed in coping with environmental demands and pressures, thus managing stressful work conditions (Bar-On, 1997; Shi et al., 2015), which lead to satisfaction and retention (e.g., Brown & Yoshioka, 2003; D'Amato & Herzfeldt, 2008; Saari & Judge, 2004). The efficiency of emotional intelligence in predicting job behaviours depends on the job types and the nature of the business.

Emotional intelligence is extensively discussed as a valid predictor of job performance (Carmeli & Josman, 2006; Cote & Miners, 2006), and particularly important for jobs that require social skills and interpersonal interactions, such as the frontline positions that involve interactions between service employees and customers (Ashkanasy & Daus, 2005; Caruso et al., 2002; Darvishmotevali et al., 2018). Employees with a high level of EI are better at dealing with the service encounter with customers and achieve better service performance.

1.4 What is Artificial Intelligence

Artificial intelligence (AI) refers to machine intelligence comprising of autonomy, the ability to learn and react, the ability to cooperate and interact with humans, embodied within humanoid or non-humanoid robots that can be programmed to think and act like a human (Rijsdijk et al., 2007; Russell et al., 2015). AI is enabled through, inter alia, machine learning, deep learning, and natural language processing (NLP). Huang and Rust (2018, 2021) classified AI as mechanical, thinking and feeling AI. Mechanical AI has been designed to undertake automated repetitive and routine tasks, which requires standardisation and consistency, such as packaging, self-service robots (van Doorn et al., 2017). Thinking AI through machine and deep learning was designed for the production and processing of information for users, through the recognition of patterns and themes (e.g., text mining, and facial recognition) for decision making. Examples include Netflix movie recommendations, Amazon cross-selling recommendations (Chung et al., 2016; Huang & Rust, 2018). Feeling AI was designed to analyse human feelings through NLP, text-to-speech technology, and recurrent neural networks (RNN). This type of AI is embedded in chatbots mimicking human speech and service robots sensing affective signals (McDuff & Czerwinski, 2018).

1.5 The Power of Artificial Intelligence

Whilst EI has been regarded as a panacea for every human problem since the onset of its induction, AI is portrayed as superpower possessed by a machine in this century. AI-powered applications such as robotics and automation can assist, facilitate and supersede humans in multiple ways as AI experts or other renown scientists have claimed. AI and its powered tools or applications can exert impact on micro, meso and macro levels, and are widely used in individual and organisational domains to facilitate personal life and business operations (e.g., Prentice et al., 2020a, 2020b; Prentice & Nguyen, 2020). In the business domain, AI not only improves operational efficiency by automating mundane tasks but also enhances customer experience (Bolton et al., 2018). For instance, large hotels rely on sophisticated computer programs that use AI to scan historical data and track patterns, resetting overbooking levels every 15 min, based on their goal reservation systems (Ma et al., 2018). Hilton Hotels & Resorts have adopted Connie as their first AI robot to provide information to tourists and improve interactions with customers. Restaurant managers use robotic servers and AI to assist self-service ordering. Chatbots and messaging allow service organisations to improve service quality in both functional and technical processes (Chung et al., 2020; Ivanov & Webster, 2017; Larivière et al., 2017).

Nonetheless, these functions and the rapid increase of AI applications in recent years sparked growing concern of replacement of human jobs. Does or can AI replace humans and take over their jobs? The following section presents estimates and predictions from experts and research institutions in chronological order.

1.6   AI Replacing Human Jobs

A McKinsey Global Institute study of eight hundred occupations in nearly fifty countries showed that more than 800 million jobs, or 20 percent of the global workforce, could be lost to robotics by the year 2030. Using the Gaussian process classifier, Frey and Osborne (2013) estimated that nearly half of all U.S. jobs are likely to be automated in the coming decades. Golonka et al. (2014) predicted that 54% of European occupations could be computerised by rapid automation. Smith and Anderson (2014) surveyed 1900 experts and stated that by 2025, a significant number of both blue and white-collar employees would be at risk of displacement by AI. Chui et al. (2015) pointed out that AI and robotics could directly displace 45% of work activities previously performed by employees. Acemoglu and Restrepo (2017) documented that an extra industrial robot per 1000 U.S. workers could reduce the employment-to-population ratio by 0.18–0.34 percentage points.

Lee (2017) applied the Frey-Osborne estimates to Asian countries and found that about one-quarter of Singaporean employment is at high risk of computerisation. Bughin et al. (2017) from Oxford University predicted that 47% of jobs could be automated by 2033. Reports from Pew Research Internet (Smith & Anderson, 2014) show that about 72 percent Americans express concern about replacement of human jobs by AI, only 33 percent are enthusiastic about capabilities of AI. The Bureau of Labour Statistics (BLS) estimates that eighty thousand fast-food jobs will disappear by 2024. A growing number of retail stores like Walmart, CVS, and McDonald's provide automated self-checkout options, likely resulting in a loss of 7.5 million retail jobs. He and Guo (2018) gauged that about 50% of financial services and insurance jobs that are related to collecting and processing data are very likely to be replaced by AI. Indeed, the pervasive use of AI has a significant influence on employee performance, job satisfaction and turnover intention (Prentice et al., 2020a). Research shows that employees who are aware of the power of AI tend to leave their jobs as they fear their jobs being replaced (Li et al., 2019).

1.7   Humans Assisting AI

Despite those predictions on AI's superseding power, in practice, researchers (Wirtz et al., 2018) assert that AI and its powered tools only replace low-level jobs and affect a limited number of employee cohorts. McKendrick (2018) indicates that AI can only replace certain tasks, not jobs. This claim concurs with that in Wirtz et al. (2018) stating only low skill and low wage jobs are likely to be automated and replaced by robots in the service industry. Other studies (Morikawa et al., 2017; Smith et al.,

2017) shows that AI and robots generally play a dominant role in low-level mundane jobs, and a very minor role in human-intensive services such as occupation-specific skills acquired by attending professional schools or holding occupational licenses (Smith et al., 2017). Jobs requiring human interactions, performing creative and emotional tasks (e.g., frontline service employees) are less likely to be replaced by AI and automation.

In reality, AI and their functions are created by humans and require human interventions and management. In most cases, AI is developed to assist human employees and facilitate their job tasks. For instance, AI-powered digital assistants need to be trained to interact with humans. Microsoft's Cortana entails extensive training and a team of experts such as poets, novelists, and playwrights to develop the right personality and skills for the bot to be able to perform the intended tasks. Similarly, Apple's Siri and Amazon's Alexa are trained by humans to behave like a human assistant. Machine-learning must be trained or supervised to analyse data and perform the work such as handling idiomatic expressions, detecting disease through medical apps, and supporting financial decision making through various recommending engines. Human experts are required to explain the results generated from AI for implementation, for instance, a law enforcer to sentence, a medical practitioner to recommend treatments, an insurer to understand the cause of the accidents.

1.8 AI Assisting Humans

Humans create AI and constantly develop extended applications and functions, which are predetermined to assist humans and facilitate task efficiency. Some researchers (e.g., Agrawal et al., 2017; Davenport & Ronanki, 2018; Ivanov, 2019; Ili & Lichtenthaler, 2017) contend that AI, instead of taking jobs, helps improve the human experience and even create new jobs. AI and robots are proved to boost employment with both low and high-skilled jobs. The European Union's new General Data Protection Regulation (GDPR) may have to create thousands of new jobs to administer the GDPR requirements as a result of implementing AI.

AI can enhance humans' analytic and decision-making abilities by providing the right information at the right time, and heighten creativity (Autodesk's Dreamcatcher). For instance, AI can be used to help designers perform the myriad calculations needed to ensure that each proposed design meets the specified criteria and identify the most appropriate designs for various users. Organizations could leverage AI and robotics to grow their businesses.

Firms, MiltonCAT, for example, have used AI to assist their human employees delegating work on demand, decreasing non-value-added travel, and focusing on value-added tasks (Lussault, 2020). Warehouses, distribution centres and manufacturing organizations extensively use AI and automation to support human workers to accomplish tasks. The industrial self-driving vehicles help thousands of organizations streamline mundane, repetitive and often dirty and dangerous tasks. AI-powered orchestration engines deliver unparalleled abilities to collect and uncover insights based on robot-specific data. This information can be used to fuel improvements, enhance real-world performance and even adapt future designs.

1.9 Emotional Intelligence, or Artificial Intelligence

Who is the winner, human or machine? Which is more powerful, human intelligence or machine intelligence? Whilst Stephen Hawking, Elon Musk or the kind claim how AI may supersede humans, humanistic protagonists have scientific faith in humans and the power of human intelligence. A plethora of books, academic and non-academic articles have explained, conceptualised, compared, argued and investigated EI and AI respectively. This book takes an objective approach to integrating human (EI) and machine (AI) intelligence and discuss how they function independently and collaboratively.

1.10 The Stance and Structure of This Book

As EI and AI have been cited to have broad effects on individuals, businesses and beyond, this book is focused on the organisational context, specifically how they affect employees and customers from a business perspective. In particular, the book takes a fresh stance and views EI and AI as services that are provided by service employees and machines as organisational offerings to customers. This stance is consistent with the conceptualisation of a service. Service is defined as a deed, process or performance that is exchanged for commercial value (Wirtz et al., 2018). This stance holds that intelligences in businesses must turn into organisational assets to manifest their values. In this service dominant logic era, compared to tangible products, service plays a key role in organisational performance and customer relationship with the organisation. Intelligence exhibited either by human or machine is not a tangible product, but can be utilised as a service to assist employees in performing tasks and delivering services as well as facilitating business transaction and customer experience. Hence, this book is structured as follows.

Chapters 2 and 3 demystify emotional and artificial intelligence, from different perspectives, including conceptualisations, the history and evolution of the concepts, how they function and where they can apply to. These discussions help readers understand what exactly these two intelligences are.

Chapters 4 and 5 analyse how emotional intelligence is related to employees and customers respectively with a focus on service organisations. Chapters 6, 7 and 8 are dedicated to anatomising AI and how it is operationalised as a service to influence employees and customers. Specifically, viewing AI as a service, Chap. 6 examines the impact of AI service quality and how it is related to employee service quality. Chapter 7 analyses the influence of AI service quality on customers. Based on the

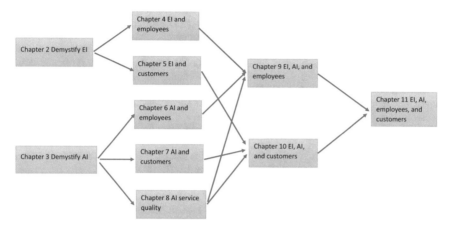

Fig. 1.1 The structure, connections and foci of the remaining chapters

discussion in Chaps. 6 and 7, Chap. 8 is extended to develop a scale to measure such AI service, named AI service quality.

The last three chapters of this book integrate EI and AI to analyse their respective impacts on employees and customers. Chapter 9 proposes EI as a moderator of AI, whereas Chap. 10 proposes AI as a moderator of EI. Chapter 11 employs service profit chain to integrate EI and AI in the chain relationship to understand their effects on both employees and customers. This chapter broadly covers the service industry with a focus on tourism and hospitality sector. The discussion on the impact of EI and AI is complemented with empirical studies conducted in tourism or hospitality context to address their effects in these sectors. The structure, connections and foci of these chapters are shown in Fig. 1.1.

References

Acemoglu, D., & Restrepo, P. (2017). Secular stagnation? The effect of aging on economic growth in the age of automation. *American Economic Review, 107*(5), 174–179.

Agrawal, A., Gans, J., & Goldfarb, A. (2017). What to expect from artificial intelligence. *MITSLoan Management Review.*

Ashkanasy, N. M., & Daus, C. S. (2005). Rumors of the death of emotional intelligence in organizational behavior are vastly exaggerated. *Journal of Organizational Behavior, 26*(4), 441–452.

Austin, E. J., Saklofske, D. H., & Egan, V. (2005). Personality, well-being and health correlates of trait emotional intelligence. *Personality and Individual Differences, 38*(3), 547–558.

Bar-On, R. (1997). *BarOn emotional quotient inventory* (Vol. 40). Multi-health systems.

Bolton, R. N., McColl-Kennedy, J. R., Cheung, L., Gallan, A., Orsingher, C., Witell, L., & Zaki, M. (2018). Customer experience challenges: Bringing together digital, physical and social realms. *Journal of Service Management, 29*(5), 776–808.

Brown, W. A., & Yoshioka, C. F. (2003). Mission attachment and satisfaction as factors in employee retention. *Nonprofit Management and Leadership, 14*(1), 5–18.

Bughin, J., Hazan, E., Ramaswamy, S., Chui, M., Allas, T., Dahlstrom, P., . Henke, N., & Trench, M. (2017). *Artificial intelligence: The next digital frontier?*

Carmeli, A., & Josman, Z. E. (2006). The relationship among emotional intelligence, task performance, and organizational citizenship behaviors. *Human Performance, 19*(4), 403–419.

Caruso, D. R., Mayer, J. D., & Salovey, P. (2002). Relation of an ability measure of emotional intelligence to personality. *Journal of Personality Assessment, 79*(2), 306–320.

Chui, M., Manyika, J., & Miremadi, M. (2015). Four fundamentals of workplace automation. *McKinsey Quarterly, 29*(3), 1–9.

Chung, J., Ahn, S., & Bengio, Y. (2016). *Hierarchical multiscale recurrent neural networks.* arXiv preprint arXiv:1609.01704.

Chung, M., Ko, E., Joung, H., & Kim, S. J. (2020). Chatbot e-service and customer satisfaction regarding luxury brands. *Journal of Business Research, 117*, 587–595.

Côté, S., & Miners, C. T. (2006). Emotional intelligence, cognitive intelligence, and job performance. *Administrative Science Quarterly, 51*(1), 1–28.

D'Amato, A., & Herzfeldt, R. (2008). Learning orientation, organizational commitment and talent retention across generations: A study of European managers. *Journal of Managerial Psychology, 23*(8), 929–953.

Darvishmotevali, M., Altinay, L., & De Vita, G. (2018). Emotional intelligence and creative performance: Looking through the lens of environmental uncertainty and cultural intelligence. *International Journal of Hospitality Management, 73*, 44–54.

Davenport, T. H., & Ronanki, R. (2018). Artificial intelligence for the real world. *Harvard Business Review, 96*(1), 108–116.

Frey, C. B., & Osborne, M. (2013). *The future of employment.*

George, J. M. (2000). Emotions and leadership: The role of emotional intelligence. *Human Relations, 53*(8), 1027–1055.

Goleman, D. (1998). *Working with emotional intelligence.* Bantam Books.

Golonka, E. M., Bowles, A. R., Frank, V. M., Richardson, D. L., & Freynik, S. (2014). Technologies for foreign language learning: A review of technology types and their effectiveness. *Computer Assisted Language Learning, 27*(1), 70–105.

Gupta, M., & Bajaj, B. K. (2017). Development of fermented oat flour beverage as a potential probiotic vehicle. *Food Bioscience, 20*, 104–109.

He, D., & Guo, M. (2018). *The impact of artificial intelligence on financial job market.* https://www.bcg.com/en-cn/the-impact-of-artificial-intelligence-ai-on-the-financial-job-market

Huang, M. H., & Rust, R. T. (2018). Artificial intelligence in service. *Journal of Service Research, 21*(2), 155–172.

Huang, M. H., & Rust, R. T. (2021). A strategic framework for artificial intelligence in marketing. *Journal of the Academy of Marketing Science, 49*, 30–50.

Ili, S., & Lichtenthaler, U. (2017). Das Ende des traditionellen Bankwesens? Hoffentlich!. *Innovationen und Innovationsmanagement in der Finanzbranche*, 21–36.

Ivanov, S. H., & Webster, C. (2017, October). Designing robot-friendly hospitality facilities. In *Proceedings of the scientific conference "Tourism. Innovations. Strategies* (pp. 13–14).

Ivanov, S. (2019). Ultimate transformation: How will automation technologies disrupt the travel, tourism and hospitality industries? *Zeitschrift Für Tourismuswissenschaft, 11*(1), 25–43.

Larivière, B., Bowen, D., Andreassen, T. W., Kunz, W., Sirianni, N. J., Voss, C., Wünderlich, N.V., & De Keyser A. (2017). "Service encounter 2.0": An investigation into the roles of technology, employees and customers. *Journal of Business Research, 79*, 238–246.

Lee, K. F. (2017). *Automation, computerisation and future employment in Singapore.* SSRN.

Li, J. J., Bonn, M. A., & Ye, B. H. (2019). Hotel employee's artificial intelligence and robotics awareness and its impact on turnover intention: The moderating roles of perceived organizational support and competitive psychological climate. *Tourism Management, 73*, 172–181.

Lussault, D. (2020). Why AI is the key to better robots and happier workers. *Robotics Business Review.* https://www.roboticsbusinessreview.com/opinion/why-ai-is-the-key-to-better-robots-and-happier-workers/

Ma, X., Wang, Y., Houle, M. E., Zhou, S., Erfani, S., Xia, S., Wijewickrema, S., & Bailey, J. (2018, July). Dimensionality-driven learning with noisy labels. In *International Conference on Machine Learning* (pp. 3355–3364). PMLR.

MacKendrick, N. (2018). *Better safe than sorry: How consumers navigate exposure to everyday toxics.* University of California Press.

Mayer, J. D., Caruso, D. R., & Salovey, P. (1997). *Emotional intelligence meets.*

Mayer, J. D., Salovey, P., Caruso, D. R., & Sitarenios, G. (2001). *Emotional intelligence as a standard intelligence.*

McDuff, D., & Czerwinski, M. (2018). Designing emotionally sentient agents. *Communications of the ACM, 61*(12), 74–83.

Morikawa, Y., Heallen, T., Leach, J., Xiao, Y., & Martin, J. F. (2017). Dystrophin–glycoprotein complex sequesters Yap to inhibit cardiomyocyte proliferation. *Nature, 547*(7662), 227–231.

Nikolaou, I., & Tsaousis, I. (2002). Emotional intelligence in the workplace: Exploring its effects on occupational stress and organizational commitment. *The International Journal of Organizational Analysis, 10*(4), 327–342.

Poon, J. M. (2004). Effects of performance appraisal politics on job satisfaction and turnover intention. *Personnel Review, 33*(3), 322–334.

Prentice, C., Dominique Lopes, S., & Wang, X. (2020a). Emotional intelligence or artificial intelligence–an employee perspective. *Journal of Hospitality Marketing & Management, 29*(4), 377–403.

Prentice, C., Dominique Lopes, S., & Wang, X. (2020b). The impact of artificial intelligence and employee service quality on customer satisfaction and loyalty. *Journal of Hospitality Marketing & Management, 29*(7), 739–756.

Prentice, C., & King, B. (2011). The influence of emotional intelligence on the service performance of casino frontline employees. *Tourism and Hospitality Research, 11*(1), 49–66.

Prentice, C., & Nguyen, M. (2020). Engaging and retaining customers with AI and employee service. *Journal of Retailing and Consumer Services, 56*, 102186.

Rijsdijk, S. A., Hultink, E. J., & Diamantopoulos, A. (2007). Product intelligence: Its conceptualization, measurement and impact on consumer satisfaction. *Journal of the Academy of Marketing Science, 35*, 340–356.

Rozell, E. J., Pettijohn, C. E., & Parker, R. S. (2004). Customer-oriented selling: Exploring the roles of emotional intelligence and organizational commitment. *Psychology & Marketing, 21*(6), 405–424.

Russell, S., Dewey, D., & Tegmark, M. (2015). Research priorities for robust and beneficial artificial intelligence. *Ai Magazine, 36*(4), 105–114.

Saari, L. M., & Judge, T. A. (2004). Employee attitudes and job satisfaction. *Human Resource Management: Published in Cooperation with the School of Business Administration, the University of Michigan and in Alliance with the Society of Human Resources Management, 43*(4), 395–407.

Schutte, N. S., Malouff, J. M., Bobik, C., Coston, T. D., Greeson, C., Jedlicka, C., Rhodes, E., & Wendorf, G. (2001). Emotional intelligence and interpersonal relations. *The Journal of social psychology, 141*(4), 523–536.

Schutte, N. S., Malouff, J. M., Thorsteinsson, E. B., Bhullar, N., & Rooke, S. E. (2007). A meta-analytic investigation of the relationship between emotional intelligence and health. *Personality and Individual Differences, 42*(6), 921–933.

Shi, X., Chen, Z., Wang, H., Yeung, D. Y., Wong, W. K., & Woo, W. C. (2015). Convolutional LSTM network: A machine learning approach for precipitation nowcasting. *Advances in neural information processing systems, 28*.

Smith, A., & Anderson, J. (2014). *AI, robotics, and the future of jobs.*

Smith, J., Anderson, S., & Fox, G. (2017). A quality system's impact on the service experience. *International Journal of Operations & Production Management, 37*(12), 1817–1839.

Van Doorn, J., Mende, M., Noble, S. M., Hulland, J., Ostrom, A. L., Grewal, D., & Petersen, J. A. (2017). Domo arigato Mr. Roboto: Emergence of automated social presence in organizational frontlines and customers' service experiences. *Journal of service research, 20*(1), 43–58.
Wirtz, J., Patterson, P. G., Kunz, W. H., Gruber, T., Lu, V. N., Paluch, S., & Martins, A. (2018). Brave new world: Service robots in the frontline. *Journal of Service Management, 29*(5), 907–931.

Chapter 2
Demystify Emotional Intelligence

Abstract Emotional intelligence (EI) has been extensively discussed in academic and non-academic communities over last three decades. The term first appeared in a German publication in 1966 (Leuner, in Praxis Der Kinderpsychologie Und Kinderpsychiatrie 15:193–203, 1966). The author discusses women who reject their social roles as having low "emotional intelligence" due to being separated at an early age from their mother but can be treated by Lysergic Acid Diethylamide (LSD). In 1983, Payne's doctoral dissertation indicates that EI can be fostered in schools by liberating emotional experience through therapy. Not until 1990s was EI brought into the mainstream psychology (Mayer et al, in J Pers Assess 54, 1990; Salovey and Mayer, in Imag Cogn Pers 9:185–211, 1990) and the academic literature. Nevertheless, Daniel Goleman was credited to popularise EI in mid 1990s. Mayer and Salovey (Emotional development and EI: educational implications. Basic Books, pp 3–34, 1997) presented a conceptual framework of emotional abilities that constitute emotional intelligence. Compared to traditional intelligence that often provides an answer to a well-defined problem in the academic world, EI is claimed and proved to predict individual wellbeing, relationships, performance, and success on both personal and professional domains that cannot be accounted for by traditional cognitive intelligence (Austin et al, in Pers Individ Differ 38:547–558, 2005; Schutte et al, in Pers Individ Diff 42:921–933, 2007). To some extent, EI has been popularised and promoted as a panacea for personal and work-related problems. This popularity leads to a variety of definitions and conceptualisations of EI, and excessive applications of these emotional abilities. This chapter discusses what exactly EI is, and how it can be applied, and in what context it functions the best.

2.1 What is Emotional Intelligence

EI has been defined and conceptualised vastly different in the academic literature and consultancy websites. The different conceptualisations for the same construct inevitably create confusion. A review of the literature shows that four EI models have generated most interests in terms of research and application and are broadly cited in various contexts. They are either classified as a state of cognitive intelligence or a trait, labelled as the ability model, mixed model, or trait EI.

Mayer and Salovey are the lead protagonists of the ability model subsuming EI in the intelligence domain and emphasising the cognitive components of emotional intelligence (Salovey & Mayer, 1990). Bar-on and Goleman extended the intelligence framework into embracing motivation, non-ability dispositions and traits, and global personal and social functioning, and blend cognitive abilities and personality traits to conceptualise and apply EI (Bar-On, 1997; Bar-On et al., 2006; Goleman, 1996, 2001). This mixed model, although overwhelmingly criticised in the academic community, is ironically popular and has been extensively used or applied in the academic literature and business contexts. Taking a conservative stance, a few English scholars led by Furnham offered two novel concepts of trait EI and ability EI to mitigate the debates on ability or trait-based models (Furnham & Petrides, 2003; Petrides & Furnhma, 2003; Petrides et al., 2007). In view of the key characteristics of each model, this book labels the ability model as the Orthodoxic EI, the mixed model as the Fancy EI, the conservative approach as Operational EI.

2.2   The Orthodox EI

EI, by its very name, should be categorised as a cognitive intelligence. This intelligence domain can be traced in social intelligence framework proposed by Thorndike and Gardener. About a century ago, Thorndike (1920) suggested that intelligence could be organised under three broad dimensions: mechanical, abstract, and social. Mechanical intelligence reflects a person's ability to manage things and mechanisms; abstract intelligence is an ability to manage and understand ideas and symbols; and social intelligence refers to "the ability to understand and manage men and women, boys and girls—to act wisely in human relations" (p. 228) (cf. Newsome et al., 2000). The last categorisation proposed by Thorndike is similar to the concept of emotional intelligence.

Gardner (1993) proposed a theory of multiple intelligences including linguistic, logical/mathematical, spatial, bodily-kinesthetic, musical, interpersonal, intrapersonal, and naturalist, intelligences. Social intelligence as a separate domain describes interpersonal and intrapersonal intelligences. Intrapersonal intelligence relates to one's ability to deal with oneself and to "symbolize complex and highly differentiated sets of feelings" (p. 239) within the self. Interpersonal intelligence relates to one's ability to deal with others and to "notice and make distinctions among other individuals and, in particular, among their moods, temperaments, motivations and intentions" (p. 239). Emotional intelligence can be viewed as a combination of the intrapersonal and interpersonal intelligence of an individual.

Relating emotional intelligence to Thorndike's social intelligence dimension, Salovey and Mayer (1990) define emotional intelligence as a form of pure intelligence, representing one's potential for achieving mastery of specific abilities in the pure intelligence domain. The authors presented a conceptual framework of emotional abilities constituting emotional intelligence. To the authors, emotional intelligence should be integrated into the domains of intelligence and emotion. It involves capacity to carry out abstract reasoning about emotional signals that convey regular and discernible meanings about relationships and a number of universal basic emotions (Mayer et al., 2002a, 2002b). This idea can be thought of as one member of an emerging group of potential hot intelligences that include social intelligence (Sternberg & Smith, 1985; Thorndike, 1920), practical intelligence (Sternberg & Caruso, 1985; Wagner & Sternberg, 1985), personal intelligence (Gardner, 1993), non-verbal perception skills (Buck, 1984; Rosenthal et al., 1979), and emotional creativity (Averill & Nunley, 1992). Each of these forgoing concepts forms coherent domains that partly overlap with emotional intelligence but divide human intelligence in distinctive ways.

To establish emotional intelligence as a pure intelligence, Mayer et al. (1999) used three criteria: conceptual, correlational and developmental. The authors assert that, conceptually, any intelligence must reflect actual mental performance rather than preferred behaviour patterns, self-esteem, or non-intellectual attainments (Mayer & Salovey, 1993). To Mayer and his colleagues, emotional intelligence does describe actual abilities. From a correlation perspective, a new "intelligence" should describe a set of closely related abilities that are similar to, but distinct from, mental abilities described by existing intelligences (Carroll, 1993). Mayer et al. regard emotional intelligence as a type of social intelligence but in a broader scope, because it does not only include reasoning about the emotions in social relationships, but also reasoning about internal emotions that are important for personal growth. Finally, from a development point of view, intelligence should develop with age and experience. The results gained by Mayer et al. showed that adults did perform at higher ability levels than do adolescents.

Subsuming emotional intelligence under the domain of intelligence, Salovey and Mayer (1990, 1997) define emotional intelligence as the ability to perceive, respond and manipulate emotional information without necessarily understanding it and the ability to understand and manage emotions without necessarily perceiving feelings well or fully experiencing them. This intelligence framework consists of four branches: Perceiving emotions, using emotions, understanding emotions, and managing emotions (Oliver, 2011).

Perceiving emotions includes the ability to identify emotion in one's physical states, feelings and thoughts, and emotions in other people, designs, artwork through language, sound, appearance, and behaviour; the ability to express emotions accurately, and the needs related to those feelings; the ability to discriminate between accurate and inaccurate, or honest versus dishonest expressions of feelings.

Using emotions includes emotion-prioritised thinking by directing attention to important information. Emotions are so sufficiently vivid and available that they can be generated as aids to judgement and memory concerning feelings. Emotional mood swings change the individual's perspective from optimistic to pessimistic, encouraging consideration of multiple points of view. Emotional states differentially encourage specific problem-solving approaches and facilitate inductive reasoning and creativity (Prentice, 2019; White, 2020).

Understanding emotions includes the ability to label emotions and recognize relations among the words and the emotions themselves, such as the relation between liking and loving; the ability to interpret the meanings that emotions convey such that sadness often accompanies a loss; the ability to understand complex feelings; the ability to recognize likely transitions among emotions, from anger to satisfaction or from anger to shame (Prentice, 2019; White, 2020).

Emotional management includes the ability to stay open to feelings, including pleasant and unpleasant ones; the ability to reflectively engage or detach from an emotion depending upon it being judged to be informative or utility; the ability to reflectively monitor emotions in relation to oneself and others, such as recognizing how clear, typical, influential or reasonable they are; the ability to manage emotion in oneself and others by moderating negative emotions and enhancing pleasant ones without repressing or exaggerating information they may convey (Prentice, 2019; White, 2020).

Mayer et al. (2001) further explain that the four branches function hierarchically with the perception of emotions acting as the most basic or bottom branch, and emotional management as the most complex or top branch. Specifically, perception of emotions is a precursor to the next three branches. If an individual lacks the ability to process the lowest level of emotional input, he or she would also lack the ability to manage emotions at a higher level described in this model. Once perception has gained, emotions can be utilised to facilitate thought consciously or unconsciously. This is supported by Levine's (1997) study which shows that different emotions are related to different problem-solving strategies. For example, sadness leads to a coping strategy where coping is the most appropriate strategy (Levine, 1997). The next step involves cognitive processing to recognize how multiple emotions can combine and to anticipate how one emotion leads to another, until they finally translate emotional knowledge into behaviour.

2.3   The Fancy EI

2.3.1   Goleman's ECI

Daniel Goleman, a psychologist and science writer who has previously written on brain and behavioural research for the *New York Times*, popularised the concept of emotional intelligence in the middle 1990s and conceptualised emotional intelligence as a general quality possessed by every normal person, a quantitative spectrum of individual differences in which people can be ranked on a type of emotional scale.

Goleman in 1995 wrote the landmark book *Emotional Intelligence*. The author describes emotional intelligence as "abilities such as being able to motivate oneself and persist in the face of frustrations; to control impulse and delay gratification; to regulate one's moods and keep distress from swamping the ability to think; to empathize and to hope." Therefore, emotional intelligence is defined as "the capacity for recognizing our own feelings and those of others, for motivating ourselves, and for managing emotions well in ourselves and in our relationships" (Goleman, 1998a, p. 317).

The model of emotional intelligence proposed by Goleman involves cognitive ability and personality factors. It focuses on the domain of work performance that is evaluated on social and emotional competencies. These competencies represent the degree to which an individual has mastered specific skills and abilities that build on emotional intelligence and allow them greater effectiveness in the workplace (Goleman, 1998a). The competency-based approach reflects a tradition emphasising the identification of competencies that can be used to predict work performance across a variety of organizational settings, often with an emphasis on those in leadership positions (Boyatzis, 1982).

In the book, *Working with Emotional Intelligence* (1998a), Daniel Goleman set out a framework of emotional intelligence based on emotional competencies that have been identified in internal research at hundreds of corporations and organizations as distinguishing outstanding performers. The author distinguishes emotional intelligence from emotional competence by defining emotional competence as "a learned capability based on emotional intelligence that results in outstanding performance at work" (Goleman, 1998b).

According to Goleman, our emotional intelligence determines our potential for learning the practical skills that underlie the emotional competence clusters; our emotional competence shows how much of that potential we have realized by learning and mastering skills and translating intelligence into on-the-job capabilities. For example, to be adept in emotional competence like customer service or conflict management requires an underlying ability in emotional intelligence fundamentals, specifically, social awareness and relationship management. Goleman (1998a) argued that emotional intelligence underlies emotional competence, and that emotional competence is a required antecedent to performance. Emotional intelligence enhances employee potential for learning, and emotional competence translates that potential into task-mastering capabilities.

Dulewicz and Higgs (2000) also distinguished emotional competencies from emotional intelligence and alleged that a competence framework appears to hold more empirical promise. In relation to organizational application, Dulewicz and Herbert (1999) demonstrate a clear linkage between competencies and elements of advancement within an organizational context. The relationship between individual attributes and differentiation between "average" and "outstanding" performance is at the heart of the case for considering emotional intelligence by tracking the career progress of General Managers over a seven-year period. The competencies of emotional awareness, accurate self-assessment, and self-confidence can be perceived as providing a road map toward making necessary adjustments on the job, managing uncontrolled emotions, motivating oneself, and assessing others' feelings, thereby developing the social skills to lead and motivate. However, existing research mainly draws on physiological research developments, educational-based research and developments in the therapy field. According to Dulewicz and Higgs (2000), research about emotional intelligence in organizational contexts has mainly been based on derivative arguments and largely anecdotal case descriptions.

From the perspective of competence, Goleman (1998a) identified four components of emotional intelligence: self-awareness, self-management, social awareness, and relationship management. According to Goleman, self-awareness is the ability to read one's emotions and recognise their impact on decision-making. Self-awareness is referred to as "knowing what we are feeling in the moment, and using those preferences to guide our decision making; having a realistic assessment of our own abilities and a well-grounded sense of self-confidence" (Goleman, 1998a, p. 318). Self-management involves controlling one's emotions and impulses and adapting to changing environments and is defined as "handling our emotions so that they facilitate rather than interfere with the task at hand; being conscientious and delaying gratification to pursue goals; recovering well from emotional stress" (Goleman, 1998a, p. 318). Social awareness is defined as "sensing what people are feeling, being able to take their perspective, and cultivating rapport and attunement with a broad diversity of people" (Goleman, 1998a, p. 318). It includes the ability to sense, understand, and react to other's emotions while comprehending social networks. Finally, relationship management entails the ability to inspire, influence, and develop others while managing conflict (Goleman, 1998a).

In an analysis of data on workplace effectiveness, Boyatzis et al. (2000) found that the four clusters are related hierarchically. According to these authors, emotional self-awareness is a prerequisite for effective self-management, which in turn predicts greater social skills. A secondary pathway runs from self-awareness to social awareness to social skill. Managing relationships well then depends on a foundation of self-management and empathy, each of which in turn requires self-awareness. Goleman believes this evidence that empathy and self-management are foundations for social effectiveness finds support at the neurological level.

From the perspective of competence, Goleman developed a measure called *Emotional Competence Inventory* (ECI) based on social and emotional competencies in organizational settings with an emphasis on those in leadership positions. The ECI is a 360-degree tool designed to assess the emotional competencies of individuals and organizations. This tool is based on emotional competencies identified by Goleman (1998a) in *Working with Emotional Intelligence* and on competencies from Hay/McBer's *Generic Competency Dictionary* (1996) as well as Richard Boyatzis's *Self-Assessment Questionnaire* (SAQ). Initial concurrent validity studies using assessments based on Goleman's model have been able to account for a larger amount of variance in work performance than emotional intelligence measures based on the Mayer and Salovey model of emotional intelligence (Bradberry & Greaves, 2003), as ECI demonstrates the utility of this approach for assessment, training, and the development of social and emotional competencies in the workplace.

The ECI can classify each respondent within the range of self and others' ratings. Evidence for content validity is reported in the technical manual through an accurate self-assessment study in which those individuals who were not aware of their strengths and weaknesses had trouble evaluating themselves on emotional intelligence competencies (Sala, 2002). Measures of criterion validity found that the emotional intelligence of college principals was significantly associated with college student retention. Other researchers (e.g., Stys & Brown, 2004) reported emotional intelligence measured by ECI was significantly positively correlated with salary, job success and life success. Construct validity was established through convergent validity studies with a variety of measures of similar constructs. Goleman's model of emotional intelligence was found to correspond significantly with the sensing/intuiting and thinking/feeling dimensions of the Myers-Briggs Type indicator and with the extroversion, agreeableness, and conscientiousness factors of the NEO Personality Inventory. A study of divergent validity found no significant correlations between the ECI and a measure of analytical/critical thinking (Sala, 2002).

2.3.2 Bar-On's EQ

Bar-On (1997) coined the term Emotional Quotient (EQ) in his doctoral dissertation as an analogue to Intelligent Quotient (IQ). His model of emotional intelligence can be viewed as a mixed intelligence, also consisting of cognitive ability and personality aspects. This model includes: the ability to be aware of, to understand, and to express oneself; the ability to be aware of, to understand and relate to others; the ability to deal with strong emotions and control one's impulses; and the ability to adapt to change and to solve problems of a personal or social nature. Emphasising its influence on general wellbeing and adaptation, Bar-On (1997) defines emotional intelligence as "an array of non-cognitive capabilities, competencies, and skills that influence one's ability to succeed in coping with environmental demands and pressures." (p. 14).

Bar-On's model of emotional intelligence relates to the potential for performance and success, rather than performance or success itself, and is considered process-oriented rather than outcome-oriented (Bar-On, 2002). It focuses on an array of emotional and social abilities, including the ability to be aware of, understand and express oneself and the ability to adapt to change and solve problems of a social or personal nature (Bar-on, 1997). This model hypothesizes that those individuals with higher than average EQ's are generally more successful in meeting environmental demands and pressures. A deficiency in emotional intelligence likely means a lack of success and the existence of emotional problems. According to Bar-On (2002), emotional intelligence and cognitive intelligence contribute equally to a person's general intelligence, which then indicates potential success in one's life.

2.4 The Operational EI

For the same construct, EI has been conceptualised as a pure intelligence or a mixed model consisting of personality and intelligence. The inconsistent frameworks led to the haphazard development of the construct and numerous conflicting findings. In recognition of the problem, Petrides and Furnham (2001) suggested the terminology "ability EI" and "trait EI" to distinguish these models based on the measurement approaches. The authors propose that, regardless of how it is conceptualised, EI should be classified as trait EI when measuring through self-report questionnaires, as ability EI when measuring through performance tests.

Based on this classification, trait EI was concerned with cross-situational consistencies in behaviour, and embedded within the personality framework, and is assessed via validated self-report inventories that measure typical behaviour (e.g., Bar-on, 1997). This approach to emotional intelligence research draws heavily on personality variables such as empathy, optimism and impulsivity. Considering the five-factor model of personality, trait emotional intelligence measures are generally found to have large significant correlations with Extraversion and Neuroticism, while smaller significant positive correlations with Openness, Agreeableness and Conscientiousness have also been found (Petrides & Furnham, 2001; Schutte et al., 1998). By contrast, the ability emotional intelligence is much more focused, as explicit as traditional intelligence and can be measured through maximal performance. Therefore, trait emotional intelligence should not be expected to correlate strongly with measures of general cognitive ability or proxies, whereas ability emotional intelligence should not be strongly correlated with factors of personality measures.

Furthermore, Petrides and Furnham (2001) clarified that the distinction between trait and ability emotional intelligence is predicated on the method used to measure the construct and not on the elements that the various models are hypothesised to encompass. As such, it is unrelated to the distinction among the models of emotional intelligence conceptualised by Mayer and Salovey, Goleman, and Bar-On. The emotional intelligence scale (EIS) developed by Schutte and her colleagues in 1998 is a good example for this clarification. EIS is a self-report measure but based on the ability model of emotional intelligence developed by Salovey and Mayer (1990). It is classified as trait emotional intelligence because it is measured through self-report questionnaires; however, it is founded on a cognitive-based conceptualisation. This distinction between ability and trait emotional intelligence sheds light on the measure-related confusion and provides basis in selecting an appropriate measure for relevant studies.

2.5   A Flexible Approach to Emotional Intelligence

The aforementioned models have been widely discussed in in the literature (see Stys & Brown, 2004). Each model from a different angle attempts to interpret and operationalise what emotional intelligence as an incepted psychological construct connotes and implies. Van Rooy and Viswesvaran (2004) commented that it is difficult to provide an operational definition for emotional intelligence accepted by all, as researchers themselves interested in this area are constantly amending their own definitions of the construct. Mayer et al.'s view has been mostly received in consensus, although some researchers (e.g., Roberts et al., 2001) show scepticism. Emmerling and Goleman (2003) indicate that it is an inherent part of the process of theory development and scientific discovery in any field as specific theories within a mature paradigm begin to emerge and differentiate. Goleman (2002) acknowledges that the existence of several theoretical viewpoints within the paradigm of emotional intelligence indicate the robustness of the field but not a weakness. As each theory represents the theoretical orientation and context in which each of these authors have decided to frame their theory, all researchers share a common desire to understand and measure the abilities and traits related to recognizing and regulating emotions in ourselves and others (Goleman, 1998a). All theories in this paradigm tend to understand how individuals perceive, understand, utilize and manage emotions in an effort to predict and foster personal effectiveness (Goleman & Emmerling, 2003).

Drawing upon the foregoing discussion, this book synthesises various definitions in both academic and non-academic arenas, and defines EI as an individual's abilities to perceive, understand, regulate and manage emotions of oneself and those of others. Fundamentally EI possessed by an individual can be used to manage oneself, and/or others in the emotional domain. Through managing the emotions of oneself, this person can rationalise his or her personal and professional life and achieve task efficiency and other set goals, such as job satisfaction and security, career success. The ability to manage others' emotions can be useful for building relationships with the parties involved in personal and professional encounters. On the personal account, this ability may nourish personal and social life. On the professional account, for instance, in the sales and marketing, this ability can be used to build rapport with customers which leads to successful business transactions. This book will be focused on business and organisational context and discusses how emotional intelligence exhibited in employees can be utilised as a tool to facilitate job-related and organisational outcomes, and how customer emotional intelligence can be employed to manage customer-related outcomes. The following section reviews what the literature has shown in these domains.

2.6 Application of Emotional Intelligence to Businesses

Emotions are prevalent in any human-intensive contexts as a fundamental and integral part of personal, business and social lives. In the organizational context, emotions are prevalent in personal encounters between co-workers (including employees and the management), between employees and customers, and between peer customers. The terms emotional dissonance, burnout, role conflict, role ambiguity, role overload, psychological stress have been popular topics to describe employees (Prentice, 2008; Prentice et al., 2013). Customer satisfaction, loyalty, commitment and retention are emotionally loaded terms describing customer emotional attachment to a firm that brings potential business profitability (Prentice & King, 2011). EI appears to be able to an intelligence that can be utilised to address these emotional related issues relating to employees and customers.

2.6.1   EI and Employees

Employees who exhibit a high level of EI can manage their own emotionally loaded issues and emotionally charged encounter with co-workers, which result in task efficiency and more positive performance evaluation. Research has extensively discussed its relationship with leadership (see McCleskey, 2014) and employees' job attitudes and behaviours (see Miao et al., 2017). A meta-analyses research (i.e., Joseph et al., 2015) shows that emotional intelligence, to a certain degree, demonstrates substantial predictive validity. The degree of the predictive validity is dependent on the study settings, selected criterion as well as the model used. In particular, emotional intelligence can be a positive predictor for jobs logically requiring a high level of emotional skills. Such jobs normally contain high emotional labour demands, for instance, the job of customer service representatives or frontline employees (Prentice et al., 2013). Emotional intelligence could also be an important factor in employee performance for jobs that have important social components (Caruso et al., 2002). Mulki et al. (2015) resonate with this view and indicate that emotional intelligence can be expected to contribute at a reasonable level of prediction of individual behaviours involving social components.

Emotional intelligence has been claimed to affect a wide variety of job attitudes and behaviours. Researchers (e.g., Cooper, 1997) allege that people with high levels of emotional intelligence experience more career success, build stronger personal relationships, lead more effectively, and enjoy better health than those with low levels of emotional intelligence. For example, emotional intelligence has been extensively discussed to exert a positive influence on job satisfaction because it influences one's ability to succeed in coping with environmental demands and pressures, thus managing stressful work conditions (Bar-On, 1997). EI is related to employee commitment because it facilitates communication. Emotionally intelligent people make others feel better suited to the occupational environment (Goleman, 1998a; Rozell et al., 2004). Emotional intelligence significantly relates to teamwork and leadership. Emotionally intelligence people have better social skills which are needed for group work (Mayer & Salovey, 1997); Leaders with higher level of emotional intelligence may affect the relationship in the work setting.

2.6.2   EI on Customers

EI exhibited in employees can also be utilised to manage emotional encounters with customers. Empirical studies on how employees' emotional intelligence affect customers' attitudes and behaviours are emerging (Prentice, 2016, 2018; Prentice & King, 2011) but rather limited. Employees' EI affect customers through managing their own emotions and behaviours when interacting with customers which affect customers' responses towards a brand or firm. For instance, employee performance during interactions with customers largely influences the latter's perception of the firm's service quality and subsequent behaviours (Zablah et al., 2016); employee commitment and retention relates to customer loyalty and retention (see Hogreve et al., 2017). Therefore, customer response towards the brand or firm can be derived from the influence of emotional intelligence on employees' job attitudes and behaviours.

EI exhibited in customers has implications for the service organisations as well as for themselves. Customers in the service dominant logic era play a role of co-producers with the service provider. The success of their encounters with the provider has impact on their service experience and transaction outcomes. Customers' EI can be conducive to their attitudes towards the business and service provider as well as to their purchase and loyalty behaviours. On the other hand, managing their own emotions may detain them from engaging in impulsive purchase or having conflict with customer-contact employees and peer customers over the service encounter. Impulsive purchase is emotionally driven and may be moderated by EI. Conflict has evidently been resolved by EI. Positive service encounter leads to the establishment and strength of customer relationship with the service provider. Such relationship has a range of financial and non-financial benefits for both customers and the provider (Prentice, 2019).

2.7 Conclusion

In view of the foregoing discussion, this book discusses how EI affects the attitudes and behaviours of employees and customers from dual perspectives. Chapter 4 focuses on how employee EI exerts influences on both employees and customers. Chapter 5 focuses on how customers' EI impacts their relationship with the firms. In particular, this book views employees' emotional competence as a service that can be offered to add value to the service organisation. The rationale for this view will be provided in the subsequent chapters. The relevant applications implications of EI as a service are elaborated to endorse this view.

References

Austin, E. J., Saklofske, D. H., & Egan, V. (2005). Personality, well-being and health correlates of trait emotional intelligence. *Personality and Individual Differences, 38*(3), 547–558.

Averill, J. R., & Nunley, E. P. (1992). *Voyages of the heart: Living an emotionally creative life.* Free Press.

Bar-On, R. (1997). Emotional intelligence. *International Journal of Sociology and Social Policy, 29*, 164–175.

Bar-On, R. (2002). *Bar-On Emotional Quotient Short Form (EQ-i: Short): Technical manual.* Toronto: Multi-Health Systems.

Bar-On, R., Handley, R., & Fund, S. (2006). The impact of emotional intelligence on performance. In *Linking emotional intelligence and performance at work: Current research evidence with individuals and groups* (pp. 3–19).

Boyatzis, R. E. (1982). *The competent manager: A model for effective performance.* New York: John Wiley & Sons

Boyatzis, R., Goleman, D., & Rhee, K. (2000). Clustering competence in emotional intelligence: Insights from the emotional competence inventory (ECI). In R. Bar-On & J. D. A. Parker (Eds.), *Handbook of emotional intelligence.* Jossey-Bass.

Bradberry, T., & Greaves, J. (2003). *Emotional intelligence appraisal: Technical manual.* San Diego: TalentSmart, Inc.

Buck, R. (1984). Rapport, emotional education, and emotional competence. *Psychological Inquiry.* 1990, *1*(4), 301–302. https://doi.org/10.1207/s15327965pli0104_4

Caroll, J. B. (1993). *Human cognitive abilities: A survey of factor-analytic studies.* New York: Cambridge University Press.

Caruso, D. R., Mayer, J. D., & Salovey, P. (2002). Relation of an ability measure of emotional intelligence to personality. *Journal of Personality Assessment, 79*, 306–320. Lawrence Erlbaum Associates.

Cooper, R. (1997). *Executive EQ.* Grosset/Putnam.

Dulewicz, S. V., & Herbert, P. J. A. (1999). Predicting advancement to senior management from competencies and personality data: A 7-year follow-up study. *British Journal of Management, 10*(1), 13–22.

Dulewicz, V., & Higgs, M. (2000). Emotional intelligence: A review and evaluation study. *Journal of Managerial Psychology, 15*(4), 341–372.

Emmerling, R. J., & Goleman, D. (2003). Emotional intelligence: Issues and common misunderstandings. *Issues and Recent Developments in Emotional Intelligence, 1*(1), 1–32.

Furnham, A., & Petrides, K. V. (2003). Trait emotional intelligence and happiness. *Social Behavior and Personality: An International Journal, 31*(8), 815–823.

Gardner, H. (1993). *Multiple intelligences: The theory in practice.* Basic Books.

Goleman, D. (1996). *Emotional intelligence: Why it can matter more than IQ.* Bloomsbury Publishing.

Goleman, D. (1998a). *Working with emotional intelligence.* New York: Bantam Books

Goleman, D. (1998b). What makes a leader? *Harvard Business Review.*

Goleman, D. (2001). Emotional intelligence: Issues in paradigm building. *The Emotionally Intelligent Workplace, 13*, 26.

Goleman, D. (2002). *Primal leadership.* Boston, MA: Harvard Business School Publishing.

Goleman, D., & Emmerling, R. J. (2003). Emotional intelligence: Issues and common misunderstandings. *The Consortium for Research on Emotional Intelligence in Organizations.*

Hogreve, J., Iseke, A., Derfuss, K., & Eller, T. (2017). The service–profit chain: A meta-analytic test of a comprehensive theoretical framework. *Journal of Marketing, 81*(3), 41–61

Joseph, D. L., Jin, J., Newman, D. A., & O'Boyle, E. H. (2015). Why does self-reported emotional intelligence predict job performance? A meta-analytic investigation of mixed EI. *Journal of Applied Psychology, 100*(2), 298.

Leuner, B. (1966). Emotional intelligence and emancipation. *Praxis Der Kinderpsychologie Und Kinderpsychiatrie, 15*, 193–203.

Levine, P. A. (1997). *Waking the tiger: Healing trauma: The innate capacity to transform overwhelming experiences.* North Atlantic Books.

Mayer, J. D., DiPaolo, M., & Salovey, P. (1990). Perceiving affective content in ambiguous visual stimuli: A component of emotional intelligence. *Journal of Personality Assessment. 54.* Lawrence Erlbaum Associates.

Mayer, J. D., & Salovey, P. (1993). The intelligence of emotional intelligence. *Intelligence, 17*(4), 433–442.

Mayer, J. D., & Salovey, P. (1997). What is emotional intelligence? In P. Salovey & D. Sluyter (Eds.), *Emotional development and EI: Educational implications* (pp. 3–34). Basic Books.

Mayer, J. D., Salovey, P., & Caruso, D. R. (1999). *MSCEIT item booklet* (Research Version 1.1). MHS Publishers

Mayer, J. D., Salovey, P., Caruso, D. R., & Sitarenios, G. (2001). *Emotional intelligence as a standard intelligence.*

Mayer, J. D., Salovey, P. & Caruso, D. (2002a). *Mayer-Salovey-Caruso Emotional Intelligence Test. (MSCEIT) user's manual.* MHS Publishers.

Mayer, J. D., Salovey, P., & Caruso, D. R. (2002b). *MSCEIT—user's manual.* Multi-Health Systems Inc.

McCleskey, J. A. (2014). Situational, transformational, and transactional leadership and leadership development. *Journal of Business Studies Quarterly, 5*(4), 117.

Miao, C., Humphrey, R. H., & Qian, S. (2017). A meta-analysis of emotional intelligence and work attitudes. *Journal of Occupational and Organizational Psychology, 90*(2), 177–202.

Mulki, J. P., Jaramillo, F., Goad, E. A., & Pesquera, M. R. (2015). Regulation of emotions, interpersonal conflict, and job performance for salespeople. *Journal of Business Research, 68*(3), 623–630.

Newsome, S., Day, A. L., & Cntano, V. M. (2000). Assessing the predictive validity of emotional intelligence. *Personality and Individual Differences, 29*(66), 1005–1016.

Oliver, L. C. (2011). *Evaluation of EQ4KIDZ, An Emotional Intelligence Program For Primary School Children in Western Australia.* https://espace.curtin.edu.au/bitstream/handle/20.500.11937/2462/163514_Oliver%20full%20.pdf?isAllowed=y&sequence=2

Petrides, K. V., & Furnham, A. (2001). Trait emotional intelligence: Psychometric investigation with reference to established trait taxonomies. *European Journal of Personality, John Wiley and Sons Ltd., 1996*(15), 425–448.

Petrides, K. V., & Furnham, A. (2003). Trait emotional intelligence: Behavioural validation in two studies of emotion recognition and reactivity to mood induction. *European Journal of Personality, 17*(1), 39–57.

Petrides, K. V., Furnham, A., & Mavroveli, S. (2007). Trait emotional intelligence: Moving forward in the field of EI. *Emotional Intelligence: Knowns and Unknowns, 4*, 151–166.

Prentice, C. (2008). *Trait emotional intelligence, personality and the self-perceived performance ratings of casino key account representatives* (Doctoral dissertation, Victoria University)

Prentice, C. (2016). Leveraging employee emotional intelligence in casino profitability. *Journal of Retailing and Consumer Services, 33*, 127–134.

Prentice, C. (2018). Linking internal service quality and casino dealer performance. *Journal of Hospitality Marketing & Management, 27*(6), 733–753.

Prentice, C. (2019). *Emotional intelligence and marketing.* World Scientific.

Prentice, C., Chen, P. J., & King, B. (2013). Employee performance outcomes and burnout following the presentation-of-self in customer-service contexts. *International Journal of Hospitality Management, 35*, 225–236.

Prentice, C., & King, B. (2011). The influence of emotional intelligence on the service performance of casino frontline employees. *Tourism and Hospitality Research, 11*(1), 49–66.

Roberts, R. D., Zeidner, M., & Matthews, G. (2001). Does emotional intelligence meet traditional standards for an intelligence? Some new data and conclusions. *Emotion, 1*(3), 196–231.

Rosenthal, R., Archer, D., Koivumaki, J. H., DiMatteo, M. R., & Rogers P. L. (1979). A sound-motion picture test for measuring sensitivity to nonverbal communication: The PONS test. In S. Chatman, U. Eco, & J. Klinkenberg (Eds.), *A semiotic Landscape: Proceedings of the First Congress of the International Association for Semiotic Studies,* Milan. Mouton.

Rozell, E. J., Pettijohn, C. E., & Parker, R. S. (2004). Customer-oriented selling: Exploring the roles of emotional intelligence and organizational commitment. *Psychology and Marketing, 21*(6), 405–424.

Sala, F. (2002). *Emotional competence inventory (ECI).* McClelland Centre for Research & Innovation.

Salovey, P., & Mayer, J. D. (1990). Emotional intelligence. *Imagination, Cognition and Personality, 9*(3), 185–211.

Schutte, N. S., Malouff, J. M., Hall, L. E., Haggerty, D. J., Cooper, J. T., & Dornheim, L. (1998). Development and validation of a measure of emotional intelligence. *Personality and Individual Differences, 25*, 167–177.

Schutte, N. S., Malouff, J. M., Thorsteinsson, E. B., Bhullar, N., & Rooke, S. E. (2007). A meta-analytic investigation of the relationship between emotional intelligence and health. *Personality and Individual Differences, 42*(6), 921–933.

Sternberg, R., & Caruso, D. (1985). Practical modes of knowing in learning and teaching the ways of knowing. In E. Eisner (Ed.). NSSE Chicago.

Stys, Y., & Brown, S.L. (2004). *A review of the emotional intelligence literature and implications for corrections.* Research Branch, Correctional Service of Canada.

Sternberg, R. J., & Smith, C. (1985). Social intelligence and decoding skills in nonverbal communication. *Social Cognition, 3*(2), 168–192.

Thorndike, E. L. (1920). Intelligence and its uses. *Harper's, 140*, 227–235.

Van Rooy, D. L., & Viswesvaran, C. (2004). Emotional intelligence: A meta-analytic investigation of predictive validity and nomological net. *Journal of Vocational Behavior, 65*(1), 71–95.

Wagner, R. K., & Sternberg, R. J. (1985). Practical intelligence in real-world pursuits: The role of tacit knowledge. *Journal of Personality and Social Psychology, 49*(2), 436–458.

White, K. R. (2020). *Emotional intelligence and psychopathic personality traits: Examination of adult male sex offenders in New Jersey.* https://scholarworks.waldenu.edu/cgi/viewcontent.cgi?article=9524&context=dissertations

Zablah, A. R., Carlson, B. D., Donavan, D. T., Maxham, J. G., III., & Brown, T. J. (2016). A cross-lagged test of the association between customer satisfaction and employee job satisfaction in a relational context. *Journal of Applied Psychology, 101*(5), 743.

Chapter 3
Demystify Artificial Intelligence

The development of full artificial intelligence could spell the end of the human race. Stephen Hawking 2014

Abstract Artificial intelligence (AI) marks a paradigm shift in every sector of the tech industry. AI-powered tools (e.g., robots) and applications (e.g., recommendation systems) have progressively permeated in almost every individual and business arena on different levels and been repeatedly hyped, particularly in Asia. Southeast Asian countries have undertaken a 200% higher adoption rate of robots than Europe or North America. China is overtaking Europe and North America in research investments on AI. Supported by government policies and a strong incentive plan, China is planning to become the leader in AI innovations by 2030. This trend is partially attributed to AI's ability to augment human intelligence with unprecedented analytics and pattern prediction capabilities to improve the quality, effectiveness, and creativity of human decisions. The amount of data that is generated by machines far outpaces humans' ability to absorb and interpret. In business, AI-powered tools or machines can uncover gaps and opportunities in the market more quickly, helping the firm introduce new products, services, channels and business models rapidly with a high level of quality. AI-powered robots can function just like or more than humans. Stephen Hawking warned that developments and advancements of AI-powered robots might be disastrous for mankind. AI experts made predictions of AI superseding or replacing humans with significant time variations: the timeline stretches between a 50% chance within 45 years and a 9% chance within the next 9 years (Grace et al, in J Artif Intell Res 62:729–754, 2018, p. 729); 30 years from Asia and 74 years by North American respondents. This chapter is intended to demystify AI by revealing the evolution of AI, what it is, how it functions, and where it can be applied. The positioning of AI as a commercial service is highlighted in this chapter.

3.1 Evolution of Artificial Intelligence

Intelligent robots and artificial beings can be sourced from ancient Greek myths and Aristotle's development of syllogism and deductive reasoning, whereas the concept of AI is knowingly originated from Turing test by Alan Turing. The test was to determine if a computer can showcase the same intelligence as a human and intended to break the Nazi's ENIGMA code during WWI. The term AI, nevertheless, first appeared on a plague at Dartmouth College in 1956 in John McCarthy's Dartmouth Summer Research Project. The project was initiated by some military computing veterans who received a fund from the Rockefeller Foundation to conduct a workshop. Herbert Simon and Allen Newell, among others attended the workshop and proposed that human minds and digital computers were "species of the same genus" on the basis that both "take symbolic information as input, manipulate it according to a set of formal rules, and in so doing can solve problems, formulate judgments, and make decisions" (Crowther-Heyck, 2005a, 2005b; Newell & Simon, 1972).

Since then, AI has evolved through three major phases. AI researchers began to identify the processes that constituted intelligent human behaviour in medical diagnosis, chess, mathematics, language processing, and so on to reproduce these behaviours by machines or automation. The first phase between 1950s and 1970s was focused on problem solving, training computers to mimic basic human reasoning, symbolic methods and neural networks that are reflective of thinking machine. The second phase between 1980s and 2010s is manifested in the rise of machine learning. The third phase from 2010s to present is popularising AI on every level of the human world with advanced deep learning, advanced algorithms, and improvements in computing power and storage. AI has progressively permeated in every domain of the human world and exerted a profound impact on individuals, organizations, and industries to a significant extent. The following table lists the major events that showcase the development of AI.

Year	Contributor/s	Major developments
1943	Warren McCullough and Walter Pitts	Published "A Logical Calculus of Ideas Immanent in Nervous Activity" Proposed the first mathematical model for building a neural network
1949	Donald Hebb	Published "The Organization of Behavior: A Neuropsychological Theory", Propose the theory that neural pathways are created from experiences and that connections between neurons become stronger the more frequently they're used

(continued)

(continued)

Year	Contributor/s	Major developments
1950	Alan Turing	Turing Test, a method for determining if a machine can demonstrate the same intelligence as a human, and for breaking the Nazi's ENIGMA code during WWII Determine if a computer Published "Computing Machinery and Intelligence"
1950	Marvin Minsky and Dean Edmonds	Built the first neural network computer: SNARC
1950	Claude Shannon	Published "Programming a Computer for Playing Chess."
1950	Isaac Asimov	Published "Three Laws of Robotics"
1952	Arthur Samuel	Developed a self-learning program to play checkers
1954	IBM	Developed the Georgetown-IBM machine translation experiment automatically translates 60 carefully selected Russian sentences into English
1956	John McCarthy, Allen Newell, J. C. Shaw, and Herbert Simon	Coined the term 'artificial intelligence', Created the Logic Theorist—the first-ever running AI software program
1958	John McCarthy	Developed the AI programming language Lisp Published "Programs with Common Sense." Proposed the hypothetical Advice Taker, a complete AI system with the ability to learn from experience as effectively as humans do
1959	Allen Newell, Herbert Simon and J. C. Shaw	Developed the General Problem Solver (GPS), a program designed to imitate human problem-solving
1959	Herbert Gelernter	Developed the Geometry Theorem Prover program
1959	Arthur Samuel	Coined the term machine learning while at IBM
1959	John McCarthy and Marvin Minsky	Found the MIT Artificial Intelligence Project
1960s	The US Department of Defense	Trained computers to mimic basic human reasoning
1963	John McCarthy	Established the AI Lab at Stanford
1966	The U.S. government	Wrote the Automatic Language Processing Advisory Committee (ALPAC) report leading to the cancellation of all government-funded MT projects

(continued)

(continued)

Year	Contributor/s	Major developments
1967	Frank Rosenblatt	Built the Mark 1 Perceptron, the first computer based on a neural network that 'learned' though trial and error
1968	Marvin Minsky and Seymour Papert	Published a book: *Perceptrons*, the landmark work on neural networks
1970s	The Defense Advanced Research Projects Agency (DARPA)	Completed street mapping projects in the 1970s
1972	Alain Colmerauer, Robert Kowalski	Created the logic programming language PROLOG
1973	The British government	Published the "Lighthill Report," leading to severe cuts in funding for artificial intelligence projects
1980	Digital Equipment Corporations	Developed R1 (also known as XCON), the first successful commercial expert system. Designed to configure orders for new computer systems
1982	Japan's Ministry of International Trade and Industry	Launched Fifth Generation Computer Systems project
1983	The U.S. government	Launched the Strategic Computing Initiative to provide DARPA funded research in advanced computing and artificial intelligence
1985	Symbolics and Lisp Machines Inc	Built specialized computers to run on the AI programming language Lisp
1991	U.S. forces	Deployed DART, an automated logistics planning and scheduling tool, during the Gulf War
1997	IBM's	Built Deep Blue Beat world chess champion Gary Kasparov
2005	The Stanley Motor Carriage Company	Made STANLEY, a self-driving car, wins the DARPA Grand Challenge
2005	The U.S. military	Boston Dynamics' "Big Dog" and iRobot's "PackBot."
2008	Google	Made breakthroughs in speech recognition Introduced the feature in its iPhone app
2011	IBM	Created Watson
2011	Apple	Released Siri, an AI-powered virtual assistant through its iOS operating system
2012	Andrew Ng	Launched Deep Learning project
2014	Google	Make the first self-driving car to pass a state driving test
2014	Amazon	Created Alexa, a virtual home is released
2015	Baidu	Created Minwa supercomputer

(continued)

(continued)

Year	Contributor/s	Major developments
2016	Google	Created DeepMind's AlphaGo d
2016	Hanson Robotics	Created the first "robot citizen", a humanoid robot named Sophia, is capable of facial recognition, verbal communication and facial expression
2018	Google	Released natural language processing engine BERT, reducing barriers in translation and understanding by machine learning applications
2018	Waymo	Launched its Waymo One service, allowing users throughout the Phoenix metropolitan area to request a pick-up from one of the company's self-driving vehicles
2020	Baidu	Released its LinearFold AI algorithm to predict the RNA sequence of the virus in just 27 s, 120 times faster than other methods

Note the information in the table is adapted from various sources on multiple sites (e.g., Javapoint; Reynoso, 2021; Tableau.). It is not the author's intention to miss citing

3.2 Conceptualising Artificial Intelligence

The term of AI was coined on the basis of the core conjecture that a machine can simulate any precisely described human learning, and any intelligent human behaviours that can be formalised and reproduced in a machine (McCarthy et al., 2006). Such simulation can be drawn from mathematical logic reasoning and philosophy aimed at formal descriptions of human thinking. On this conjecture, AI has been defined variously by academics and industry practitioners with nuanced foci on automation, machine learning, language processing or beyond since its first appearance in 1950s.

The founders of AI, John McCarthy, Marvin Minsky, Nathaniel Rochester and Claude Shannon defined AI as *machines that are enabled to use language, form abstractions and concepts, solve problems for humans as well as improving themselves.* Winston (1992) refers to AI as algorithms that support models connecting thinking, perception and action together. Russell and Norvig (2002) define AI as computer systems that can think humanly and rationally, act humanly and rationally. Thinking refers to thought processes and reasoning. Acting refers to best outcomes achieved by machines. The authors later deepened this concept and indicate that AI can be applied to machines to display human-like intelligence in two essential ways. First, it focuses on acting intelligently, such as perceiving, learning, memorising, reasoning and problem-solving towards goal-directed behaviour. Second, AI is referred to as computational agents in information systems that can perceive the environment and act upon this environment (Norvig and Intelligence 2002; Russell et al., 2015; Russell & Norvig, 1995). McCarthy and Wright (2004) defines AI as the science and engineering of making intelligent machines, especially intelligent computer programs, and using computers to understand human intelligence. Kaplan and Haenlein (2019) also refer to AI as computational agents that act intelligently and define AI as a system's ability to interpret and learn from external data correctly, to achieve specific goals and tasks.

In the non-academic community, AI is defined on the basis of problem solving and applications in businesses and industries. From customer service and supply chain perspectives, Accenture regards AI as a constellation of technologies including machine learning, deep learning and natural language processing that work together to achieve business goals in combination with data, analytics and automation to enable machines/computers to sense, comprehend, act, and learn with human-like levels of intelligence (https://www.accenture.com/au-en/insights/artificial-intelligence).

Despite the variety of conceptualising, essentially AI is a branch of computer science, more so an interdisciplinary science with multiple approaches that endeavour to replicate or simulate human intelligence in machines. AI is able to mimic or reproduce intelligent human behaviours, in some cases, to bypass human intelligence or behaviours, for instance, the automated gameplaying systems. The level of intelligence and capabilities varies and manifests in the following forms.

3.2.1 Reactive Non-memory Machines

A reactive machine cannot store a memory or rely on past experiences to inform decision making in real-time. This type of machine follows the most basic of AI principles and, is capable of only using the computational systems to perceive and react to the stimuli. These AI systems have no memory and are task specific. The reactive machines are designed to complete only a limited number of specialised duties. Nevertheless, this type of AI reacts to the same stimuli the same way each time reliably, and can attain a level of complexity, and offers reliability to fulfill repeatable tasks.

Deep blue is an example of a reactive machine. This machine was designed by IBM in the 1990s as a chess-playing supercomputer and defeated international grandmaster Gary Kasparov in a game. Deep Blue was capable of identifying the pieces on a chess board, knowing how each piece should move based on the rules of chess, acknowledging each piece's present position, and determining what the most logical move would be at that moment. The computer was not pursuing future potential moves by its opponent or trying to put its own pieces in better position. Every turn was viewed as its own reality, separate from any other movement that was made beforehand. Another example of a game-playing reactive machine is Google's AlphaGo. AlphaGo relies on its own neural network to evaluate developments of the present game, giving it an edge over Deep Blue in a more complex game. AlphaGo trumped world-class competitors of the game, and defeated champion Go player Lee Sedol in 2016. However, like Deep Blue, AlphaGo is incapable of evaluating future moves (Schroer, 2022).

3.2.2 Limited Memory AI

Some AI systems have memory, albeit limited, are able to gather information, store previous data, weigh potential decisions, make predictions, inform future decisions using past experiences. Limited memory AI utilises three major machine learning models: (1) Reinforcement Learning, which learns to make better predictions through repeated trial-and-error; (2) Long Short-Term Memory (LSTM), which utilizes past data to help predict the next item in a sequence. LTSMs view more recent information as most important when making predictions and discounts data from further in the past, though still utilizing it to form conclusions; (3) Evolutionary Generative Adversarial Networks (E-GAN), which evolves over time, growing to explore slightly modified paths based on previous experiences with every new decision. This model is constantly in pursuit of a better path and utilizes simulations and statistics, or chance, to predict outcomes throughout its evolutionary mutation cycle (Schroer, 2022).

AI with limited memory presents greater possibilities and is more complex than reactive machines. Machine learning techniques are utilised in limited memory AI. This type of AI is trained to analyse and utilise new data in a system that models are built and automatically trained and renewed in a cycle of creating training data, creating the machine learning model that is able to make predictions, and receive human or environmental feedback which is stored as data. Self-driving car is based on this type of AI systems that draws on the past to predict the future.

3.2.3 Narrow AI

Narrow AI or weak AI draws upon machine learning and deep learning and is regarded as most successful realization of artificial intelligence to date (Schroer, 2022). This type of AI simulates human intelligence but operates within a limited context under constraints and limitations. Although labelled as narrow or weak, these AI systems have immense transformational power that influence how the human world function multidimensionally. This type of AI excels in performing a single task or a set of related tasks efficiently, and have experienced massive breakthroughs over last decade. Examples include

- Autonomous vehicles
- Interactive apps
- Industrial robots

- Google search
- Image recognition software
- Digital and virtual personal assistants such as Apple's Siri, Amazon's Alexa, IBM Watson (Burns et al., 2023).

3.2.4 Future AI

Future AI refers to strong AI or artificial general intelligence (AGI). It is labelled as future AI as this type of AI is still the theory of minds with no practical examples in use today. In theory, AGI can be programmed to replicate the cognitive abilities of the human brain. When presented with an unfamiliar task, a strong AI system can use fuzzy logic to apply knowledge from one domain to another and find a solution autonomously (Burns et al., 2023). The concept is based on the psychological premise of understanding that other living things have thoughts and emotions that affect the behaviour of oneself. Strong AI could comprehend how humans, animals and other machines feel and make decisions through self-reflection and determination, and then will utilise that information to make decisions of their own. Essentially, machines would have to be able to grasp and process the concept of "mind," the fluctuations of emotions in decision making and a litany of other psychological concepts in real time, creating a two-way relationship between people and artificial intelligence (Burns et al., 2023).

This type of AI is theorised to have self-aware consciousness, understands its own existence, and has social and emotional abilities that can be used to solve problems, learn, and plan for the future. Another type of AI is referred to as artificial super intelligence (ASI), also known as superintelligence, is visioned to surpass the intelligence and ability of the human brain. This AI often appears in sci-fi films, where sentient machines emulate human intelligence, thinking strategically, abstractly and creatively, with the ability to handle a range of complex tasks. While machines can perform some tasks better than humans (e.g. data processing), this fully realized vision of general AI does not yet exist outside the silver screen (Burns et al., 2023; Schroer, 2022).

3.3 Operationalising Artificial Intelligence

With advancements of cloud processing and computing power, AI systems function by combining and ingesting large amounts of data with fast, iterative processing and intelligent algorithms, analysing the data for correlations and patterns, and using these patterns to make predictions about future states (Schroer, 2022). In short, AI reasons on input of data and explains on output. For example, a chatbot can learn to produce lifelike exchanges with people by feeding examples of text chats. An image recognition tool can learn to identify and describe objects in images by reviewing millions of examples (Accenture, 2023).

AI is embedded in various types of technologies such as automation, robotics and machine version. Automation, or robotic process automation, differs from IT automation and can be programmed to perform high-volume, repeatable tasks like humans. Self-driving cars are an example of automating safe driving using computer vision, image recognition and deep learning capabilities (Burns et al., 2021). Robotics are generally used to perform mundane tasks requiring low-level social interactions (e.g., assembling lines in manufacturing). Machine vision captures and analyses visual information using cameras and digital signal processes such as human eyesight, which can be used, for example, in signature identification and image analysis. Computer vision applies machine learning models to images used widely such as selfie filters and medical imaging (Accenture, 2023).

AI programming focuses on three cognitive skills: learning, reasoning and self-correction. Learning processes of AI programming focus on acquiring data and creating algorithms for how to turn the data into actionable information and how to complete a specific task. Reasoning processes of AI programming focus on choosing the right algorithm to reach a desired outcome. Self-correction processes of AI programming are designed to continually fine-tune algorithms and ensure they provide the most accurate results possible (Accenture, 2023).

AI learning is exhibited in machine learning and deep learning: learning from data and results in near real time, analysing new information accurately from many sources and adapting accordingly (e.g., product recommendations). Machine or deep learning enables computers to automate predictive analytics and act without programming, and generate results in near real time, including supervised, unsupervised and reinforcement learning (Bulchand-Gidumal, 2022).

Both deep learning and machine learning are sub-fields of artificial intelligence, and deep learning is a sub-field of machine learning. Machine and deep learning functions on artificial neural networks that are similar to human neurons. Artificial neural networks are networks of a large amount of simple artificial neurons, each of which imitate a human neuron, and connected similarly to the way that human neurons are connected. The theory of neural networks is that as the magnitude of connected neurons approaches that of humans (approximately 1011), artificial and natural systems can perform similarly. The main use of neural networks has been related to forecasting (Claveria et al., 2015).

3.3.1 Machine Learning

Machine learning automates analytical model building, and uses methods from neural networks, statistics, operations research and physics to find hidden insights in data without explicitly being programmed (Šukjurovs et al., 2019). Machine learning feeds a computer data and uses statistical techniques to help it "learn" how to get progressively better at a task, without having been specifically programmed for that task, eliminating the need for written code. Machine learning is a set of algorithms through which the machines learn, as they repeat certain processes and obtain feedback on how they performed in those processes (Dubey, 2021). This feedback can be provided by humans or developed by the machine after observing the results of previous processes. There are three types of machine learning algorithms:

- Supervised learning: Data sets are labelled so that patterns can be detected and used to label new data sets.
- Unsupervised learning: Data aren't labelled and are sorted according to similarities or differences.
- Reinforced learning: Data sets aren't labelled but render feedback after performing an action or several actions (Khpcahoba, 2022).

For example, a machine may be taught to choose the best picture from a set of similar pictures of a travel memory (Bulchand-Gidumal, 2022). After observing whether the user engages with that chosen picture or album, the machine can improve the selection process for future instances. Uber has become one of the largest companies in the world by using computer software to connect riders to taxis. It utilises sophisticated machine learning algorithms to predict when people are likely to need rides in certain areas, which helps proactively get drivers on the road before they're needed. Google use machine learning to understand how people use their services and constantly make improvements. Since 2017, Google has become one of the largest players for a range of online services and operated as an "AI first" company.

3.3.2   Deep Learning

Deep learning, also known as "scalable machine learning" or supervised learning (Lex Fridman, MIT), is a type of machine learning that comprised of neural networks and runs inputs through a biologically-inspired neural network architecture (Hounguè et al., 2022). The neural networks contain a number of hidden layers through which the data is processed, allowing the machine to go "deep" in its learning, making connections and weighting input for the best results. Deep learning uses neural networks with many layers of processing units, taking advantage of advances in computing power and improved training techniques to learn complex patterns in large amounts of data (Hounguè et al., 2022). "Deep" in deep learning refers to a neural network comprised of more than three layers—which would be inclusive of the inputs and the output—can be considered a deep learning algorithm. "Deep" machine learning can leverage labelled datasets but not necessarily require a labelled dataset. It can ingest unstructured data in its raw form (e.g. text, images), and automatically determine the hierarchy of features which distinguish different categories of data from one another.

Deep learning differs from machine learning on the basis of how each algorithm learns and whether require human intervention to process data (IBM, https://www.ibm.com/artificial-intelligence). Deep learning automates much of the feature extraction piece of the process, eliminating some of the manual human intervention and enabling the use of larger data sets. Unlike machine learning, where the algorithm is provided with a large set of rules, in deep learning, the computer is given a model than can evaluate examples and a small set of instructions on how to modify the model to make it stronger and more accurate. Thus, the analysis starts at a superficial level but moves onto more complex and deep layers in successive approaches (Melián-González & Bulchand-Gidumal, 2016). Common applications include image or object detection through computer vision and speech recognition (natural language processing (LeCun et al., 2015).

Deep learning is embedded in computer vision or machine vision for capturing images or videos, processing, analysing and understanding images in real time and interpreting their surroundings. In short, computer vision is focused on machine-based image processing. This AI technology, powered by convolutional neural networks enables computers and systems to derive meaningful information from digital images, videos and other visual inputs, and inform decisions or provide recommendations based on those inputs. Computer vision often conflated with machine vision, captures and analyses visual information using a camera, analogue-to-digital conversion and digital signal processing. It functions like human eyesight but is more capable than biological eyes manifested in boundless visions such as seeing through walls. The common use of computer and machine vision includes signature identification, medical image analysis, photo tagging in social media, radiology imaging in healthcare, and self-driving cars within the automotive industry.

3.3.3 Natural Language Processing (NLP)

Natural Language Processing (NLP) is an AI program based on machine learning to enable machines or computers to generate, analyse and understand the human language and speech, and enables machines to communicate with humans in text or verbal manner through natural language interaction. Natural language processing (NLP) processes human language via a computer program including text translation, sentiment analysis and speech recognition (e.g., spam detection which determines a junk or spam mail based on the subject line and the text.

Human language is complex with homonyms, homophones, sarcasm, idioms, metaphors, grammar and usage exceptions, variations in sentence structure. NLP are developed to make machines to generate, analyse, and understand human language. Behind the scenes, NLP analyses the grammatical structure of sentences and the individual meaning of words, then uses algorithms to extract meaning and deliver outputs. In other words, it makes sense of human language to automatically perform different tasks. NLP combines computational linguistics—rule-based modelling of human language—with statistical, machine learning, and deep learning models. Together, these technologies enable computers to process human language in the form of text or voice data and to 'understand' its full meaning, complete with the speaker or writer's intent and sentiment (Kulkarni et al., 2021).

NLP drives computer programs that translate text from one language to another, respond to spoken commands, and summarize large volumes of text rapidly—even in real time, in the form of, for instance, voice-operated GPS systems, digital assistants like Google Assist, Siri, and Alexa, speech-to-text dictation software, customer service chatbots, and other consumer conveniences. NLP also plays a growing role in helping streamline business operations increase employee productivity and simplify mission-critical business processes. The following are common NLP tasks, albeit not conclusive (IBM, https://www.ibm.com/topics/natural-language-processing).

Speech recognition is the task of converting voice data into text data. It is also known as automatic speech recognition (ASR), computer speech recognition, or speech-to-text. This function uses natural language processing (NLP) to process human speech into a written format (Kulkarni et al., 2021). Many mobile devices incorporate speech recognition into their systems to conduct voice search, for instance, Siri, or provide more accessibility around texting. Speech recognition is required for any application that follows voice commands or answers spoken questions. Virtual agents such as Apple's Siri and Amazon's Alexa use speech recognition to recognize patterns in voice commands and natural language generation to respond with appropriate action or helpful comments. Voice recognition, coupled with simulated human dialog, is the first point of interaction in a customer service inquiry. Higher-level inquiries are redirected to a human. Call centres use Virtual customer assistance (VCA). VCA to predict and respond to customer inquiries outside of human interaction. Speech recognition can be challenging as human talks can be fast, slurry with varying emphasis and intonation, in different accents and incorrect grammar (RingCentral, https://www.ringcentral.com/gb/en/blog/5-predictions-for-the-new-age-of-voice/).

Text recognition is used in online chatbots replacing human agents along the customer journey. They answer frequently asked questions (FAQs) around topics, or provide personalised advice, cross-sell products or suggest sizes for users (Digital Transform, https://sidni.in/home/). This function has transformed customer engagement across websites and social media platforms. Examples include messaging bots on e-commerce sites with virtual agents and messaging apps (e.g., Slack and Facebook Messenger). When a customer initiates a dialog on a webpage via chat (chatbot), this customer is often interacting with a computer running specialised AI. If the chatbot can't interpret or address the question, a human employee intervenes to communicate directly with the customer. These noninterpretive instances are fed into a machine-learning computation system to improve the AI application for further interactions. Another example of text recognition is used to detect spam or phishing emails. Spam detection use NLP's text classification capabilities to scan emails for language that often indicates spam or phishing (Digital Transform, https://sidni.in/home/; IBM, https://www.ibm.com/topics/natural-language-processing). These indicators can include overuse of financial terms, characteristic bad grammar, threatening language, inappropriate urgency, misspelled company names, and more.

Sentiment analysis: NLP has become an essential business tool for uncovering hidden data insights from social media channels. Sentiment analysis can analyse language used in social media posts, responses, reviews, and more to extract attitudes and emotions in response to products, promotions, and events. Companies can use such information in product designs, advertising campaigns, and more.

Text summarisation uses NLP techniques to digest huge volumes of digital text and create summaries and synopses for indexes, research databases, or busy readers who don't have time to read full text. The best text summarisation applications use semantic reasoning and natural language generation (NLG) to add useful context and conclusions to summaries.

Topic Classification manifests in organising unstructured text into categories. It is used to gain insights from customer feedback by analysing myriads of open-ended responses to NPS surveys such as numbers of responses mentioning the topic of customer support; the frequently words used in the responses. Topic classification can be used to automate the process of tagging incoming support tickets and automatically route them to the right audience.

3.4 Application of Artificial Intelligence to Businesses

AI technologies are applied in industries and businesses to facilitate operations, accelerate innovation, improve customer experience, and reduce costs. In education, AI has been used to automate grading, track students' progress, and support tutors and students. AI could change where and how students learn. In retailing, AI can support inventory management (e.g., Amazon's analytical AI) (Liu et al., 2018). And in tourism, AI-powered robots can serve as tour guides to improve tourist participation (Ivanov et al., 2017). In human resource management, AI assists in screening and selecting suitable candidates (Agarwal et al., 2023).

In health care, AI can solve some of the greatest medical challenges through machine learning, computer vision, natural language processing, and forecasting and optimisation (Jiang et al., 2017). AI technologies have been used to predict, fight and understand the recent pandemic COVID-19. AI evolution enables health care organisations to improve patient outcomes, empower physicians with more accurate diagnostics (e.g., personalized medicine and X-ray readings) and targeted prevention capabilities, control costs by improving the operational performance of hospitals, optimising staffing resources, and taking action to reduce the number of hospital readmissions. Online virtual health assistants or chatbots help patients and other healthcare customers find medical information, schedule appointments, understand the billing process and complete other administrative processes.

In finance and banking, AI can enhance the speed, precision and effectiveness of human efforts. AI is used to collect biodata for the provision of financial advice for clients (e.g., Intuit Mint or TurboTax), monitor and identify fraudulent transactions in real time, adopt fast and accurate credit scoring, automate manually intense data management tasks. Banks use AI to improve their decision-making for loans, and to set credit limits and identify investment opportunities. AI virtual assistants are being used to improve and cut the costs of compliance with banking regulations, and handle transactions that don't require human intervention.

3.5 Conclusion

AI manifests in different forms and shapes with widespread applications. This book is focused on the service sector and its associations with human employees and customers in service organisations. Whilst arguably AI may replace, complement or supplement human employees, this book is not intended to debate on those and takes a stance that AI in general reinforces the role of humane employees to drive growth and boost labour productivity. In practice, AI in service organizations has functioned as part of service offerings provided to employees and customers primarily for facilitating employee task efficiency and improving customer experience (Prentice & Nguyen, 2020; Prentice et al., 2020a, 2020b, 2020c). The subsequent chapters on AI will elaborate how AI is associated with employees and customers.

References

Accenture. (2023). *What is artificial intelligence.* https://www.accenture.com/au-en/insights/artifi cial-intelligence-summary-index?c=acn_glb_brandexpressiongoogle_12088831&gclid=Cjw KCA&n=psgs_0321

Agarwal, S., Gupta, A., & Roshani, P. (2023). Redefining HRM with artificial intelligence and machine learning. In *The Adoption and Effect of Artificial Intelligence on Human Resources Management, Part A* (pp. 1–13). Emerald Publishing Limited.

Bulchand-Gidumal, J. (2022). Impact of artificial intelligence in travel, tourism, and hospitality. *Handbook of e-Tourism* (pp. 1943–1962). Springer International Publishing.

Burns, E., Laskowski, N., & Tucci, L. (2021). What is artificial intelligence. *Search Enterprise AI*.

Burns, E., Laskowski, N., & Tucci, L. (2023). *What is artificial intelligence (AI).* https://www.tec htarget.com/searchenterpriseai/definition/AI-Artificial-Intelligence?_gl=1*6mcqk7*_ga*NDI 4NTc5Ni4xNjM4MDI0MTU3*_ga_TQKE4GS5P9*MTYzODA1

Claveria, O., Monte, E., & Torra, S. (2015). Tourism demand forecasting with neural network models: Different ways of treating information. *International Journal of Tourism Research, 17*(5), 492–500.

Crowther-Heyck, H. (2005a). Mind and network. *IEEE Annals of the History of Computing, 27*(3), 104–104.

Crowther-Heyck, H. (2005b). *Herbert A. Simon: The bounds of reason in modern America.* JHU Press.

DigitalTransfrom. *Managing Sap S/4 HANA Greefield Implementation with Activate Methodology.* Think Beyond Tomorrow—Making Digital Transformation Simple. https://sidni.in/home/

Dubey, A. (2021). Digital learning in 2021 and its exciting benefits. *Anuragspace.* http://anurag space.com/page/3/

Grace, K., Salvatier, J., Dafoe, A., Zhang, B., & Evans, O. (2018). When will AI exceed human performance? Evidence from AI experts. *Journal of Artificial Intelligence Research, 62*, 729–754.

Hounguè, P., & Bigirimana, A. G. (2022). Leveraging pima dataset to diabetes prediction: Case study of deep neural network. *Journal of Computer and Communications, 10*(11), 15–28.

IBM. *What is natural language processing.* https://www.ibm.com/topics/natural-language-proces sing

IBM. *AI for customer service.* https://www.ibm.com/artificial-intelligence

Impact of Artificial Intelligence in Travel, Tourism, and Hospitality

Ivanov, S. H., Webster, C., & Berezina, K. (2017). Adoption of robots and service automation by tourism and hospitality companies. *Revista Turismo & Desenvolvimento, 27*(28), 1501–1517.

Java Point. *History of artificial intelligence.* https://www.javatpoint.com/history-of-artificial-intell igence. Accessed Feb 20, 2023

Jiang, F., Jiang, Y., Zhi, H., Dong, Y., Li, H., Ma, S., Wang, Y., Dong, Q., Shen, H., & Wang, Y. (2017). Artificial intelligence in healthcare: Past, present and future. *Stroke and Vascular Neurology, 2*(4), 230–243.

Kaplan, A., & Haenlein, M. (2019). Siri, Siri, in my hand: Who's the fairest in the land? On the interpretations, illustrations, and implications of artificial intelligence. *Business Horizons, 62*(1), 15–25.

Khpcahoba, H. B. (2022). *Professional English for software developers.* https://ugatu.su/media/upl oads/MainSite/Ob%20universitete/Izdateli/El_izd/2022%E2%80%90117.pdf

Kulkarni, A., Kariyal, A. V., Dhanush, V., & Singh, P. N. (2021, September). Speech to Indian Sign Language Translator. In *3rd International Conference on Integrated Intelligent Computing Communication & Security (ICIIC 2021)* (pp. 278–285). Atlantis Press.

LeCun, Y., Bengio, Y., & Hinton, G. (2015). Deep learning. *Nature, 521*(7553), 436–444.

Liu, C., Zoph, B., Neumann, M., Shlens, J., Hua, W., Li, L. J., Fei-Fei, L., Yuille, A., Huang, J. and Murphy, K., & Murphy, K. (2018). Progressive neural architecture search. In *Proceedings of the European conference on computer vision (ECCV)* (pp. 19–34).

McCarthy, J., Minsky, M. L., Rochester, N., & Shannon, C. E. (2006). A proposal for the dartmouth summer research project on artificial intelligence, august 31, 1955. *AI Magazine, 27*(4), 12–12.

McCarthy, J., & Wright, P. (2004). Technology as experience. *Interactions, 11*(5), 42–43.

Melián-González, S., & Bulchand-Gidumal, J. (2016). Worker word of mouth on the internet: Influence on human resource image, job seekers and employees. *International Journal of Manpower, 37*(4), 709–723.

NetApp. *What is artificial intelligence.* https://www-origin.netapp.com/artificial-intelligence/what-is-artificial-intelligence/

Newell, A., & Simon, H. A. (1972). *Human problem solving* (Vol. 104, No. 9). Prentice-hall.

Norvig, P. R., & Intelligence, S. A. (2002). *A modern approach.* Prentice Hall.

Prentice, C., & Nguyen, M. (2020). Engaging and retaining customers with AI and employee service. *Journal of Retailing and Consumer Services, 56*, 102186.

Prentice, C., Dominique Lopes, S., & Wang, X. (2020a). The impact of artificial intelligence and employee service quality on customer satisfaction and loyalty. *Journal of Hospitality Marketing & Management, 29*(7), 739–756.

Prentice, C., Dominique Lopes, S., & Wang, X. (2020b). Emotional intelligence or artificial intelligence–an employee perspective. *Journal of Hospitality Marketing & Management, 29*(4), 377–403.

Prentice, C., Weaven, S., & Wong, I. A. (2020c). Linking AI quality performance and customer engagement: The moderating effect of AI preference. *International Journal of Hospitality Management, 90*, 102629.

Reynoso, E. (2021). *A complete history of artificial intelligence.* https://www.g2.com/articles/his tory-of-artificial-intelligence. Accessed Feb 20, 2023.

RingCentral Team. *5 predictions for the new age of voice.* https://www.ringcentral.com/gb/en/blog/ 5-predictions-for-the-new-age-of-voice/

Russell, S., Dewey, D., & Tegmark, M. (2015). Research priorities for robust and beneficial artificial intelligence. *Ai Magazine, 36*(4), 105–114.

Russell, S., & Norvig, P. (1995). A modern, agent-oriented approach to introductory artificial intelligence. *Acm Sigart Bulletin, 6*(2), 24–26.

Russell, S. & Norvig, P. (2002). *Artificial intelligence: A modern approach* (2nd ed.). New Jersey: Prentice Hall.

Schroer, A. (2022). *What is artificial intelligence.* https://builtin.com/artificial-intelligence?fbclid= IwAR3nPrSkaiHeKlz_vC-qOMB91KnFmp8CtoQsBDICMHWMY27QjTi_TFAfaI4

Šukjurovs, I., Zvirgzdiņa, R., & Jeromanova-Maura, S. (2019, June). Artificial intelligence in workplaces and how it will affect employment in Latvia. In *Environment. Technologies. Resources. Proceedings of the international scientific and practical conference* (Vol. 2, pp. 154–158).

Tableau. *What is the history of artificial intelligence.* https://www.tableau.com/data-insights/ai/history. Accessed Feb 20, 2023.

Winston, P. H. (1992). *Artificial intelligence.* Addison-Wesley Longman Publishing Co., Inc.

Chapter 4
Leveraging Emotional Intelligence for Employees

Abstract Since the incept of emotional intelligence (EI) in early 1990s, the concept has been extensively discussed in business and academia as an individual' intelligence in the emotional domain. This intelligence is often viewed as a predictor of personal achievements on both personal and professional accounts. Prentice's book "emotional intelligence and marketing" published in 2019 has reconceptualised this concept as a marketing strategy from a marketing perspective and how frontline service employees can use this strategy to achieve optimal marketing performance. Taking a similar stance, this book approaches from the perspectives of both employees and customers and discusses how emotional intelligence can be utilised as a service offered by customer-contact employees to shape their attitudes and behaviours in the business context. Employees are often referred to as internal customers and are equally important as external customers for the organisation as one of the key contributors of value creation in the service dominant logic era. Their emotional intelligence can be treated as internal service for themselves and external service to customers. The current chapter discusses how employees' EI as internal service can be used for better wellbeing and job-related outcomes with a focus on those who have virtual and physical contact with external customers. To understand how EI functions for these intended outcomes, the chapter first analyses the job nature of service employees, then discussed the relationship between EI and employees. Two empirical studies are conducted in the hospitality sector to support this discussion.

4.1 Emotional Work

Service employees in the service industries generally perform a necessary communications function between customers and the firm and play a significant role in influencing customer attitudes and behaviours which affect business performance and organizational effectiveness (Prentice, 2013a, 2013b). Situated in boundary spanning positions, however, these employees are caught between the demand of customers for attention and quality service provision and organizational demands for efficiency and productivity. The most challenging part of the job as customer-contact employees in the service industry is to manage customers' emotions. When service fails to deliver as expected, customers could be harsh and critical towards the service employee. This response is often exacerbated when customers experience some unpleasant encounters. At such times they could be wildly emotional and abusive. The customer-contact employees might be severely accused or abused, even if they have done nothing wrong (Prentice, 2013a, 2013b). However, they still have to behave in a friendly manner and present a smiling face towards the abusive customers and try their best to serve them. In other words, they perform emotional labour constantly dealing with customers' emotional outburst. In most cases, particularly in hospitality and tourism sector, service employees are generally underpaid, under-trained, overworked, stressed, and susceptible to burnout (Singh, 2000). Despite this status quo, they are required to perform emotional labour in accordance with organisational display rules (Prentice et al., 2013). Emotional labour is the nature of their work and stipulated in these employees' job description.

4.2   Emotional Labour

Emotional labour refers to managing emotions for a wage, involving enhancing, faking, or suppressing emotions to modify the emotional expression (Hochschild, 1979). According to Hochischild (1979), emotional labour is performed as an act, either surface or deep acting. Surface acting involves simulating and feigning emotions that are not actually felt or experienced, and often performed by the labourer complying with display rules. Deep acting refers to experiencing or feeling the emotions that one wishes to display.

Emotional labour has its salient benefits for both organizations and individuals. The display feelings during service interactions have a strong impact on the quality of service transactions, the attractiveness of the interpersonal climate, and the experience of emotion itself (Hochischild, 1979). Performing emotional work is not only conducive to providing the service employee with a prescribed set of responses and patterns of behaviour that can facilitate the dynamic encounter communication, but also to selling more products, dealing with customer complaints adequately, ensuring the smooth-running communicative interactions.

Despite the benefits of emotional labour, researchers suggest that managing emotions for pay can be detrimental to the employees. The pivot on which emotional labour revolves is the fact that there is a discrepancy between emotions expected and those actually experienced. "What is functional for the organization may well be dysfunctional" for the actor (Ashforth and Humphrey (1993, p. 96). Portraying emotions that are not felt (surface acting) creates the strain of emotive dissonance that is akin to cognitive dissonance. The dissonance may cause the labourer to feel false and hypocritical. Ultimately, such dissonance leads to personal and work-related maladjustment, such as poor self-esteem, depression, cynicism and alienation from work (cited by Ashforth & Humphrey, 1993). On the other hand, deep acting may distort these reactions and impair one's sense of authentic self, and ultimately lead to self-alienation and may impair one's ability to recognize or even experience genuine emotion (Ashforth & Humphrey, 1993).

When a person is unable to express script emotions, a condition of burnout may be experienced. Emotional labour has been overwhelmingly cited as a detrimental factor of employee burnout. The incidence of burnout has negative consequences such as low employee self-esteem, health problems, absenteeism, turnover, job dissatis-faction and poor performance with serious consequences for both individuals and organisations. Managing burnout would revoke those negative consequences. What is burnout?

4.3 Burnout

Burnout in the organizational context is a psychological syndrome resulting from chronic stress at work that occurs when an employee's emotional and energy resources are depleted. Job burnout is one of the two psychological processes of job demands-resources model (JD-R). According to Maslach et al. (2001), there are three components of burnout syndrome, namely: emotional exhaustion, depersonalization, and inefficiency. The state of emotional exhaustion is the depletion of emotion and energy in an employee from interactions with others (e.g., co-workers, customers). Depersonalisation refers to the disconnection of feeling and the display of callous behaviour in employees towards others (e.g., customers). Inefficiency or reduced personal accomplishment is the feeling of low professional morale and reduction in productivity or capability of the employee.

Prior research suggests that emotional exhaustion and depersonalization are highly correlated (Johnson & Spector, 2007). The components of emotional exhaustion and depersonalization tend to arise from the stressors from work and social interaction exertion that depletes resources, whereas the sense of inefficiency emerges from a lack of job resources to complete the job function (e.g., inadequate information, time scarcity, or undersupply of tools). One would first experience emotional exhaus-tion, which would further develop into depersonalization as a maladaptive coping behaviour to deal with the exhausted resources in order handle the job demands. However, the other dimension—inefficiency is found to be developed indepen-dently from emotional exhaustion and depersonalization and have a relatively low correlation with the latter two.

Hobfoll's (1989) conservation of resources (COR) theory explains how burnout is an individual's reaction to the loss or threat of loss to their emotional resources and their lack of regaining those resources following its expenditure. In the case of service employees, the frequency of interactions with customers leads to constant emotional exertion from these employees which leads to job burnout. The theory indicates that employees work to conserve resources. However, the constant exposure to work related interactions will cause them to deplete resources until they feel no longer having' sufficient resources left to handle the confronted stressors and thus experiencing burnout.

4.4 Emotional Labour and Burnout

Both surface acting and deep acting causes service employees to deplete resources as they require conscious effort and focus from them to exert the required actions. Surface acting involves two strategies, suppressing felt emotions and faking the display of unfelt emotions. The actions taken to surface act causes emotional dissonance to be experienced amongst employees. This refers to the structural discrepancy between felt emotions and the emotional display that is both required and appropriate in their working context. This display of inauthentic emotions over a period of time can result in employees feeling detached from their true feelings and the feelings of others around and the true emotion to be divulged, which gradually lead to job burnout experienced by employees.

Although both surface acting and deep acting require employees to expand resources in regulating emotions, be it felt, expressed or both, the authenticity of emotions both felt and expressed of the deep acting process has been consistently demonstrated to realign the experienced emotional dissonance and lead to depersonalisation. For instance, when handling an unpleasant customer, employees may be initially disturbed by the customer's behaviour before internalizing the thought that the customer may have had a negative experience during the day, causing them to replace the initial negative emotions towards the customer with sympathy and compassion. This example of deep acting depicts the realignment of felt and displayed emotions, resulting in only the need for resources to be invested to follow display rules and not the excess management of experienced emotional dissonance. Although it requires more resources to be expanded to regulate inner emotions, deep acting can be offset by resources gained from reduced emotional dissonance experienced and positive reactions from customers who are able to perceive the authentic expressions. Emotional intelligence has been evidently proved to moderate or ameliorate the negative consequences of emotional labour (Prentice et al., 2013).

4.5 Emotional Intelligence and Emotional Work

4.5.1 Leveraging Emotional Intelligence for Emotional Labour

Studies have been undertaken to demonstrate and confirm the important relationships between emotional intelligence and emotional labour in both laboratory and field studies. Conceptualised into four hierarchical branches, emotional intelligence may be capable of adjusting the EL process. For example, the first branch may influence surface acting (simulating emotions that are not actually felt). This contention may be explained as follows. Emotions can only be simulated effectively in circumstances where the perception is accurate, thereby allowing the simulation to fit the context. A nurse may for example simulate sympathy for a patient who has deep concerns about his or her health. In this circumstance the process of simulation is dependent on the nurse possessing the required perception of the patient's concerns. The fourth branch can facilitate deep acting (attempts to experience or feel the emotions that one wishes to display). Mayer et al. (2001) indicated that the four branches function hierarchically. The perception of emotions acts as both the most basic branch and as a precursor to the other three. Since it occupies the top branch, emotional management may be viewed as the most complex. Once a perception has been acquired, emotions may be deployed in order to facilitate conscious or unconscious thought. Emotional knowledge can subsequently be transferred to behaviours (Mayer et al., 2001).

With simulated customer service representatives, Daus (2002) found that people who could read emotions in faces felt less of an emotional load from the job, and people who could better manage emotions in themselves felt more of such load. In actual customer service representatives and sales personnel, Cage et al. (2004) found that with respect to the dimensions of emotional intelligence, understanding emotions was positively related with the faking positive aspect of emotional labour, whereas expressing negative emotions was negatively associated with actual sales performance. Employing police officers as a sample, Daus et al. (2004a, 2004b) quantitatively demonstrated a definitive link between aspects of emotional labour and emotional intelligence. Based on these studies, Daus and Ashkanasy (2005) concluded that emotional intelligence and its four branches proposed by Mayer and Salovey (1997) were significantly associated with deep acting of emotional labour; while the branch understanding emotions was associated with surface acting, the other three branches were significantly related to suppressing negative emotions; finally, using emotions was related to faking positive emotions.

4.5.2   Leveraging Emotional Intelligence for Burnout

Prior studies suggest that emotionally intelligent employees are aware of the expected emotions to display in a given interpersonal interaction and are more adaptive and flexible in regulating emotions to fit the situation. EI is argued to play an important role in assisting employees to accurately perceive situational demands through being able to better empathise with customers and having superior awareness and regulation competency over their own emotions. All of which are the necessary social skills needed to manage the interactions and the motivation to push themselves to effectively serve the customers. These skills and competencies are crucial to deep act, since engaging the deep acting process requires a clear understanding of the appropriate emotions to internalize for each respective customer, and the ability to effectively convey felt emotions. In this sense, employees with a high level of EI are able to correctly identify the required emotions to internalize and have the ability to better communicate with the customer. This in turn furnishes the FLE with a higher ability to replenish or attain emotional resources that is necessary to potentially increase job engagement and further attenuate job burnout.

Employees with a high level of EI are potentially able to strength job engagement and moderate appropriate acting and weaken its effect on job burnout. For example, in a classic spy film such as Mission Impossible, the villain is typically shown to seemingly befriend the protagonist, only to be revealed as a "plot twist" in a later part of the film of his/her antagonist nature. As viewers, we are able to identify that these characters are surface acting as we know that behind their friendly behaviour hides inner feelings of negative emotions and opposing ideologies. These villains are typically shown to have high EI as they are aware of their own emotions and emotions of others, which they use to suemployeessfully establish relationships with the rest of the cast. Throughout this, though some may show signs of emotional dissonance, they are shown to be consistently engaged in their antagonistic role, which is reinforced especially after each suemployeessful antagonistic deed.

Consistent with Hobfoll's (2002) COR theory, which suggests that the more resources one possesses are more likely to experience better outcomes than those with fewer resources, EI can be viewed as a resource capacity to buffer and better protect employees from the depletion of resources as a result of engaging in emotional labour behaviour. In addition, surface actors may further attain resources from handling customers due to having superior self-awareness, self-regulation, social skills and empathy. Coupled with the expectation of lower loss of resources, higher levels of EI increase the potential to increase job engagement, achieve a surplus of resources while surface acting, and reducing burnout. By the same token, having high EI will also enable employees to be more engaged in their jobs, having more successful interactions with customers, and perform deep acting, consequently strengthening weakening its effect on job burnout.

To support the foregoing discussion, an empirical study was conducted to understand the relationship between emotional intelligence, emotional labour, and burnout. The hotel setting is opted for this study as service employees in the hotel sector perform emotional work and have intensive interpersonal contact with hotel clients. The sample and data collection procedures are detailed in the following section.

4.6 Empirical Study 1

4.6.1 Sample and Data Collection Procedure

The respondent sample has been drawn from service employees working in hotel resorts. Five resorts participated in this study with assistance from their respective human resources managers. The paper-and-pencil surveys were either delivered to the participants or made available in the employee refreshment area. The human resources manager disseminated a message announcing a draw of raffle tickets for two $100 gift cards to employees with a view to encouraging participation.

Of the 1000 surveys distributed, 578 usable responses were returned (58%). Of the total usable sample, 260 (45%) were male, and 318 (55%) were female. The participants ranged from 18 to 55 years and above, with most in the age group between 18 and 25 (56%), followed by the 26–35 group (26%), by 36–55 group (12%), and finally those over 55 (4%). Almost 48% of the respondents had some college education. Over 65% of respondents earned less than $40,000 a year, indicative that service employees are relatively poorly paid. The respondents occupied a variety of positions including bar tenders, bellman, cashier, concierge, front desk agent, server, and sales representative. About one-third of the respondents had been employed by their current organization for three to five years, with 5% having more than 20 years of experience.

4.6.2 Instruments

A self-report questionnaire was developed using a paper–pencil test to collect information. The questions investigated EL, burnout, emotional intelligence. Since the present study involved a survey of hospitality organisations, the research used the Hospitality Emotional Labour Scale (HELS) first developed by Chu and Murrmann (2006). This scale was developed specifically to measure the EL presentation of hospitality employees and consists of three factors: surface acting, genuine acting and deep acting. To be consistent with the two acting strategies of the original EL concept, the two items that had been developed to measure genuine acting were excluded from the present investigation. To estimate emotional intelligence, the present study used the self-report EI Test (SREIT) designed by Schutte et al. (1998), which was based on Salovey and Mayer's ability model (1990). The 33-item self-report measure includes items such as "By looking at their facial expression, I recognize the emotions people are experiencing" and "I easily recognize my emotions as I experience them." To measure participant burnout the researchers used the Maslach Burnout Inventory (MBI). The inventory is a scale consisting of three dimensions, namely emotional exhaustion (9 items), diminished personal accomplishment (7 items), and depersonalisation (6 items). In the case of emotional exhaustion the sample item that was provided is "I feel emotionally drained from my work"; for diminished personal accomplishment "I can't deal effectively with the problems of my recipients"; and for depersonalisation; "I have become more callous towards people since I took this job," Although originally designed for service workers, the MBI has been applied to other occupations including computer professionals and police officers.

4.6.3 Findings and Discussion

Emotional labour and burnout. The study shows that both surface acting and deep acting had significant effects on three dimensions of burnout: the beta values for surface/deep acting—emotional exhaustion are 0.39 ($p < 0.0005$) and 0.08 ($p < 0.05$), 0.11 ($p < 0.05$) and 0.12 ($p < 0.0005$) for surface/deep acting—diminished personal accomplishment, and 0.37 ($p < 0.0005$) and 0.14 ($p < 0.005$) for surface/deep acting—depersonalisation. Although some studies have reported that only surface acting is related to burnout, this finding supported Ashforth and Humphrey's (1993) proposition and the findings of Mikolajczak et al.'s (2007) study. The inconsistency may have arisen as a result of differences between the sampling frames. Given the intensifying competition that has been prevalent in recent years and the organizational restructuring which has affected the hospitality industry, service employees face the threat of retrenchment as well as excessive job demands (see Lo & Lamm, 2005). In order to keep their jobs, they may feel obliged to follow organizational rules to "act." Lack of spontaneity and unwillingness in their acting may eventually lead to job dissatisfaction and burnout. If these employees perceive that it is necessary to act genuinely (deep acting) but are unable or unwilling to do so (due to low wages), they may suffer low self-esteem or self-alienation, eventually leading to burnout.

The study provides new insights into deep acting strategies and suggests that researchers should be cautious about promoting deep acting. This finding is consistent with Ashforth and Humphrey's argument that EL is dysfunctional and that ultimately "deep acting may ultimately lead to self-alienation … the masking or reworking of authentic emotions that one would otherwise prefer to express has been linked to psychological and physical dysfunctions" (see Ashforth & Humphrey, 1993, p 97).

4.6.4 *Leveraging Emotional Intelligence for Emotional Labour and Burnout*

The testing of moderation has shown that emotional intelligence reduced all three dimensions of burnout through surface or deep acting. Specifically, emotional intelligence significantly reduced the levels of surface/deep acting—emotional exhaustion ($\beta = -0.36, p < 0.0005$; $\beta = -0.18, p < 0.05$), surface/deep acting—diminished personal achievement ($\beta = -0.16, p < 0.0005$; $\beta = -0.09, p < 0.05$), surface/deep acting—depersonalisation ($\beta = -0.19, p < 0.0005$; $\beta = -0.19, p < 0.0005$).

The results from the moderation analyses indicate that the incorporation of emotional intelligence as a moderator can be a remedy for reducing EL-caused burnout. Emotional intelligence moderates the relationship between the two EL acting processes and burnout. This finding is consistent with the Daus and Ashkenansy (2005) assertion that emotional intelligence plays a significant role in jobs such as customer service representative which demand high EL. Service encounters between employees and customers often involve a strong emotional component due to unpredictable situational factors and demanding customers (see Ashforth & Humphrey, 1993). Employee emotional intelligence may facilitate service transactions by facilitating the management of one's own emotions and those of others. Smooth transactions lead to fewer customer complaints and consequently to low employee stress which is a precursor of burnout.

4.6.5 *Leveraging Emotional Intelligence for Employee Satisfaction and Loyalty*

Given that employee EI can be utilised to moderate the negative consequence of performing emotional labour, despite the constant pressure of dealing with emotional encounter, this emotional competence can exert influence on job satisfaction and retention/loyalty. This can be construed by emotional contagion theory. Emotions are contagious. According to Hatfield et al. (1993), one person's emotions can affect others through automatic mimicry and expression synchronization. Facing someone expressing an emotion can evoke similar emotions in oneself in an unconscious manner (Goleman, 1995).

In the case of the interpersonal interactions between service employees and customers, emotions manifested in customers will inevitably affect employees who become affected by customers' emotions. Emotional exhaustion is often inevitable for employees with a low level of emotional competence. Employees with a higher level of emotional intelligence generally perform better and receive less complaints from customers through managing emotions associated with the service encounter (Chiva & Alegre, 2008; Joseph et al., 2015; Prentice & King, 2011a, 2011b, 2013; Wolfe & Kim, 2013; Sy et al., 2006). Consequently, employee emotional intelligence affects employee job satisfaction (Brunetto et al., 2012; Kafetsios & Zampetakis, 2008; Sy et al., 2006). Job satisfaction influences employee retention or loyalty (Stempien & Loeb, 2002).

Job satisfaction generally refers to an emotional state resulting from one's job experiences or the level of content that an employee feels about his or her work (Locke, 1976; Spector, 1997). This is often reflected in financial (e.g., salary, promotion) and non-financial facets (e.g., communication, job conditions; Spector, 1997). Job satisfaction has been widely discussed as an antecedent of employee performance, turnover intention, and job retention (e.g., Abbas et al., 2014; Carsten & Spector, 1987; Harris et al., 2009). Employees with a high level of emotional intelligence tend to enjoy their job, happy employees likely achieve more and receive better monetary and non-monetary benefits/rewards (compliments by customers), consequently these employees are less likely to leave their job. Highly emotional intelligent employees are better able to regulate and manage emotions (Prentice et al., 2013).

To gain insight into this discussion, a second study was conducted in the casino to understand how emotional intelligence affects employee satisfaction and retention. The casino sector is a people-intensive business that service employees are required to perform emotional labour during interactions with customers. The procedures of the empirical study are documented as follows.

4.7   Empirical Study 2

4.7.1   Sample

The study was undertaken with service employees in casinos with a focus on dealers. These employees are in frontline positions directly dealing with customers. The data were collected randomly from dealers working in one of the casinos in Macau. After 4 weeks, 738 usable match-up responses were received. Of the total usable dealer sample, 51.8% of respondents were male, and 48.2% were female. The age of participants ranged from 21 to 55 years old and above. Fifty-two percent of respondents fell in the age group of 26–35, 31% in the 36–45 group, 13% in the 21–25 group, and only 2% in the 46–55 group. The majority (66%) only had high school education; about 15% graduated from colleges.

4.7.2   Instruments

Job satisfaction was measured by using MacDonald and MacIntyre's (1997) generic job satisfaction scale. The items were consulted with several casino managers and a human resource senior executive to ensure suitability. The items that were used to assess dealer satisfaction include, for instance, "I receive recognition for a job well done;" "I feel secure about my job at this casino." A seven-point Likert scale was used to show respondents' degree of agreement (1—strongly disagree to 7—strongly agree). Items that had loadings below 0.50 were excluded from further analysis. The reliability for this scale was 0.884.

Employee retention was assessed by adapting Kelloway et al. (1996) measure asking the respondent to indicate their intention to leave the job and explore other career opportunities within next 12 months. For example, "How likely do you think you would get out of your current job within next 12 months;" and "How likely it is that you would explore other career opportunities within next 12 months." A seven-point Likert scale was used to show respondents' degree of agreement (1—strongly disagree to 7—strongly agree). The reliability value for this scale was 0.790.

4.7.3   Findings and Discussion

The results show that dealer emotional intelligence has a significant effect on their job satisfaction ($\beta = 0.609$, $p < 0.0005$) and retention ($\beta = 0.494$, $p < 0.001$). The study also shows that job satisfaction mediates the relationship between employee emotional intelligence and retention and indicates that individual emotional abilities are important to maintain a positive job attitude. The results are shown in Table 4.1.

Table 4.1 Results for relationships between the study variables

Variables	Job satisfaction	Employee retention	Retention with satisfaction as mediator
Gender	0.053*	0.047	–
Age	−0.038	0.037	–
Tenure	0.028	0.072	–
EI	0.609***	0.494***	0.09
Job satisfaction		0.652**	
Employee retention			

Note $*p < 0.05$, $**p < 0.001$, $***p < 0.0005$

The results indicate that the dealer needs these emotional abilities to ensure positive interactions with gaming customers, hence, to enjoy and remain in the croupier occupation, as emotional intelligence refers to one's abilities to appraise, utilize and manage emotions, Job satisfaction is reflective of job security, support, and recognition from the management. Dealers work in a very emotionally charged environment. Each encounter with gamblers has high emotional contents due to the nature of gambling and emotions associated with gambling outcomes. The dealer must be able to understand and manage the emotional encounters to appreciate this occupation. Underlying such emotional abilities is the potential to receive recognition from both customers and the management. Income and recognition therefore influence dealer job satisfaction which encourages dealers to stay in this occupation.

4.8 Implications and Conclusion

The current chapter positions emotional intelligence as an internal service for employees to manage their emotional work and job satisfaction and retention. Study 1 in this chapter demonstrates the capacity of emotional intelligence to reduce the incidence of burnout that is associated with acting. Since training and development can provide effective means of enhancing activity, the relevant training should be provided for existing frontline employees, particularly in the case of those who perform emotional labour but are unable to act appropriately. It is evident that higher levels of emotional intelligence can reduce the likelihood of burnout and may improve performance. Emotional intelligence testing can also be used for the purposes of recruitment and selection. The conduct of such testing could help human resource managers to identify suitable candidates.

As shown in the second study of this chapter, employee emotional intelligence significantly influences job satisfaction and retention. Assessment of emotional competence should also be included when recruiting service employees. Some firms have included emotional competence in job recruitment. Emotional intelligence training is rather limited.

Employee loyalty and retention has financial implication for the organization as recruiting and training new staff is rather costly. Research also shows that employee retention often results from, inter alia, job satisfaction and supervisor support. Hence, it is imperative to identify the factors that affect employee attitude. Employee emotional intelligence, as shown in this chapter, is a significant factor. Practitioners should look into appropriate service offerings catered for customers. Different segments of customers differ in their service expectations and demands (Prentice, 2013a, 2013b). The management should work closely with service employees who are in direct contact with customers in order to better understand and satisfy customer expectations.

References

Abbas, M., Raja, U., Darr, W., & Bouckenooghe, D. (2014). Combined effects of perceived politics and psychological capital on job satisfaction, turnover intentions, and performance. *Journal of Management, 40*(7), 1813–1830.

Ashforth, B. E., & Humphrey, R. H. (1993). Emotional labor in service roles: The influence of identity. *Academy of Management Review, 18*(1), 88–115.

Brunetto, Y., Teo, S. T., Shacklock, K., & Farr-Wharton, R. (2012). Emotional intelligence, job satisfaction, well-being and engagement: Explaining organisational commitment and turnover intentions in policing. *Human Resource Management Journal, 22*(4), 428–441.

Carsten, J. M., & Spector, P. E. (1987). Unemployment, job satisfaction, and employee turnover: A meta-analytic test of the Muchinsky model. *Journal of Applied Psychology, 72*(3), 374–381.

Chiva, R., & Alegre, J. (2008). Emotional intelligence and job satisfaction: The role of organizational learning capability. *Personnel Review, 37*(6), 680–701.

Goleman, D. (1995). *Emotional Intelligence.* Bloomsbury.

Harris, K. J., Wheeler, A. R., & Kacmar, K. M. (2009). Leader–member exchange and empowerment: Direct and interactive effects on job satisfaction, turnover intentions, and performance. *The Leadership Quarterly, 20*(3), 371–382.

Hatfield, E., Cacioppo, J. T., & Rapson, R. L. (1993). Emotional contagion. *Current Directions in Psychological Science, 2*(3), 96–100.

Hochschild, A. R. (1979). Emotion work, feeling rules, and social structure. *American journal of sociology,* 551–575.

Johnson, H. A. M., & Spector, P. E. (2007). Service with a smile: Do emotional intelligence, gender, and autonomy moderate the emotional labor process? *Journal of Occupational Health Psychology, 12*(4), 319.

Joseph, D. L., Jin, J., Newman, D. A., & O'Boyle, E. H. (2015). Why does self-reported emotional intelligence predict job performance? A meta-analytic investigation of mixed EI. *Journal of Applied Psychology, 100*(2), 298.

Kafetsios, K., & Zampetakis, L. A. (2008). Emotional intelligence and job satisfaction: Testing the mediatory role of positive and negative affect at work. *Personality and Individual Differences, 44*(3), 712–722.

Locke, E. A. (1976). The nature and causes of job satisfaction. In M. D. Dunnette (Ed.), *Handbook of industrial and organizational psychology* (pp. 1297–1349). Rand McNally.

Macdonald, S., & MacIntyre, P. (1997). The generic job satisfaction scale: Scale development and its correlates. *Employee Assistance Quarterly, 13*(2), 1–16.

Mayer, J. D., & Salovey, P. (1997). What is emotional intelligence? In P. Salovey & D. Sluyter (Eds.), Emotional development and emotional intelligence: Educational implications. New York: Basic Books.

Mayer, J. D., Salovey, P., Caruso, D. R., & Sitarenios, G. (2001). Emotional intelligence as a standard intelligence.

Prentice, C. (2013a). Service quality perceptions and customer retention in casinos. *International Journal of Contemporary Hospitality Management., 25*(3), 49–64.

Prentice, C. (2013b). Emotional labour and its consequences: The moderating effect of emotional intelligence. In *Individual Sources, Dynamics, and Expressions of Emotion* (Vol. 9, pp. 187–201). Emerald Group Publishing Limited.

Prentice, C., Chen, P. J., & King, B. (2013). Employee performance outcomes and burnout following the presentation-of-self in customer-service contexts. *International Journal of Hospitality Management., 35*(2013), 225–236.

Prentice, C., & King, B. (2011a). Emotional intelligence and the service performance of casino frontline employees. *Tourism and Hospitality Research., 11*(1), 49–66.

Prentice, C., & King, B. (2011b). Relationship marketing in the casino industry. *Journal of Vacation Marketing., 17*(1), 51–63.

Salovey, P., & Mayer, J. D. (1990). Emotional intelligence. *Imagination, Cognition and Personality, 9*(3), 185–211.

Singh, J. (2000). Performance productivity and quality of frontline employees in service organizations. *Journal of Marketing, 64*(2), 15–34.

Spector, P.E. (1997). *Job satisfaction: Application, assessment, causes and consequences.* Thousand Oaks, CA: SAGE

Stempien, L. R., & Loeb, R. C. (2002). Differences in job satisfaction between general education and special education teachers: Implications for retention. *Remedial and Special Education, 23*(5), 258–267.

Sy, T., Tram, S., & O'Hara, L. A. (2006). Relation of employee and manager emotional intelligence to job satisfaction and performance. *Journal of vocational behaviour, 68*(3).

Wolfe, K., & Kim, H. J. (2013). Emotional intelligence, job satisfaction, and job tenure among hotel managers. *Journal of Human Resources in Hospitality & Tourism, 12*(2), 175–191.

Chapter 5
Leveraging Emotional Intelligence for Customers

Abstract This chapter analyses how emotional intelligence (EI) demonstrated by service employees as external service can be incorporated into the personal service encounter in the service sector to enhance customer experience and relationship with the service provider. This chapter focuses on service operations in the service industry to support contributions to theory of the antecedents and outcomes of achieving high employee emotional intelligence. This chapter first discusses the link of service quality to business profitability. Second, the characteristics of service encounter and the role of service employees are analysed. The discussion extends to how emotional intelligence exhibited by employees can induce a successful encounter and garner positive service experience, followed by explaining the role of customers' emotional intelligence in service experience and other related outcomes.

5.1   Linking Service Quality and Business Profitability

The marketing literature shows that customer acquisition is an expensive process. The firm often benefits when marketers nurture on-going relationships with acquired customers with intention to build a long-term business relationship with them, ultimately achieve customer loyalty, and retention. Customer retention is a more cost-effective approach and has direct impact on company profitability (e.g., Hallowell, 1996; Prentice, 2013; Rust & Zahorik, 1993). According to Reichheld (1996), a five percent increase in customer retention can lead to a 25–85% increase in a firm's general revenue. The rate of increase depends on the industry.

Given the link between customer retention and business profitability, the factors that lead to customer retention have impact on profitability. Customer service-quality perceptions and customer satisfaction are commonly acknowledged to affect customer loyalty and company profitability (see Hallowell, 1996; see Prentice, 2013; Zeithaml et al., 1996). Service quality has been widely acknowledged as an important key to competitive advantage and customer loyalty (e.g., Caruana, 2002; Zeithaml et al., 1996). Service quality in the service industry is particularly regarded as an important factor in customer satisfaction and retention (Johnson & Beale, 2002;

C. Prentice, *Leveraging Emotional and Artificial Intelligence for Organisational Performance*, https://doi.org/10.1007/978-981-99-1865-2_5

Prentice, 2013), and in seeking a competitive advantage. "Perceived service quality" is a consumer's judgement or perception of an entity's overall excellence or superiority, often as a result of comparing expectations with perceived performance (Parasuraman et al., 1988).

As an antecedent of customer satisfaction, service quality can be measured at the encounter level to predict encounter satisfaction, or measured as a function of multiple experiences to predict overall service satisfaction. The evaluation of one encounter may be correlated with the measures of overall satisfaction, which is correlated with overall perceptions of service quality (Bitner & Hubbert, 1994). Although overall service quality predicts customer loyalty and ultimately a firm's profitability, every service encounter experience adds up to the cumulative perception and judgement.

Numerous studies have provided empirical evidence of a chain relationship between service quality, customer satisfaction, and loyalty (e.g., Olorunniwo et al., 2006; Prentice, 2013; Shi et al., 2014). However, service quality is not necessarily directly related to customer satisfaction, as the level of overall quality service is expected unless some service elements (tangible or intangible) exceed customer expectations and are transferred into memorable experiences (Prentice, 2013). Consumers opt to purchase and consume the service to acquire such experiences (Sandström et al., 2008). These memorable events that occur during service encounters affect their attitudes (e.g., satisfaction) and behaviours (e.g., purchase, loyalty behaviours) toward the service provider (Williams et al., 2020). Therefore, customers' memorable experiences likely play a role in the relationship chain of service quality, customer satisfaction, and loyalty. Customer experience results from service encounter interactions through pre, during and post-purchase or consumption journey between customers and service providers. From a marketing perspective, customer experience is largely resulted from service quality delivered through the service encounter (Mossberg, 2007).

A successful company usually dominates the quality dimension by not only supplying a quality tangible product, but also by fostering good interactions between customers and employees. In people-intensive industries such as hospitality and tourism, a successful personal encounter between service employees and customers is key to overall service quality assessment and positive customer experience (e.g., Farrell et al., 2001; Vada et al., 2020).

5.2 The Role of Service Encounter in Service Quality

The importance of dyadic encounters between buyer and seller–client and service provider in service marketing lies in the interpersonal contact during service encounter being a factor in customers' perception of service quality and determining customer experience and satisfaction (Bitner et al., 1994). Other researchers (e.g., Prentice, 2013, 2016) also point out that interpersonal contact between frontline service employees and customers is vital to customers' service experience and perception of a company's service quality. Personal interactions involve dynamic bargaining and communication processes that can dramatically change the attitudes, intentions, and behaviours of the parties involved. A close examination of the scale items for each dimension of service quality by Parasuraman et al. (1988) reveals that a majority of the items relate directly to the human interaction element of service delivery.

A personal service encounter refers to personal interactions between employees and customers (Bitner et al., 1990). Although tangible products and situational factors (e.g. Buhalis & Amaranggana, 2015; Chandralal & Valenzuela, 2013; Mossberg, 2007) are common antecedents of customer experience, revisit intentions and product/brand attachment (Chandralal & Valenzuela, 2013; Vada et al., 2019), research in services marketing and management has emphasised the role of frontline employees in service industries and shows that these employees' behaviours and performance over each service encounter with customers influence customer decision making in purchase and loyalty behaviours (Liao, 2017).

Nevertheless, based on service co-production and value co-creation principles, customers must endeavour to co-produce the service to create positive memorable experiences and achieve desirable value for themselves (Etgar, 2008; Ordanini & Pasini, 2008; Voorberg et al., 2015), which subsequently leads to customer satisfaction and loyalty. In other words, both employees and customers pay important roles in a co-production process and service encounter. The encounter that involves humans has emotional characteristics. Emotional intelligence from each party involved is important to create a successful service encounter.

5.3   The Role of Service Employees in Service Encounter

Customer service representatives or frontline service employees, normally in the marketing-oriented boundary spanning positions, are the first and primary contact point for the customer before, during and after the service process. They play an important role in affecting customers' perceptions of any service encounter (Bitner et al., 1990). Customers often base their impression of the firm largely on the service received from customer contact employees (Singh et al., 1994). In an exploratory study, Parasuraman et al. (1985) indicated that frontline service employees are pivotal in forming a customer's level of perceived service quality. These employees' behaviours and performance over the service encounter form customers' perceptions of service quality, which further leads to customer satisfaction (Hartline & Ferrell, 1996).

Other researchers (e.g., Bitner, 1990; Surprenant & Solomon, 1987) uncovered the importance of customer contact employee's behaviour in affecting customer satisfaction. A few survey-based studies, from customer satisfaction point of view, indicated the significant role of the frontline employees during the service delivery process, and the association of their service performance and customer satisfaction or dissatisfaction. For example, Crosby and Stephen (1987) found the service performance of the customer contact person is the significant predictor of overall satisfaction of the service. In another study, Crosby et al. (1990) revealed that the employees' relationship selling behaviours are the major determinants of relationship quality composed of two dimensions: trust and customer satisfaction. A similar finding was reported by Boles and Babin (1996). As indicated in prior context, customer satisfaction, preceded by service quality, is an important antecedent of customer retention; hence, frontline employees in people-based service contexts become a key factor in customer retention.

The role of frontline employees in customer satisfaction and loyalty is important in tourism and hospitality. Taking the example of casinos, Johnson and Beale (2002) used the critical incident technique (CIT) to identify very satisfactory and very dissatisfactory service encounters from the customer's point of view. The results suggested that customer satisfaction is directly or indirectly related to service employees in the casino, for example, how employees respond to service delivery systems failure, how employees respond to customer needs and requests, and how much attention employees pay to regular visitors.

In the high-end gaming sector, the preferred mode of marketing to key customer accounts is one-on-one marketing. It is largely up to the casino frontline employees and their human relationship skills to determine the length of their relationship with a casino. Galletti and Giannotti (2002) claims that frontline employees play a primary role in establishing relationships with customers through interacting with, influencing and servicing the target. A repeated visit is often attributed to customer-contact staff who form the critical component of customer service such as greeting customers, diagnosing customer problems, showing empathy, handling customer complaints, serving customers, communicating with customers, responding to customers properly, answering customer questions properly, usually consistently ensuring a good customer experience and establish rapport. Such customer service is critical to gain customer loyalty and a competitive advantage for service organisations in the midst of increased competition.

Given the critical role of service employees in service encounter that forms service quality assessment, how these employees conduct themselves over those personal service encounter has implications for customer retention and company profitability. Their performance can be largely influenced by, inter alia, the level of their emotional intelligence. This can be accounted for by the emotional nature of the service encounter.

5.4   Emotional Service Encounter

Service encounter, according to Hartel et al. (1999), is characterised as an emotional event. For example, service encounter behaviours, those suggested in the SERVQUAL model by Parasuraman et al. (1988) for service employees, the employee showing concern for customer, demonstrating awareness and empathy of customer needs, have clear emotional contents (Bardzil & Slaski, 2003). The emotions that are associated with the service encounter can be accounted for by the emotional benefits of the services; customers' emotions and emotional contagion.

5.4.1 Seeking Emotional Benefits of Services

Customers enter and exit service encounters with associated cognitions and emotions. These cognitions and emotions are largely the result of the cognitive and affective information processing initiated by the service event. In investigating customer emotional responses to service encounter, Price et al. (1995) indicate that service encounter can be classified as low-affect contexts such as bank transactions or hotel check-in, and high affect content, referred to emotional encounter. The authors distinguish two service encounter contexts that have high affective content. First, the consumer is motivated by the expected functional benefits of service encounters, emotional content is nonetheless an important part of interaction and service satisfaction, for example, psychological reactance (bill collectors); invasive procedures on the self (e.g., tattooing); and risk associated with credence goods (e.g., financial advising). In the second type, the consumer is motivated by the affective benefits offered by the service. Examples include martial arts training, and adventure recreations (Arnould & Price, 1993; Siehl et al., 1992).

In these contexts, customers seek emotional benefits of services. The service employees convey the affective content of events through their own engagement, emotions, sense of drama and skills (Deighton, 1992; Grove & Fisk, 1992). Competence and efficiency will be expected of service providers (Arnould & Price, 1993). Under these circumstances, customers expect the employee to interact with them on the basis of their emotional state, rather than according to a standardized script by the management (Price et al., 1995).

The second type of emotional events associated with the encounter may take place in the low-affect context. In this context, customers' emotions may be caused by service employees' encounter behaviours. The emotions may be sourced from role conflict, role ambiguity, and role overload, based on the role theory (Bateman & Strasser, 1984; Hrebiniak 1974; Hartline & Ferrell, 1996), as well as from customers because of the interactive nature of the service encounter. Employees' emotions may affect their service behaviours, which subsequently affect customers' attitudes.

Tourism, for example, is such a context with tourists seeking pleasure and memorable experiences that are offered by tourism representatives (e.g. travel agents, tour guide, tourism provider) for business profitability (Vada et al., 2019). Over last few decades, tourism has experienced continued expansion and diversification to become one of the largest and fastest-growing economic sectors in the world; and has increasingly been regarded as the key to local economic development and tourist well-being (UNWTO, 2016). Emotions permeates in tourism journey and plays a key role in tourists' experiences (Hosany et al., 2015). Such experience may result from consuming tourism products and interacting with tourism service representatives (e.g. tour guides or leaders). Tourism products include, inter alia, festivals, theme parks, unique tourist attractions, and adventures. These services are emotionally loaded with tourists being emotionally motivated to opt for these products (Cetin & Yarcan, 2017). The options result in tourists enter and exit these services with associated cognitions and emotions. These cognitions and emotions are largely the result of the cognitive and affective information processing initiated by the service event (Prentice, 2016). The service encounter associated with these services involve high affect context since tourists are motivated by the expected functional benefits of tourism offerings with emotional contents being an important part of interaction and the affective benefits offered by the destination, for instance, spiritual tourism, and adventure recreations. In this case, tourists seek emotional benefits of services.

The tourist experience plays a vital role in tourism as such experience influences customer satisfaction and behavioural intentions (Chen & Chen, 2010; Hosany & Witham, 2010; Williams & Soutar, 2009). People often feel happier, healthier and more relaxed after a vacation (Nawijn et al., 2010). These positive feelings result from experiences with tourism-associated offerings including tourism products and representatives (Mossberg, 2007). Whilst tourism offerings such as spa tourism (Voigt et al., 2011), religious and spiritual travel (Chamberlain & Zika, 1992), sport tourism (Filo & Coghlan, 2016) and volunteer tourism (Crossley, 2012) can be a core component of tourism experience, it is the service encounter with frontline personnel (i.e. tourism representatives) that differentiates customers'/tourists' experience (Prentice et al., 2013; Prentice 2016) since other factors offers limited differentiation and novelty with emerging technologies (e.g. experiencing the destination without visiting) and facilitation of digitalisation (e.g. Google search of the destination).

5.4.2 Leveraging Employee Emotional Intelligence for Emotional Services

In the case of customers seeking emotional services, employee emotional intelligence may be able to moderate the customer's attitudes and behaviours resulting from the employees' encounter behaviours (Hartel et al., 1999). As emotional intelligence constitutes abilities of displaying strong self-awareness and high levels of interpersonal skills, and emotional intelligent individuals are empathetic, and adaptable (e.g., Bar-On, 2002; Boytzis et al, 2000; Sjoberg & Littorin, 2003), highly emotionally intelligent employees are more likely to harness the emotional level of the encounter (Fineman, 1996).

5.4.3 Emotional Response Toward Service Representative

In identifying five-service encounter dimensions: mutual understanding, extra attention, authenticity, competence and minimum standards of civility, Price et al. (1995)

examines customers' emotional responses to employees' service encounter performance. The results show that mutual understanding, extras, authenticity and competency are the significant factors in positive emotional responses to service encounter. However, failure to meet minimum standards of civility negatively affects positive feelings; whereas failing to meet minimum standards of civility is the most important predictor of negative feelings; mutual understanding is a significant predictor of negative emotions.

Employees in the service sector, tourism and hospitality in particular, are generally lowly paid, and highly stressed (Prentice et al., 2013). Their jobs involve high social components and contains intensive emotional labour demand. In the case of tourism service representatives such as tour guides or leaders, they lead the tour, coordinate with travel agents, destination managers, local tour operators, and tourists. They play multiple roles such as organisers, instructors, motivators, ambassadors, coordinators, consultants (Heung, 2008). These roles conceive hassles for these representatives, manifested in irritating, frustrating, or distressing experiences (Tsau & Lin, 2014). For instance, they have to deal with tourists' complaints possibly resulted from poor organizations by tour operators and unreasonable demands from tourists. It may be irrelevant to their prescribed tasks; these service representatives who have direct contact with tourists perform emotional labour acting strategies to ensure positive tourist experience.

5.4.4 Leveraging Employee Emotional Intelligence for Customer Response

In the case of customer emotional response toward services, service employee's emotional intelligence may be able to influence customer's quality perception and service experience. First, through the aspect of perceiving, understanding and managing the employee's own emotions, emotional intelligence exerts effect on preventing the detrimental side of emotional labour that may affect the labourer's performance over the encounter with customers, thus influences the customer's perceptions towards the firm's service quality. On the other hand, emotional intelligence, through the aspect of utilising and regulating customer's emotions, can be served as a vehicle by which service providers can affect a customer's emotion formation and appraisal process in service encounters (Prentice, 2016).

5.4.5 Emotions Aroused by Customer Attributions

Researchers (e.g., Bitner et al., 1990; Hartel et al., 1999) indicate that emotions are not only affected by the service encounter and the employee's behaviours, but also by the customer's attributions concerning the encounter. In other words, a customer may bring his or her own emotions into a service encounter which affects the experience and satisfaction level (a honeymoon maker or a sad divorcee). Unsatisfactory service encounters may be due to inappropriate customer behaviours. Their study provides empirical evidence that these emotional customer types do exist and in fact can be the source of their own satisfaction or dissatisfaction. In some service industries, problem customers are the source of 22% of the dissatisfactory incidents. This group may be even larger in industries in which the customer has greater inputs into the service delivery process. Tourists are involved in the whole service/travel process. Their dissatisfaction may result from their own bad choice of the service products (e.g., wrong tour or tourism events), or personal situations such as relationship breakup or family loss which prompt them to engage in service consumption such as travelling as an escaping mechanism from the dismay (Hosany et al., 2015; Tsaur & Lin, 2014).

5.4.6   Leveraging Employee Emotional Intelligence for Customer Attribution

In the case of emotions from customers' attribution, frontline employee's emotional competencies can be important factors in solving customers' problems (Bitner et al., 1990), achieving customer satisfaction (Bardzil & Slaski, 2003). In a few qualitative studies, Bitner (1990) and Bitner et al. (1990) show that customers have positive emotions towards service encounters when employees possess emotionally competent behaviours. Bitner et al. also found that an employee's ability to adapt to special needs and requests enhances customers' positive perceptions of the service encounter. Furthermore, several studies have shown that the friendliness, enthusiasm and attentiveness of contact employees positively affect customers' perceptions of service quality (e.g., Bowen & Schneider, 1985). These behaviours are under influence of employee emotional intelligence (Bar-On, 1997).

5.4.7   Emotional Contagion

Emotions are contagious, despite who is the transmitter (Hatfield et al., 2014). Emotional contagion is the interactions that people automatically and continuously tend to mimic and synchronize their movements with the facial expressions, voices, postures movements, and the instrumental behaviours of others. Many scholars have suggested that emotions affect the dynamics of a conversation between a customer-contact employee and customer (e.g., Liljander et al., 1995). Verbal cues, and especially nonverbal cues from the part of sender, which set the emotional tone in a conversation, make up for this process of impression (Weitz et al., 1999). Once a person is in contact with another, this person arouses the other person. This process of arousal also takes place in the opposite direction. Seeing someone express an emotion can evoke that mood regardless of the facial expression mimicking. People become influenced in an unconscious manner (Goleman, 1995).

Customer's emotional feelings sometimes inevitably translate into difficult behaviours that the customer-contact employees have to encounter with (Prentice et al., 2013). Customers are not always right, but the management requires the front-line employees to treat them as if they are (Bitner, 1990). This sometimes leads to emotional dissonance of the contact employees and thus affects their encounter behaviours, which further leads to customer emotional reactions and behavioural intentions.

5.4.8 Leveraging Employee Emotional Intelligence for Emotional Contagion

In the case of emotional contagion, highly emotional intelligent employees may be less susceptible to burnout and hence able to manage the interactions with customers. According to the emotional contagion theory, each individual is different in one's abilities to infect another person or to become infected by another person's emotions. For example, when people mimic and synchronize reactions with one another, some might be powerful transmitters of emotions (they are able to infect others with their emotions) and others might be powerful catchers of emotions (they assume the senders' emotions) (Hatfield et al., 2014). Transmitters, those who by their innate bodily circuitry transmit their emotions to others, are charismatic, colourful and entertaining, scored high on dominance, affiliation, and exhibition (Hatfield et al., 2014). In many cases, being able to transmit positive emotions to another person might cause this other person to become more accessible to the intention of the conversation (Isen & Means, 1983). On the other side, those susceptible to the emotions of others are people whose attention tends to be riveted to others. Therefore, they are more likely to be affected by other people's emotions.

According to Goleman (1995), those who can infect others or be infected by others' emotions without suffering burnout or emotional dissonance could be perceived as emotionally intelligent people, while burnout and emotional dissonance have been empirically evidenced to be negatively related to one's behaviour and performance, which affect customer attitudes and behaviours. Consequently, emotional intelligence can have a significant influence on managing service encounter where emotional contagion is prevalent.

5.5   Leveraging Customer Emotional Intelligence for Customer Experience

Most service research considers the provider's perspective to elucidate how customers evaluate the services and what services can be offered to generate customers' positive attitudes and behaviours. Customers' personal traits and attributes also contribute to their service experience and attitudes towards the provider. Despite the motto 'the customer is always right' that is to exhort service employees to prioritise customers to execute successful business transactions, the reality is that the customer is not always right, and they can sometimes be emotional, demanding, abusive, and bullying (Grandey et al., 2004). Although frontline employees are supposed to perform emotional labour, and their emotional intelligence (EI) can be exhibited to manage emotional encounters with customers (Prentice, 2013), such performance has detrimental effects on employees who are equally subject to emotional vulnerability (Prentice et al., 2013). Customers should equally make endeavour to ensure a successful business transaction when interacting with the supplier.

Such endeavours can include their abilities and efforts to understand and manage their own emotions and those of others, referred to as EI. Customers' EI may affect their perceptions, service experience, attitudes, and behaviours towards the service provider. This concept has rarely been employed to explain customer satisfaction and loyalty although a few studies have examined how the level of EI exhibited by frontline employees may affect customer satisfaction (Kernbach & Schutte, 2005), service encounter (Prentice, 2013).

5.5.1   Leveraging Customer Emotional Intelligence for Co-production and Co-creation

From the service provider's perspective, EI is important in managing emotional encounters for successful business outcomes (Prentice, 2013, 2016; Prentice & King, 2012). Similarly, customers' EI is equally important to ensure a happy encounter. This can be construed as a value co-creation principle. The S–D logic dictates that service organisations and customers participate in the service production and delivery processes to co-produce a desirable service and achieve values for the parties involved (Grönroos, 2008; Vargo & Lusch, 2004). Therefore, to co-produce a successful encounter that contains emotional events, customers should demonstrate emotional competence to manage their own emotions and avoid conflicts with peer customers or service employees. This leads to their overall satisfaction with the provider and subsequent loyalty behaviours. In other words, customers' EI plays a significant role in the relationship between service quality, customer satisfaction and loyalty.

5.5.2 Leveraging Customer Emotional Intelligence for Employees

In the case of employee attitudes and behaviours contributing to the emotional encounter, rather than complaining to the employee, an emotionally intelligent customer could empathise with the employee, understanding the demanding and stressful nature of the frontline position and forgive their negatively connoted emotions and behaviours, and endeavouring to cooperate with the employee to facilitate service production and delivery. This initiative results in a memorable encounter experience. In the case of an emotional encounter resulting from customers' emotions (e.g., depression and loneliness experienced by geriatric customers), emotionally intelligent customers can regulate and manage their own emotions by understanding that one's predicament should not be resorted to blame shifting. Such an endeavour may be appreciated by the service employee who may make extra effort to create a memorable encounter experience for the customer. Based on reciprocity theory (Falk & Fischbacher, 2006), according to which people tend to reward the kind actions of others and punish for the unkind ones, the customer would continue to patronage and stay loyal to this service provider. Hence, customers' EI plays a significant moderating role in the relationship between service quality and memorable experience and customer loyalty.

5.6 Implications and Conclusion

This chapter has discussed how EI exhibited by employees and customers can exert influences on customers. Although emotional intelligence is a personal competency, this paper positions it as an external service to manage the service encounter for enhancing the customer experience which has marketing implications in regard to customers' attitudes and loyalty behaviours (Chi & Qu, 2008; Gallarza & Saura, 2006). As a result, this chapter bridges marketing, psychology, and human resource to reveal how a psychological construct can be approached from marketing perspective to manage service personnel and consumer behaviours through the service encounter manifested in the moment of truth.

Although services include both tangible elements, and the intangible elements of the services performed by frontline employees, it is the intangible component that appears to most attract customer patronage and loyalty. Second, the service encounters between frontline employees and customers are characterised as emotional events, so both employees' and customers' emotional competencies are critical in shaping customer perceptions of service quality and service experience. In other words, employees' emotional abilities affect their performance over the encounters that lead to customer service quality judgements. Equally, customers' emotional intelligence facilities their own service experience by having pleasant interactions with the service provider. This suggests that both parties are a key factor of customer loyalty and retention. Their emotional competence influences customer experience and company profitability.

Admittedly emotional intelligence is not a panacea for business revenue growth. Marketing promotions including all customer acquisition means and other impersonal retention strategies (i.e., loyalty programs) are still important for business depending on location and the development stage of the business. Research (e.g., Prentice & Wong, 2015; Wong & Prentice, 2015) shows that service environment and other tangible offerings play a significant role in customer satisfaction and loyalty. Emotional intelligence may add to the relationship chain through its impact on employee performance and productivity.

The discussion has practical implications for marketing and human resource practitioners as well as for service personnel working in the service industry. Marketers and other relevant parties often endeavour to create all fancy packages and provide unique products to attract customers and strive for competitive advantage. These offerings can be easily matched by competitors. However, the personal competency such as emotional intelligence demonstrated by service representatives differentiates one from the other organization (Prentice, 2016). Hiring and training these representatives would be a key competitive strategy for human resource practitioners. Indeed, Tsaur and Ku (2019) has attempted to understand how EI demonstrated by service representatives affects customer responses. The authors confirm that these representatives perform emotional labour and indicates necessity of further research on the impact of emotional intelligence on customers. The current chapter concurs with this view and suggests utilising emotional intelligence as a service to enhance customer experience. Possessing emotional intelligent skills by the representatives is not only conductive to enhancing customer experience but also beneficial to their wellbeing since they perform emotional labour which has negative consequences to the labourer as discussed before. Emotional intelligent individuals are less prone to these consequences.

Understanding the influence of customers' emotional intelligence provides an additional venue for service organisation to enhance business performance and financial growth. More optimistically, emotional intelligence is measurable and developable. Individual emotional intelligence can be measured. Therefore, emotional intelligence tests should be incorporated within the recruitment and selection processes, as well as a venue for educating customers. The longitudinal studies conducted by Boyatzis and Kolb (1995) provide the most persuasive evidence that emotional intelligence can also be developed and improved. Results of another study by Slaski and Cartwright (2002), which involved the conduct of 6-weeks of emotional intelligence training for 60 managers from a large retail chain, show that participants in the programme increase their level of emotional intelligence after the training. In addition, the findings of LeDoux's (1996) effective neuroscience also provide evidence for the potential to extend the application of emotional intelligence. Therefore, emotional intelligence training would be a worthwhile initiative for firms to adopt to optimise their business performance.

References

Arnould, E. J., & Price, L. L. (1993). River magic: Extraordinary experience and the extended service encounter. *Journal of Consumer Research, 20*(1), 24–45.

Bardzil, P., & Slaski, M. (2003). Emotional intelligence: Fundamental competencies for enhanced service provision. *Managing Service Quality: An International Journal, 13*(2), 97–104.

Bar-On, R. (1997). *BarOn emotional quotient inventory.* Multi-Health Systems.

Bar-On, R. (2002). BarOn Emotional Quotient Inventory. *Technical Manual, 3.*

Bateman, T. S., & Strasser, S. (1984). A longitudinal analysis of the antecedents of organizational commitment. *Academy of Management Journal, 27*(1), 95–112.

Bitner, M. J. (1990). Evaluating service encounters: The effects of physical surroundings and employee responses. *Journal of Marketing, 54*(2), 69–82.

Bitner, M. J., Booms, B. H., & Mohr, L. A. (1994). Critical service encounters: The employee's viewpoint. *Journal of Marketing, 58*(4), 95–106.

Bitner, M. J., Booms, B. H., & Tetreault, M. S. (1990). The service encounter: Diagnosing favorable and unfavorable incidents. *Journal of Marketing, 54*(1), 71–84.

Bitner, M., & Hubbert, A. (1994), Encounter satisfaction versus overall satisfaction versus quality. In R. Rust & R. Oliver (Eds.), *Service quality: New directions in theory and practice* (pp. 72–94). CA: Sage Publications.

Boles, J. S., & Babin, B. J. (1996). On the front lines: Stress, conflict, and the customer service provider. *Journal of Business Research, 37*(1), 41–50.

Boyatzis, R. E., Goleman, D., & Rhee, K. (2000). Clustering competence in emotional intelligence: Insights from the Emotional Competence Inventory (ECI). *Handbook of Emotional Intelligence, 99*(6), 343–362.

Boyatzis, R. E., & Kolb, D. A. (1995). From learning styles to learning skills: The executive skills profile. *Journal of Managerial Psychology, 10*(5), 3–17.

Buhalis, D., & Amaranggana, A. (2015). Smart tourism destinations enhancing tourism experience through personalisation of services. In *Information and communication technologies in tourism 2015* (pp. 377–389). Springer.

Caruana, A. (2002). Service loyalty: The effects of service quality and the mediating role of customer satisfaction. *European Journal of Marketing, 36*(7/8), 811–828.

Cetin, G., & Yarcan, S. (2017). The professional relationship between tour guides and tour operators. *Scandinavian Journal of Hospitality and Tourism, 17*(4), 345–357.

Chamberlain, K., & Zika, S. (1992). Stability and change in subjective well-being over short time periods. *Social Indicators Research, 26,* 101–117.

Chandralal, L., & Valenzuela, F. R. (2013). Exploring memorable tourism experiences: Antecedents and behavioural outcomes. *Journal of Economics, Business and Management, 1*(2), 177–181.

Chen, C. F., & Chen, F. S. (2010). Experience quality, perceived value, satisfaction and behavioral intentions for heritage tourists. *Tourism Management, 31*(1), 29–35.

Chi, C. G. Q., & Qu, H. (2008). Examining the structural relationships of destination image, tourist satisfaction and destination loyalty: An integrated approach. *Tourism Management, 29*(4), 624–636.

Crosby, L. A., Evans, K. R., & Cowles, D. (1990). Relationship quality in services selling: An interpersonal influence perspective. *Journal of Marketing, 54*(3), 68–81.

Crosby, L. A., & Stephens, N. (1987). Effects of relationship marketing on satisfaction, retention, and prices in the life insurance industry. *Journal of Marketing Research, 24*(4), 404–411.

Crossley, É. (2012). Poor but happy: Volunteer tourists' encounters with poverty. *Tourism Geographies, 14*(2), 235–253.

Deighton, J. (1992). The consumption of performance. *Journal of Consumer Research, 19*(3), 362–372.

Etgar, M. (2008). A descriptive model of the consumer co-production process. *Journal of the Academy of Marketing Science, 36,* 97–108.

Falk, A., & Fischbacher, U. (2006). A theory of reciprocity. *Games and Economic Behavior, 54*(2), 293–315.

Farrell, P. M., Kosorok, M. R., Rock, M. J., Laxova, A., Zeng, L., Lai, H. C., Hoffman, G., Laessig, R. H., Splaingard, M. L., & Wisconsin Cystic Fibrosis Neonatal Screening Study Group. (2001). Early diagnosis of cystic fibrosis through neonatal screening prevents severe malnutrition and improves long-term growth. *Pediatrics, 107*(1), 1–13.

Filo, K., & Coghlan, A. (2016). Exploring the positive psychology domains of well-being activated through charity sport event experiences. *Event Management, 20*(2), 181–199.

Fineman, S. (1996). Emotional subtexts in corporate greening. *Organization Studies, 17*(3), 479–500.

Gallarza, M. G., & Saura, I. G. (2006). Value dimensions, perceived value, satisfaction and loyalty: An investigation of university students' travel behaviour. *Tourism Management, 27*(3), 437–452.

Galletti, C., & Giannotti, E. (2002, January). Multiloop kinematotropic mechanisms. In *International Design Engineering Technical Conferences and Computers and Information in Engineering Conference* (Vol. 36533, pp. 455–460). American Society of Mechanical Engineers.

Goleman, D. (1995). *Emotional intelligence: Why it can matter more than IQ.* Bantam.

Goleman, D. (1998). *Working with emotional intelligence.* Bantam.

Grandey, A. A., Dickter, D. N., & Sin, H. P. (2004). The customer is not always right: Customer aggression and emotion regulation of service employees. *Journal of Organizational Behavior: THe International Journal of Industrial, Occupational and Organizational Psychology and Behavior, 25*(3), 397–418.

Grönroos, C. (2008). Service logic revisited: Who creates value? And who co-creates? *European Business Review, 20*(4), 298–314.

Grove, S. J., & Fisk, R. P. (1992). The service experience as theater. *ACR North American Advances.*

Hallowell, R. (1996). The relationships of customer satisfaction, customer loyalty, and profitability: An empirical study. *International Journal of Service Industry Management.*

Hartel, C. E., Barker, S., & Baker, N. J. (1999). The role of emotional intelligence in service encounters: A model for predicting the effects of employee-customer interactions on consumer attitudes, intentions, and behaviours. *Australian Journal of Communication, 26*(2), 77.

Hatfield, E., Bensman, L., Thornton, P. D., & Rapson, R. L. (2014). New perspectives on emotional contagion: A review of classic and recent research on facial mimicry and contagion. *Interpersona: An International Journal on Personal Relationships, 8*(2).

Hartline, M. D., & Ferrell, O. C. (1996). The management of customer-contact service employees: An empirical investigation. *Journal of Marketing, 60*(4), 52–70.

Hrebiniak, L. G. (1974). Effects of job level and participation on employee attitudes and perceptions of influence. *Academy of Management Journal, 17*(4), 649–662.

Heung, V. C. S. (2008). Effects of tour leader's service quality on agency's reputation and customers' word-of-mouth. *Journal of Vacation Marketing, 14*(4), 305–315.

Hosany, S., & Witham, M. (2010). Dimensions of cruisers' experiences, satisfaction, and intention to recommend. *Journal of Travel Research, 49*(3), 351–364.

Hosany, S., Prayag, G., Deesilatham, S., Cauševic, S., & Odeh, K. (2015). Measuring tourists' emotional experiences: Further validation of the destination emotion scale. *Journal of Travel Research, 54*(4), 482–495.

Isen, A. M., & Means, B. (1983). The influence of positive affect on decision-making strategy. *Social Cognition, 2*(1), 18–31.

Johnson, K. M., & Beale, C. L. (2002). Nonmetro recreation counties: Their identification and rapid growth. *Rural America.*

Kernbach, S., & Schutte, N. S. (2005). The impact of service provider emotional intelligence on customer satisfaction. *Journal of Services Marketing, 19*(7), 438–444.

LeDoux, J. (1996). Emotional networks and motor control: A fearful view. *Progress in Brain Research, 107*, 437–446.

Liao, Y., Deschamps, F., Loures, E. D. F. R., & Ramos, L. F. P. (2017). Past, present and future of Industry 4.0—A systematic literature review and research agenda proposal. *International Journal of Production Research, 55*(12), 3609–3629.

Liljander, V., & Strandvik, T. (1995). The nature of customer relationships in services. *Advances in Services Marketing and Management, 4*(141), 67.

Olorunniwo, F., Hsu, M. K., & Udo, G. J. (2006). Service quality, customer satisfaction, and behavioral intentions in the service factory. *Journal of Services Marketing, 20*(1), 59–72.

Ordanini, A., & Pasini, P. (2008). Service co-production and value co-creation: The case for a serviceoriented architecture (SOA). *European Management Journal, 26*(5), 289–297.

Mossberg, L. (2007). A marketing approach to the tourist experience. *Scandinavian Journal of Hospitality and Tourism, 7*(1), 59–74.

Nawijn, J., Marchand, M. A., Veenhoven, R., & Vingerhoets, A. J. (2010). Vacationers happier, but most not happier after a holiday. *Applied Research in Quality of Life, 5*(1), 35–47.

Parasuraman, A., Zeithaml, V. A., & Berry, L. L. (1985). A conceptual model of service quality and its implications for future research. *Journal of marketing, 49*(4), 41–50.

Parasuraman, A., Zeithaml, V. A., & Berry, L. (1988). SERVQUAL: A multiple-item scale for measuring consumer perceptions of service quality. *1988, 64*(1), 12–40.

Prentice, C. (2013). Service quality perceptions and customer loyalty in casinos. *International Journal of Contemporary Hospitality Management.*

Prentice, C. (2016). Leveraging employee emotional intelligence in casino profitability. *Journal of Retailing and Consumer Services, 33*, 127–134.

Prentice, C., Chen, P. J., & King, B. (2013). Employee performance outcomes and burnout following the presentation-of-self in customer-service contexts. *International Journal of Hospitality Management, 35*, 225–236.

Prentice, C., & King, B. E. (2012). Emotional intelligence in a hierarchical relationship: Evidence for frontline service personnel. *Services Marketing Quarterly, 33*(1), 34–48.

Prentice, C., & Wong, I. A. (2015). Casino marketing, problem gamblers or loyal customers? *Journal of Business Research, 68*(10), 2084–2092.

Price, L. L., Arnould, E. J., & Tierney, P. (1995). Going to extremes: Managing service encounters and assessing provider performance. *Journal of Marketing, 59*(2), 83–97.

Reichheld, F. F. (1996). Learning from customer defections. *Harvard Business Review, 74*(2), 56–67.

Rust, R. T., & Zahorik, A. J. (1993). Customer satisfaction, customer retention, and market share. *Journal of Retailing, 69*(2), 193–215.

Sandström, S., Edvardsson, B., Kristensson, P., & Magnusson, P. (2008). Value in use through service experience. *Managing Service Quality: An International Journal, 18*(2), 112–126.

Schneider, B., & Bowen, D. E. (1985). Employee and customer perceptions of service in banks: Replication and extension. *Journal of Applied Psychology, 70*(3), 423.

Shi, Y., Prentice, C., & He, W. (2014). Linking service quality, customer satisfaction and loyalty in casinos, does membership matter? *International Journal of Hospitality Management, 40*, 81–91.

Siehl, C., Bowen, D. E., & Pearson, C. M. (1992). Service encounters as rites of integration: An information processing model. *Organization Science, 3*(4), 537–555.

Singh, J., Goolsby, J. R., & Rhoads, G. K. (1994). Behavioral and psychological consequences of boundary spanning burnout for customer service representatives. *Journal of Marketing Research, 31*(4), 558–569.

Sjöberg, L., & Littorin, P. (2003). Emotional intelligence, personality and sales performance. *Center for Risk Research Stockholm School of Economics-SSE/EFI. Working Paper Series in Business Administration, 8.*

Slaski, M., & Cartwright, S. (2002). Health, performance and emotional intelligence: An exploratory study of retail managers. *Stress and Health: Journal of the International Society for the Investigation of Stress, 18*(2), 63–68.

Surprenant, C. F., & Solomon, M. R. (1987). Predictability and personalization in the service encounter. *Journal of Marketing, 51*(2), 86–96.

Tsaur, S. H., & Ku, P. S. (2019). The Effect of Tour Leaders' Emotional Intelligence on Tourists' Consequences. *Journal of Travel Research, 58*(1), 63–76.

Tsaur, S. H., & Lin, W. R. (2014). Hassles of tour leaders. *Tourism Management, 45*, 28–38.

United Nations World Tourism Organization (UNWTO), Blomberg-Nygard, A., & Anderson, C. K. (2016). United Nations world tourism organization study on online guest reviews and hotel classification systems: An integrated approach. *Service Science, 8*(2), 139–151.

Vada, S., Prentice, C., & Hsiao, A. (2019). The influence of tourism experience and well-being on place attachment. *Journal of Retailing and Consumer Services, 47*, 322–330.

Vada, S., Prentice, C., Scott, N., & Hsiao, A. (2020). Positive psychology and tourist well-being: A systematic literature review. *Tourism Management Perspectives, 33*, 100631.

Vargo, S. L., & Lusch, R. F. (2004). Evolving to a new dominant logic for marketing. *Journal of Marketing, 68*(1), 1–17.

Voigt, C., Brown, G., & Howat, G. (2011). Wellness tourists: In search of transformation. *Tourism Review, 66*(1/2), 16–30.

Voorberg, W. H., Bekkers, V. J., & Tummers, L. G. (2015). A systematic review of co-creation and co-production: Embarking on the social innovation journey. *Public Management Review, 17*(9), 1333–1357.

Weitz, B. A., & Bradford, K. D. (1999). Personal selling and sales management: A relationship marketing perspective. *Journal of the Academy of Marketing Science, 27*, 241–254.

Williams, E., Bond, K., Zhang, B., Putland, M., & Williamson, D. A. (2020). Saliva as a noninvasive specimen for detection of SARS-CoV-2. *Journal of Clinical Microbiology, 58*(8), e00776–e820.

Williams, P., & Soutar, G. N. (2009). Value, satisfaction and behavioral intentions in an adventure tourism context. *Annals of Tourism Research, 36*(3), 413–438.

Wong, I. A., & Prentice, C. (2015). Multilevel environment induced impulsive gambling. *Journal of Business Research, 68*(10), 2102–2108.

Zeithaml, V. A., Berry, L. L., & Parasuraman, A. (1996). The behavioral consequences of service quality. *Journal of Marketing, 60*(2), 31–46.

Chapter 6
Leveraging Artificial Intelligence for Customer Satisfaction and Loyalty

Abstract Do customers prefer employee service or artificial intelligence (AI) powered services? This chapter provides answers to this question by proposing AI-powered applications as service and discusses how employee and AI services influence overall service quality and customer response, particularly customer satisfaction and loyalty which is related to business profitability and sustainability. The chapter begins with reviewing the relevant literature on the link of service quality to customer satisfaction and loyalty then hypothesises an association of AI service quality with customer response. To provide a better insight into this association, employee service quality is included as a comparison. An empirical study in the hotel sector is undertaken to test the proposed relationships. The methodology, results and discussion of the case study findings are elaborated subsequently. Implications of these finding are highlighted and conclude this chapter.

6.1 Three Pillars of Customer Service

An organisation's service offerings include tangible and intangible components (Parasuraman et al., 1995). The tangible component refers to all physical elements including marketing promotions and communication material, equipment, and the appearance of physical facilities (e.g., servicescape) and personnel associated with the service provider. These elements comprise physical environment for a service to take place, which is referred to as servicescape. The intangible component generally refers to services provided by employees.

With the rapid development of technologies and digitalisation in recent years, artificial intelligence (AI) has permeated the wider community, particularly service industries such as hospitality and tourism, in the quest for enhancing business operational efficiency and customer experience (Bowen & Morosan, 2018; Ivanov & Webster, 2017; Naumov, 2019; Prentice et al., 2019). The service provided by AI-powered tools such as service robots, chatbots, recommender systems are becoming more prevalent in managing the service encounter with customers. In practice, the digital and robotic services powered by AI has been offered to customers to facilitate their purchase and consumption journey and progressively permeated in every service encounter (Gursoy, 2018; Lu et al., 2019; Prentice et al., 2020). The "Hotel of the Future" in Hangzhou China is run by robots. The hotel allows guests to manage reservations and payments entirely from a mobile app and enter rooms using facial-recognition technology while robots serve food and toiletries etc.

To a great extent, AI-powered applications in business and organisations can be referred to as commercial services that are offered to generate benefits and value for relevant stakeholders (e.g., customers, service providers) as discussed in the previous chapter. This view is consistent with the definition of services in the marketing literature as "economic activities offered by one party to another..." (Wirtz et al., 2013, p. 15). AI services in the organisational context can be regarded as value-added activities that are offered to facilitate employees' job efficiency such as managing inventory, writing articles, and answering customer queries (Bolton et al., 2018; Chung et al., 2018), and enhance customer experience through the whole customer journey (Prentice et al., 2019; Van Belleghem, 2017). Consequently, this chapter refers to these AI-powered application as AI service and argues that AI service can be regarded as a service product and an addition to service offering to create value for the service provider.

In reality, servicescape, employee service, AI-powered applications in today's competitive environment have become three main pillars of customer service provided by a service firm to shape customer experience and attitudes in order to attract them to purchase/repurchase, and consume/re-consume, ultimately become loyal customers. Whilst servicescape or the physical environment is considered the presumptive basic that is expected of a service provider, employee service has been traditionally regarded as a differentiator for the provider to attract customers' positive attitudes and loyalty behaviours as well as gaining competitive advantage (Prentice, 2013, 2014, 2019). The role of AI service as an addition to service offering to customers is empirically unclear as AI is generally associated with information technology.

6.2 AI Service Quality

Artificial intelligence (AI) refers to machine intelligence that can be applied in various contexts (e.g., businesses) to achieve certain goals (e.g., improve and enhance operational efficiency) (e.g., Kaplan & Haenlein, 2019; Russell & Norvig, 2009). AI functions like humans and performs cognitive tasks to achieve defined goals and tasks through computers, robots, and machines based on automation, big data, and machine learning (Kaplan & Haenlein, 2019). AI-powered tools permeate individuals' daily lives (Apple's Siri providing voice-activated assistance to mobile users), and are common in businesses, organisations, and industries. Unlike human intelligence that is innate and possessed by individuals, AI is represented by humanoid and non-humanoid machines and programmed by humans to serve human and business purposes.

Although service organisations (e.g., hotels) provide AI service to improve business efficiency and customer experience, a review of the relevant literature shows that very little academic research has attempted to understand how consumers/customers respond to such services. The value of any commercial service is manifested in customers' evaluations. Such service evaluation is reflective of service quality. Service quality has been extensively discussed as an antecedent of customer satisfaction and behaviour in the marketing and management literature (e.g., Prentice, 2013; Shi et al., 2014; Zeithaml et al., 1996). This concept refers to customers' perceptions and assessments of service offerings by a business entity (Parasuraman et al., 1995). Service quality generally consists of a value judgement of tangible (e.g., physical setting, service environment) and intangible services offered by employees (Parasuraman et al., 1995). This chapter integrates AI service quality into overall service quality perception and assessment to understand its impact on customers.

6.3 Leveraging AI Service Quality for Customer Satisfaction and Loyalty

Given that AI service quality is technologically based, customer response is likely dependent upon their attitudes and experiences with technologies. Previous research shows that technology-based services can influence customer satisfaction and loyalty. Using a critical incident technique, Mueter et al. (2000) found that self-service technologies (SST) generated both positive and negative incidents for different customers. Positive incidents include SST solved intensified needs, performed better than service personnel, were easy to use, and were cost and time-efficient. However, the study also found that customers were frustrated with technology failure and ineffective designs. Customer relationship management (CRM) is another technology-based application used to manage information about customers and service encounters for optimal financial outcomes (e.g., customer purchase and loyalty behaviours) (Kumar, 2010). CRM technologies and applications entail a huge financial investment. Nevertheless, research (e.g., Mithas et al., 2005) shows that such investment is financially worthwhile as CRM applications are positively related to customer satisfaction, which leads to customer loyalty. McKecnie et al. (2011) included technology-based services in a service quality assessment of the banking industry. The authors identified four technology-based service quality dimensions (i.e., customer service, technology security and information quality, technology convenience, and technology easiness and reliability) and found that two of these are significantly related to customer satisfaction and loyalty.

Subsuming AI applications under the service domain, this chapter view AI service as a component of the total service quality that has financial implications for the organisation. Service quality indicates the excellence of services offered to meet and exceed customers' expectations and is often assessed by customers' perceptions of the organisation's service offerings (Parasuraman et al., 1995). Service quality is widely acknowledged as an antecedent of customer satisfaction and loyalty (e.g., Prentice, 2013, 2014; Shi et al., 2014; Zeithaml et al., 1996). Consequently, it is plausible to posit that

AI service quality is significantly related to customer satisfaction and loyalty; and customer satisfaction with AI service quality is significantly related to customer loyalty to the service provider.

6.4   Leveraging Employee Service Quality for Customer Satisfaction and Loyalty

Although service organisations endeavour to utilise AI to improve operational efficiency and provide convenience to customers, a CGS report (see Elliott (2018) demonstrated that customers prefer humans to robots. Holding a similar view, Wirtz and colleagues (2018) indicated that customers prefer to deal with "people", not AI-powered robots. The endeavours to offer AI services by service organisations and customer experience with these services may form a knowledge gap manifested in the difference between what management believes customers expect and what customers actually need and expect (Cronin & Taylor, 1994).

In people-intensive industries such as the tourism and hospitality sector, the intangible services performed by employees over the service encounter with customers offer a competitive advantage, as these interpersonal interactions form customers' perceptions of a company's service quality (Prentice, 2013, 2014). The service experience with employees distinguishes one service organisation from another, as a result of the unique interaction between the customer and employee (Prentice, 2019).

Frontline service employees are the first and primary contact point for the customer before, during, and after the service process. They play an important role in affecting customers' perceptions of any service encounter (Prentice, 2013). Customers often base their impression of the firm largely on the service received from customer contact employees. Frontline service employees are pivotal in forming a customer's level of perceived service quality. The widely applied service quality measure—SERVQUAL (Parasuraman et al., 1991) has five core dimensions: reliability, assurance, empathy, responsiveness, and tangibles, the first four dimensions correspond to the service delivery performed by the employees with emphasis on service promptness, accuracy, consistency, and employee friendliness and caring. The last dimension corresponds to the physical setting of the service premises, that includes employees' appearance. Facilities may be spotless, and the service delivered on time as ordered, however, the customer may leave with a negative impression from the attitude of an employee with other efforts overlooked (Prentice, 2013, 2019).

The employees' behaviour and performance within the service encounter form customers' perceptions of service quality, which further leads to customer satisfaction and retention (Delcourt et al., 2013). This relationship chain is documented in the service profit chain model, which was originally developed by Heskett et al.

(1994). The model indicates that business profit and growth are stimulated primarily by customer loyalty; loyalty is a direct result of customer satisfaction; satisfaction is largely influenced by employee service performance and productivity. These employee behaviours and performance over the service encounter constitute the customer experience and form customers' perceptions of service quality, which further leads to their involvement and commitment with the firm and is manifested in their engagement and loyalty behaviours (Delcourt et al., 2013). Hence. The following hypotheses are offered:

Employee service quality is significantly related to customer satisfaction and loyalty to the service provider; and customer satisfaction with employee service quality is significantly related to customer loyalty.

Whilst both AI and employee service quality have important implications for customer satisfaction and loyalty, it's unclear of the difference of variance accounted by AI or employee service. Studies (Ivanov & Webster, 2017; Murphy et al., 2019) indicate that the adoption of such service is dependent upon customers' readiness and awareness. Very little research has been undertaken to understand customers' responses to services performed by AI versus employees. Some anecdotal blogs and news items suggest that customers prefer to deal with employees and tend to be frustrated by AI service (e.g., Glaser, 2017; Sentence, 2018). This may affect their overall quality assessment of the firm and subsequent purchasing behaviour. This discussion leads to posit that:

Employee service quality accounts for more variance in overall service quality than AI service quality does for overall service quality; and employee service quality accounts for more variance in customer loyalty than AI service quality.

6.5 Empirical Study

6.5.1 The Study Context

A study in the hotel sector was undertaken to test these relationships. AI services are particularly pervasively applied in the hotel industry to assist hotel guests and shape their experience. For example, Connie (an AI entity like Apple's Siri) in Hilton Hotels & Resorts can perform tasks such as greeting in different languages, recommending interesting sites and attractions, answering customer queries, refining responses based on the frequency of customer interactions, and assisting with checking-in (Solomon, 2016). The Wynn Casino in Las Vegas is integrating Amazon Echo to digitalise hotel rooms to offer guests voice control of room lighting, temperature, TV, and draperies, in addition to offering multiple facilities leveraging Echo's personal assistant services. The Clarion Hotel Amaranten in Stockholm also uses Amazon Echo as a powered chatbot butler to help guests with ordering taxi's, room service, assisting with online information and so on. Rose, an AI-powered concierge in the Cosmopolitan (where?) acts as a voice-activated assistant with a calling card to assist guests at check in and can manage customers' queries and requests on entertainment options and information on local sites and hotel specialties. Rose can also convey complicated queries to hotel staff. The **Edwardian Hotels also offer chatbot services where the customer** can simply type "Edward" (into what?) to request assistance on finding local restaurants, bars, and to find information on famous tourist sights. The Henna na Hotel in Japan uses humanoid female and dinosaur-personified robots at the front desk to greet and assist guests. The hotel also uses robotic porters to carry customers' luggage to their rooms or to store them as requested. These examples are taken from Makadia (2018).

AI services include, inter alia, concierge robots, digital assistance, and travel experience enhancers to assist customer purchases, travel choices, designing journey patterns and itineraries, as well as facilitating location preferences and payment options (Li et al., 2019). AI services in hotels are not only provided for guests in-house but throughout the customer journey to facilitate customer purchase/consumption and experience (Li et al., 2019). In the pre-purchase stage, AI is used to gather information about customers on their previous purchases and travel choices, destination preferences, journey patterns, and payment methods. AI applications manifest in various online channels, including assisting with personalised options and recommendations, saving user preference and page visits, travel bookings and suggestions for safe routes, room bookings, and reservations, as well as advanced food and beverage preferences (Maruti Techlabs, 2018, https://marutitech.com/artificial-intell igence-in-hospitality/). At the purchase/consumption stage, AI-powered tools can assist guests to check in, check out, and process payment. For example, the Marriott Hotel allows guests to use a mobile app to perform these services without queuing at the hotel front desk. After check-in, hotel customers can use special mobile devices to interact with AI-powered chatbots to order and schedule meals, control room temperature and lighting, plan travel journeys, and recommend sightseeing (Maruti Techlabs, 2018). These AI-powered applications manifest service offerings by the organisation. The following section describes the method of this study.

6.5.2   The Sample and Data Collection

The study was undertaken at hotels in Portugal. These hotels use various AI tools to support their business and provide services to customers. Examples include chatbots, concierge robots, digital assistance, voice-activated services, and travel experience enhancers. Data were collected from customers who had stayed at the surveyed hotels and had just finished the check-out process. Only those who understood and used AI-powered services from the hotel were invited to participate in this survey.

After a detailed discussion with the AI experts from the various hotels in relation to the original questionnaire relating to AI dimensionality prior to the survey, a pilot test was conducted with 20 randomly selected customers who had used the hotel's AI services to confirm the face validity of the questionnaire (Tabachnick et al., 2007) and ensure a survey completion time of less than 15 min to minimise respondents' fatigue. As a result, some items were modified for clarity.

The management from different hotels were contacted to seek for permission to conduct the survey. The hotel customers who were departing the hotel after check-out were invited to participate in this study. The questionnaires were conducted using the SurveyMonkey platform. Those who agreed to participate were provided with an iPad to assist in completing the survey. This method is cost-effective, easy to complete, and can encompass a wide range of question styles (Brickman Bhutta, 2012). To overcome response bias and reduce the overall non-completion rate, participants were blocked from previewing or skipping questions (Baltar & Brunet, 2012). A small gift was offered to encourage participation. Of the total usable sample, 42.7% of respondents were male, and 57.3% were female. The age of participants ranged from 18 to 55 years old and above. About 20% of respondents fell in the age group of 18–24, 21% from the age group of 25–34, 15% in the 35–44 group, 19% in the 45–54 group, and 21% in the 55 or above group. Nearly half of the respondents had university degrees.

6.5.3 Instruments

AI services vary across the study contexts. As this study is focused on hotels, the items that were used to assess AI service quality were adopted from Makadia (2018). This measure is reflective of AI-powered services provided to hotel guests by all of the surveyed hotels. To ensure the content validity, a review was conducted on AI services used by these hotels and consulted AI experts from the hotels to confirm these services. As a result, the following are the AI services that were used by all hotels and were included in this study: concierge robots, digital assistance, voice-activated services, travel experience enhancers, and automatic data processing. A total of 15 items were generated to reflect AI service quality in the hotel context. Participants were asked to rate the degree to which they were satisfied with certain services provided by the AI tools (1 = strongly disagree to 7 = strongly agree).

Employee service quality was measured by adapting Parasuraman et al.'s (1991) four dimensions in SERVQUAL, namely reliability, assurance, empathy, and responsiveness corresponding to the services performed by the employees. These dimensions empathise service promptness, accuracy, consistency, and employee friendliness and caring. Six items were used to measure responsiveness with a Cronbach's alpha value of 0.88, such as "the hotel's employees served me in a reasonable amount of time", and "the hotel employees quickly corrected anything that was wrong". Five items were used to measure reliability with a Cronbach's alpha value of 0.88, including "the hotel's employees were dependable and consistent", and "the hotel employee followed through on their promises". Eight items were used to measure assurance with a Cronbach's alpha value of 0.92, for example, "the hotel employees made me feel comfortable and confident in my dealings with them", and "the hotel employee made me feel personally safe". Five items were used to measure empathy with a Cronbach's alpha value of 0.86, including "the hotel employees made me feel special", and "the hotel employees could anticipate my individual needs and wants". There was also an item to measure customers' perception of overall service quality.

Customer satisfaction with AI and employee service quality was measured using three items adopted from Bogicevic et al. (2017) and Cronin et al. (2000). The items addressed overall satisfaction with AI and employee services, respectively. For example, "overall I am satisfied with services provided by AI/employees". The reliabilities were 0.80 and 0.76 for AI and employee service quality, respectively. Customer loyalty was measured by adapting Kandampully and Suhartanto's (2003) items to include customers' willingness to give referrals, to provide positive word-of-mouth communication, intention to return, and pay a premium price for service, with a reliability score of 0.83.

6.5.4 Findings and Discussion

6.5.4.1 AI and Employee Service in Service Quality

To understand how AI and employee service affect customer satisfaction and loyalty, these two constructs were treated as a second-order factor to examine their overall effects, and then as a first-order factor to assess the effect of each dimension on the outcomes of interest. Five dimensions of AI service quality that are offered by hotels to enhance customer experience were identified, including concierge robot service, digital assistance, voice-activated services, travel experience enhancers, and automatic data processing service and examined how they affect customer satisfaction and loyalty. As service quality, AI explains a significant portion of the variance in overall service quality. This finding indicates AI service quality is an important component of hotel service quality assessment.

When assessing unique variance by each dimension, only concierge robots, voice-activated services, and travel experience enhancers significantly explain overall service quality. This finding is plausible as customers have direct interactions with these services. Among these three services, voice-activated services had the most significant effect. The results show that when consumers have positive experiences with voice-activated services, they are more likely to develop favourable attitudes toward hotel services overall. However, when these services cannot answer consumers' questions sufficiently, they tend to have less favourable attitudes. Consumers are thus less likely to trust voice-activated services with something involving money (e.g., order meals) where AI may not be able to understand their questions well. On the other hand, digital assistance and automatic data processing often operates in the background and are less able to be directly assessed by users/customers.

The study shows that employee service quality explains a significant and substantial variance in overall service quality assessment. Among the four selected employee

Table 6.1 The respective effects of AI/employee service quality dimensions on customer-related outcomes

AI service quality	SQ	CSAIS	CL	Employee service quality	SQ	CSES	CL
Concierge robots	0.16*	0.25***	0.17*	Responsiveness	−0.03	−0.00	0.07
Digital assistance	−0.09	0.05	−0.02	Reliability	0.22**	0.21*	0.17
Voice-activated services	0.28***	0.05	0.08	Empathy	0.11*	−0.01	0.15
Travel experience enhancers	0.23**	0.03	0.10	Assurance	0.52***	0.23*	0.09
Automatic data processing	−0.04	0.10	−0.02				
R^2	0.19	0.16	0.06	R^2		0.18	0.21

Note * $p < 0.05$; ** $p < 0.01$; *** $p < 0.001$
SQ overall service quality, *CSAIS* customer satisfaction with AI service, *CL* customer loyalty, *CSES* customer satisfaction with employee service

services, responsiveness has an insignificant and negative effect. This result indicates that employees probably do not respond to customer requests as promptly as AI-powered tools do. Indeed, AI services are available around the clock as they are computer and internet-based, whereas, in most hotels, especially those of a small scale, employee services are often only accessible during office hours.

In relation to how AI and employee service quality are related to overall service quality, the results show that AI explains 19%, whereas employee service quality explains a 63% variance in the hotel's service quality assessment. Evidently, employee services play a primary role in this assessment. When assessing the unique variance contributed by each dimension, digital assistance and automatic data processing had no influence in the case of AI, whereas responsiveness did not contribute to the quality assessment in the case of employee services. When regressing all AI and employee service quality in one equation, interestingly, the effect of AI service quality becomes negative ($\beta = -0.09$, $p < 0.05$), nevertheless employee service quality has increased ($\beta = 0.83$, $p < 0.001$). The results are shown in Table 6.1.

6.5.4.2 The Impact of AI Service Quality on Customer Satisfaction and Loyalty

When testing AI's impact on customer satisfaction and loyalty, the study shows that AI service quality is significantly related to customer satisfaction, which has a substantial effect on customer loyalty. Overall, AI has a significant direct and

Fig. 6.1 The relationships between AI service quality, customer satisfaction with AI service and loyalty

indirect effect on customer loyalty, indicating a partial mediation role for customer satisfaction. This result demonstrates that customers loyalty behaviours can be a direct response to AI service quality. The results are shown in Fig. 6.1.

However, when examining the effect of each service quality dimension on customer satisfaction and loyalty, only the concierge robot service is significantly related to both customer satisfaction and loyalty. The robot can recommend interesting tour sights, answer customers' queries, and amuse them like a human employee. The other dimensions, namely digital assistance, voice-activated services, travel experience enhancers, and automatic data processing services, are computer-based without a humanoid representation like a concierge robot. This finding indicates that customers prefer to deal with human-like robots rather than pure technologies. As shown in Murphy et al. (2019), human-like robots have more influence on consumers accepting AI service. The other AI service dimensions are rather common and offer no novelty or differentiation from competitors. These services are expected of any service provider in this digital era. The results are shown in Table 6.1.

6.5.4.3   The Impact of Employee Service Quality on Customer Satisfaction, and Loyalty

When assessing the impact of employee service quality on customer satisfaction and loyalty, reliability, and assurance are significantly related to customer satisfaction. Responsiveness and empathy have almost zero effect. Reliability indicates employees perform and deliver service dependently as expected, and assurance refers to employees' credibility, professionalism, and friendliness. The significant effects exerted by these two dimensions show that hotel guests expect a certain level of service that symbolises the hotel quality, is manifested in employees' dependence and credible skills and together represent the uniqueness of the hotel. These findings are consistent with those in Prentice (2013). Responsiveness refers to employees' promptness and wiliness to help customers. The insignificant relationship may indicate that employees are not as responsive as expected or that customers are indifferent

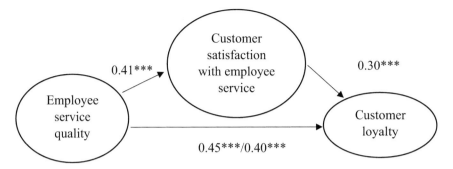

Fig. 6.2 The relationships between employee service quality, customer satisfaction with employee service, and loyalty

in this regard as they can access digital services at their discretion. Empathy indicates employees' approachability and empathy. The non-significant finding possibly shows that customers are used to digital services and are ready to access the necessary services from AI-powered tools. Customers may prefer to be left alone to enjoy the hotel facilities or sightseeing where the hotel is just perceived as a sleeping lodge. Most hotel guests may have minimal interaction with employees and hence require little attention from them.

Interestingly, none of these dimensions had a significant direct effect on customer loyalty, although overall employee service quality did. The results contrast to those in previous studies (e.g. Kandampully & Suhartanto, 2000; Liat et al., 2014). Such a finding may indicate that employee service is important to attract customer loyalty. Every aspect of employee service and every interpersonal encounter account for customers' responses. Suggesting that one unhappy encounter with an employee may affect the customers' assessment of overall service quality and satisfaction (Fig. 6.2).

6.6 Comparing the Influence of AI and Employee Service Quality

When the analysis included all AI and employee service quality in the regression equation, surprisingly, AI service quality has a negative effect on the overall service quality assessment, whilst employee service quality made a substantially significant contribution to this assessment. This outcome may be a result of "net suppression" (Cohen & Cohen, 1975) in that the significant relationship between AI service quality and overall service quality is accounted for by employee service. In other words, the primary role of AI service quality in overall quality is to suppress the error variance, rather than explaining more variance. When assessing each service quality dimension, employees' reliability, empathy, and assurance made unique variances in overall service quality. None of the AI service quality dimensions did. When the equation is extended to explain customers' loyalty, only employee empathy had a significant effect. These findings are interesting and are consistent with those of Naumov (2019). Since AI-powered tools and applications are becoming more popular in businesses and organisations for the purpose of enhancing operational efficiency and customer experience, they appear to have little or no influence in comparison to employee services. Service quality is regarded as a competitive tool to attract customer satisfaction and loyalty. These results may also imply that AI services cannot be regarded as a critical component of a competitive strategy that differentiates one organisation from the other.

6.7   Implications and Conclusion

Subsuming AI-powered applications as a component of service quality, the chapter discusses how it relates to customer satisfaction and loyalty. This initiative extends AI research into the services marketing domain and enriches service quality and customer loyalty research by incorporating an additional dimension to the overall service quality assessment.

A case study was conducted in the hotel sector to understand the respective impact of AI and employee service quality on customer satisfaction and loyalty. This study examines AI services as part of the hotel's service quality and reveals how AI and employee services contribute to overall service quality and how they are related to customer satisfaction and loyalty. The study adopts commonly used AI services in hotels and employee service quality is assessed based on reliability, responsiveness, assurance, and empathy. In particular, the study identifies five dimensions of AI services in the hotel industry. This AI service quality scale may be extended to other hospitality organisations to measure AI services.

The results show that both AI and employee service quality explain significant variance in the overall service quality assessment. When regressing them in one equation, AI service quality has a negative effect, whereas employee service quality explains a significantly substantial variance in the overall service quality assessment. When analysing them separately, both AI and employee service quality are significantly related to customer satisfaction and loyalty to the hotel, respectively. This study shows that customers still prefer employee services. The findings caution researchers and practitioners to seek or provide more empirical evidence before making any claims.

The study has important practical implications for hotel practitioners. Whilst AI-powered tools provide convenience for customers, these services do not represent a competitive advantage that gains favourable customer response. Employee services are still critical in the overall service quality assessment and customer satisfaction. However, it was also noted that customers seem to enjoy interacting with robots. Other AI-powered services may be taken for granted and offer no differentiation from other hotels. However, the results do indicate that AI services are important in the overall service quality assessment when employee services are not taken into account. The insignificant effect from employee responsiveness may caution hotel management to look into employees' promptness in response to customers' requests and investigate whether employees' responsiveness can be replaced by AI tools.

When integrating AI and employee services to assess their impact on customers' loyalty, employee empathy trumps all. Empathy is indicative of employees' approachability, communicative skills, and capacity to pay individualised attention to customers. Hotel management must ensure that employees demonstrate these traits and abilities. Empathy is a personal trait that differentiates one from the other employee. As compared to robot services, empathy is more reflective of human service and can shape customers' experiences at the hotel.

In conclusion, the chapter is intended to understand how machine/computer and employees contribute to the overall service quality and customers' responses, respectively. This option responds to various claims made in the wider community that AI-powered robots and machines may replace humans. The empirical study supports that AI-powered applications can be referred to as commercial services that service organisations (hotels) provide to customers to enhance their service experience at the hotels.

References

Baltar, F., & Brunet, I. (2012). Social research 2.0: Virtual snowball sampling method using Facebook. *Internet Research, 22*(1), 57–74.

Bogicevic, V., Bujisic, M., Bilgihan, A., Yang, W., & Cobanoglu, C. (2017). The impact of traveler-focused airport technology on traveler satisfaction. *Technological Forecasting and Social Change, 123*, 351–361.

Bolton, C., Machova, V., Kovacova, M., & Valaskova, K. (2018). The power of human-machine collaboration: Artificial Intelligence, business automation, and the smart economy. *Economics, Management, and Financial Markets, 13*(4), 51–56.

Bowen, J., & Morosan, C. (2018). Beware hospitality industry: The robots are coming. *Worldwide Hospitality and Tourism Themes, 10*(6), 726–733.

Brickman Bhutta, C. (2012). Not by the Book: Facebook as a Sampling Frame. *Sociological Methods & Research, 41*(1), 57–88.

Chung, M., Ko, E., Joung, H., & Kim, S. J. (2018). Chatbot e-service and customer satisfaction regarding luxury brands. *Journal of Business Research.*

Cohen, J., & Cohen, P. (1975). *Applied multiple regression/correlation analysis for the behavioral sciences.* Erlbaum.

Cronin, J. J., & Taylor, S. A. (1994). Servperf versus Servqual: Reconciling performance-based and perceptions-minus-expectations measurement of service quality. *Journal of Marketing, 58*(1), 125–131.

Cronin, J. J., Brady, M. K., & Hult, T. M. (2000). Assessing the effects of quality, value, and customer satisfaction on consumer behavioral intentions in service environments. *Journal of Retailing, 76*(2), 193–218.

Delcourt, C., Gremler, D., van Riel, A., & van Birgelen, M. (2013). Effects of perceived employee emotional competence on customer satisfaction and loyalty. *Journal of Service Management, 24*(1), 5–24.

Elliott, C. (2018). Chatbots are killing customer service, here's why. Published on 27 August 2018. https://www.forbes.com/sites/christopherelliott/2018/08/27/chatbots-are-killing-customer-service-heres-why/#79c1a77113c5

Glaser, A. (2017). When robots make us angry, humans pay the price. https://slate.com/business/2017/09/customers-who-get-angry-at-robots-take-out-their-frustrations-on-human-employees.html

Gursoy, D. (2018). Future of hospitality marketing and management research. *Tourism Management Perspectives, 25*, 185–188.

Heskett, J. L., Jones, T. O., Loveman, G. W., Sasser, W. E., & Schlesinger, L. A. (1994). Putting the service-profit chain to work. *Harvard Business Review, 72*(2), 164–174.

Ivanov, S. H., & Webster, C. (2017). Adoption of robots, artificial intelligence and service automation by travel, tourism and hospitality companies—A cost-benefit analysis. In *International Scientific Conference "Contemporary Tourism—Traditions and Innovations"*, Sofia University.

Kandampully, J., & Suhartanto, D. (2000). Customer loyalty in the hotel industry: The role of customer satisfaction and image. *International Journal of Contemporary Hospitality Management, 12*(6), 346–351.

Kandampully, J., & Suhartanto, D. (2003). The role of customer satisfaction and image in gaining customer loyalty in the hotel industry. *Journal of Hospitality & Leisure Marketing, 10*(1–2), 3–25.

Kaplan, A., & Haenlein, M. (2019). Siri, Siri, in my hand: Who's the fairest in the land? On the interpretations, illustrations, and implications of artificial intelligence. *Business Horizons, 62*(1), 15–25.

Kumar, V. (2010). Customer relationship management. In *Wiley international encyclopedia of marketing*.

Li, J., Bonn, M. A., & Ye, B. H. (2019). Hotel employee's artificial intelligence and robotics awareness and its impact on turnover intention: The moderating roles of perceived organizational support and competitive psychological climate. *Tourism Management, 73*, 172–181.

Liat, C. B., Mansori, S., & Huei, C. T. (2014). The associations between service quality, corporate image, customer satisfaction, and loyalty: Evidence from the Malaysian hotel industry. *Journal of Hospitality Marketing & Management, 23*(3), 314–326.

Lu, L., Cai, R., & Gursoy, D. (2019). Developing and validating a service robot integration willingness scale. *International Journal of Hospitality Management, 80*, 36–51.

Makadia, M. (2018). How cutting-edge hotels use artificial intelligence for a great guest experience. Published on 7 February 2018. PhocusWire. https://www.phocuswire.com/How-cutting-edge-hotels-use-artificial-intelligence-for-a-great-guest-experience

Maruti Techlabs (2018). https://marutitech.medium.com/the-future-of-insurance-customer-service-whatsappchatbots-391298f05652.

McKecnie, S., Ganguli, S., & Roy, S. K. (2011). Generic technology-based service quality dimensions in banking. *International Journal of Bank Marketing, 29*(2), 168–189.

Mithas, S., Krishnan, M. S., & Fornell, C. (2005). Why do customer relationship management applications affect customer satisfaction? *Journal of Marketing, 69*(4), 201–209.

Mueter, M. L., Ostrom, A. L., Roundtree, R. I., & Bitner, M. J. (2000). Self-service technologies: Understanding customer satisfaction with technology-based service encounters. *Journal of Marketing, 64*(3), 50–64.

Murphy, J., Gretzel, U., & Pesonen, J. (2019). Marketing robot services in hospitality and tourism: The role of anthropomorphism. *Journal of Travel & Tourism Marketing, 36*(7), 784–795.

Naumov, N. (2019). The impact of robots, artificial intelligence, and service automation on service quality and service experience in hospitality. In Ivanov, S. and Webster, C. (Ed.) *Robots, artificial intelligence, and service automation in travel, tourism and hospitality* (pp. 123–133). Emerald Publishing Limited.

Parasuraman, A., Berry, L. L., & Zeithaml, V. A. (1991). Refinement and reassessment of the SERVQUAL Scale. *Journal of Retailing, 67*(4), 420–450.

Parasuraman, A., Zeithaml, V. A., & Berry, L. L. (1995). Reassessment of expectations as a comparison standard in measuring service quality: Implications for further research. *Journal of Marketing, 58*(1), 111–124.

Prentice, C. (2013). Service quality perceptions and customer loyalty in casinos. *International Journal of Contemporary Hospitality Management, 25*(1), 49–64.

Prentice, C. (2014). Who stays, who walks, and why in high-intensity service contexts. *Journal of Business Research, 67*(4), 608–614.

Prentice, C. (2019). *Emotional intelligence and Marketing*. World Scientific Publishing Co. Pte, Ltd., Singapore. ISBN 978-981-120-354-1

Prentice, C., Lopes, S. D., & Wang, X. (2019). Emotional intelligence or artificial intelligence—An employee perspective. *Journal of Hospitality Marketing & Management*, 1–27.

Prentice, C., Weaven, S., & Wong, I. A. (2020). Linking AI quality performance and customer engagement: The moderating effect of AI preference. *International Journal of Hospitality Management, 90*, 102629.

Russell, S. J., & Norvig, P. (2009). *Artificial intelligence: A modern approach*. Prentice Hall.

Sentence, R. (2018). Robots or humans: Which provide a better customer experience. https://econsultancy.com/robots-or-humans-which-provide-a-better-customer-experience/

Shi, Y., Prentice, C., & He, W. (2014). Linking service quality, customer satisfaction and loyalty in casinos, does membership matter? *International Journal of Hospitality Management, 40*, 81–91.

Solomon, M. (2016, March 18). Technology invades hospitality industry: Hilton robot, Domino delivery droid, Ritz-Carlton mystique. Forbes. Retrieved from https://www.forbes.com/sites/micahsolomon/2016/03/18/high-tech-hospitality-hilton-robot-concierge-dominos-delivery-droid-ritz-carlton-mystique/#25a0730b120b

Tabachnick, B. G., Fidell, L. S., & Ullman, J. B. (2007). *Using multivariate statistics* (Vol. 5). Pearson.

Van Belleghem, S. (2017). *Customers the day after tomorrow—How to attract customers in a world of AI, bots and automation*. LannooCampus.

Wirtz, J., Chew, P., & Lovelock, C. (2013). *Essentials of services marketing*. Pearson Education.

Wirtz, J., Patterson, P. G., Kunz, W. H., Gruber, T., Lu, V. N., Paluch, S., & Martins, A. (2018). Brave new world: Service robots in the frontline. *Journal of Service Management, 29*(5), 907–931.

Zeithaml, V. A., Berry, L. L., & Parasuraman, B. A. (1996). The Behavioral consequences of service quality. *Journal of Marketing, 60*(2), 31–46.

Chapter 7
Leveraging Artificial Intelligence for Customer Engagement

Abstract This chapter discusses how customers' preference for AI services affects their satisfaction with multidimensional elements associated with service derived from AI-powered tools, as well as their affinity for the service organisation that offers AI service. Such affinity is manifested in customers' engagement with the service organisation. *Qui me amat, amat et canem meum—Saint Bernard of Clairvaux.* The chapter begins with operationalising AI and proposes its relationship with customer engagement. An empirical study is conducted in Australian hotels to support these hypotheses. The findings of the case study are elaborated. The implications of these findings conclude this chapter.

7.1 Diagnosing Artificial Intelligence

AI generally embodies machine simulations of human intelligence for performing human tasks operated through the interpretation and understanding of imputed data which are used for predetermined goals and tasks (Russell & Norvig, 2009). AI is embedded in various types of technologies: for instance, (1) automation, such as robotic process automation, which differs from IT automation and can be programmed to perform high-volume, repeatable tasks like humans; (2) machine or deep learning, which enables computers to automate predictive analytics and act without programming, including supervised, unsupervised and reinforcement learning; (3) machine vision, which captures and analyses visual information using cameras and digital signal processes such as human eyesight, which can be used, for example, in signature identification and image analysis; (4) natural language processing (NLP), which is based on machine leaning and processes human language via a computer program including text translation, sentiment analysis and speech recognition (e.g., spam detection which determines a junk or spam mail based on the subject line and the text); (5) robotics that are used to perform mundane tasks requiring low-level social interactions (e.g., assembling lines in manufacturing); (6) self-driving cars, which automate safe driving using computer vision, image recognition and deep learning capabilities (Burns & Laskowski, 2018).

AI has progressively infiltrated the commercial world to facilitate internal business operations for the organisation and external transactions with customers in both personal and impersonal service encounters (Prentice et al., 2019a, 2019b, 2019c). For instance, AI can be used in personnel recruitment by combining face recognition and natural language processing technologies during interviews; training and development using robots and visual scanning technologies; and salary evaluation through neural network functioning (Jia et al., 2018). Amazon and Netflix routinely utilise AI to analyse customer data and customise products for customers (Walch, 2019).

AI has evolved rapidly from performing simple tasks (e.g., Siri) to undertaking more sophisticated social functions such as recognising customers' emotions for subsequent intervention (Prentice et al., 2019a). AI can be effectively utilised in reasoning, explaining, modelling, predicting and forecasting. The evolution of AI has presented unprecedented convenience (24-h automated services) to customers in the service sector. In practice, AI (e.g. robots) is extensively used in customer service to engage customers and enhance the service experience by providing convenience and flexibility (e.g., 24-h automated services; concierge robots). Industry practitioners and IT consultants are the most prominent protagonists who promote and reinforce the role of AI in customer-centric businesses (e.g., Kannan & Bernoff, 2019; Walch, 2019; Walchuk, 2019).

This chapter positions AI-powered tools (e.g., concierge robots in hotels, travel enhancers, chatbots) as computer/machine-enabled services that cater to customers in a fashion similar to other commercial services (e.g., employee service) and benefit all involved parties (e.g., the organisation, customers) (de Kervenoael et al., 2020).

As in any commercial service, the value of AI services is revealed in customer perceptions and assessments of such services. In the service-marketing literature, service quality often reflects customers' perceptions and value-judgments of a service (Yuan & Jang, 2008). Service quality captures service excellence that is deemed to meet or exceed customer expectations (Parasuraman 1995; Prentice, 2013; Shi et al., 2014). Equally, the quality of AI services is manifested in customers' perceptions and assessments.

7.2 Operationalising Artificial Intelligence

Given that AI is operated through machines and computer programs, the level of AI service is dependent upon both imputed data and programming capability. The service derived with AI-powered tools is multidimensional, involving tangible (e.g., butler service from concierge robots) and intangible (e.g., information from chatbots) elements. Unlike other services offered by organizations, AI as a technology-based service involves information and system characteristics that influence information and system quality perceptions and, ultimately, user satisfaction (Wixom & Todd, 2005). Hence, AI service quality can be operationalised into informational and systematic quality.

Information quality is pertinent to accuracy, currency, presentation and completeness of AI service provision (Wixom & Todd, 2005). The information provided by AI-powered applications such as Siri, chatbots and other automated messaging tools must be as accurate and timely as possible to effectively address users/customers' queries (Hong et al., 2001). For example, AI-powered E-travel agents manage travel planning, sightseeing, car rentals and hotel bookings. The information relating to these activities must be reflective of customer requests and demands (Zanker et al., 2008). The activities recommended by AI-powered intermediaries must be consistent with tourists' preferences and requirements (García-Crespo et al., 2011; Zanker et al., 2008). The accuracy of destination information by Smart Tourist Information Points is important for tourists' decision-making pertaining to destination choice (Garrido et al., 2017).

System quality is predicated on the responsiveness of AI-powered tools and flexibility of the system adapted to a variety of user/customer demands (Wixom & Todd, 2005). For instance, restaurants use AI to assist customers in ordering food, which varies across customers. AI tools must respond to customers in a timely manner and provide sufficient flexibility in line with customer demands. These AI services are deemed as object indicators that influence object-based beliefs, while service quality is based on customers' perceptions and assessments; hence AI services regarded as object-based beliefs. The foregoing discussion informs the hypothesis:

AI service is significantly related to AI information quality and system quality.

7.3   AI Service Quality and Customer Satisfaction

Service quality is related to an individual's object-based attitude, which is manifested in the level of satisfaction with service quality based on the theory of planned behaviour (Ajzen, 1980; Wixom & Todd, 2005). Customer satisfaction, deemed as a post-consumption response, is defined as an overall feeling of pleasure or disappointment emerging from comparisons of perceived performance of a service with pre-service expectations (Oliver, 1980). Customer satisfaction can be measured as transaction-specific with discrete elements or events (e.g., AI information quality, AI system quality), or as overall satisfaction reflecting a holistic assessment of all experience encounters (Cronin et al., 2000; Gustafsson et al., 2005; Veloutsou, 2015). Overall satisfaction with a service is relevant to the attributes of the provided service (Chow, 2014).

Service quality and customer satisfaction are generally regarded as discrete constructs and modelled separately (Cronin & Taylor, 1992; Hu & Huang, 2011; Yoon & Uysal, 2005; Yuan & Jang, 2008). Service quality perceptions are cognitive reactions to the experience, whereas customer satisfaction represents an affective reaction to that experience (Tosun et al., 2015). Service quality is an antecedent to customer satisfaction (Cronin et al., 2000; Rust et al., 1995; Woodside et al., 1989; Zeithaml et al., 1996). Consistent with the aforementioned two-dimensional service quality, customer satisfaction can be operationalised into information and system dimensions. The services marketing literature confirms that service quality is widely recognised as an antecedent of satisfaction and behavioural intentions that leads to organisational profitability (Cronin et al., 2000; Kim et al., 2016; Zeithaml et al., 1996), and such a relationship shall also be present in AI applications. Hence, the following hypothesis can be made:

AI information quality and system quality are positively and significantly related to customer satisfaction with AI service.

7.4   Customer Satisfaction and Engagement

Customer engagement captures customers' affective, cognitive and behavioural involvement with the service organisation (Hollebeek, 2011; So et al., 2016). Customer engagement indicates the process of customers' "reaching out" to the organization, demonstrated in their cognitive, emotional, behavioural, sensorial, and social responses (Lemon & Verhoef, 2016). Customer engagement can also be referred to as state of mind or a psychological process that generates customer loyalty (Bowden, 2009; Kumar & Pansari, 2016). Customer engagement includes co-creation, social influence through word of mouth, customer referrals, purchasing behaviour, influencing, and knowledge behaviours (Verhoef et al., 2010).

Customer engagement reflects co-creation between the service providers and customers; and the level of engagement with the service organization and its associated businesses has financial implications for the organization as well as for customers (Brodie et al., 2011; Hoyer et al., 2010; Nambisan & Nambisan, 2008). Van Doorn et al. (2010) provided a comprehensive conceptual framework detailing the antecedents, components and consequences of customer engagement. The model indicates customer satisfaction is proposed as a customer-based predictor of customer engagement.

Relevant marketing and management literature shows that customer satisfaction is a universal antecedent of behavioural intentions and behaviours (Bowen & Chen, 2001; Kandampully & Suhartanto, 2000; Yuksel et al., 2010). These studies show that a high level of satisfaction influences customer patronage and retention. However, many empirical studies also demonstrate that this relationship is not significant (e.g., Bitner & Hubbert, 1994; Kivela et al., 2000; Rust et al., 1995). Neal (1999) argued that satisfaction on its own cannot predict customers' purchase behaviour or loyalty, but could possibly improve customer involvement with the organization or the brand. For example, although a satisfied customer may not return to the business on account of financial constraints or other situational factors, this customer can still be engaged with the organization as a source of referrals. Similarly, an extremely dissatisfied passenger might engage with the organization in the sense of spreading negative word of mouth communication, or continue to be engaged in other ways that may be available.

In reality, AI has been used in customer services to engage customers. For instance, chatbots as the first point of contact could identify customer needs and problems and transfer customers to human agents when necessary. Chatbots sometimes engage customers by providing a positive and consistent level of interaction with customers and continuous service to promote seamless service experiences (Walch, 2019). A concierge robot can interact with hotel guests for an extended period of time (Rodriguez-Lizundia et al., 2015). Interactive experience is an important means to enhance customer engagement in the service organization (Hayes & MacLeod, 2007; Vivek et al., 2014). Customers tend to be more engaged when they receive pleasant and memorable experiences with AI services. Such experience motivates customers to have more physical, mental, social, and emotional engagement with the brand or the associated organisation (Carù & Cova, 2003; Hayes & MacLeod, 2007; Ullah et al., 2018). This discussion informs the hypothesis:

Customer satisfaction with AI service quality is positively and significantly related to customer engagement with the service organisation.

7.5 Customers' Preference Matters

Each individual customer has different requests and demands (Prentice, 2013). Some customers may opt for employee services, others may prefer dealing with AI service (Prentice et al., 2019a, 2019b, 2019c). Numerous studies have shown that employee service is pivotal in determining customers' attitudes and behaviours (e.g., Delcourt et al., 2013; Prentice, 2013). Customers prefer personal interactions with service employees who are reliable, responsive, professional, and empathetic as shown in SERVQUAL measures (Parasuraman et al., 1991; Prentice, 2013). It is imperative for service organisations to understand customers' preferences in order to cater for individual needs and create optimal customer experience. From a customer's perspective, such preference can lead to positive attitudes and affinity for the service organisation. As the saying goes: *Qui me amat, amat et canem meum* or "love me so love my dog," a sermon used by Saint Bernard of Clairvaux, indicating that if you love someone, you must accept their good and bad as well as everything associated with them.

In the social sciences, the notion of preferences is derived from rational choice theory, which refers to an optimal choice based on the decision-maker's best interest and the relative utility of given alternatives (Blume & Easley, 2016). The premise of the theory is that humans act as rational agents who consider the costs and benefits of a task carefully and behave consistently with self-determined choices (Tversky & Kahneman, 1986). Preference represents customers' disposition to favour services provided by an organization. Prior research shows that preference is related to customer-related outcomes such as purchase intention, willingness to buy and becoming a referral (Bagozzi, 1992). However, Tversky and Thaler (1990) indicate that preference is a context-dependent process by means of choice, and hence labile. Customers who have a preference for AI services may hold more positive object-based attitudes (manifested in satisfaction with AI) and tend to be more engaged with object-related entities—the service organisation. This proposition accords with rational choice theory in that an individual would be able to better enjoy experience with AI services, and hence be more engaged with such "self-determined choice," when the quality of the AI service is superior and the consumer holds a high level of interest.

These relationships can be accounted for by the affordance theory (Gibson & Nobel, 1986). The theory considers environmental objects around an organism (e.g., an animal, a human) as an opportunity for action (Gibson, 2000). Although the theory originated in the ecological literature, the affordance concept has been widely applied to organisations to understand how technologies can be utilised to achieve organizational outcomes including operational efficiency, customer satisfaction and engagement (e.g., Cabiddu et al., 2014; Ganguli & Roy, 2011).

In essence, AI-powered tools in service organisations are manifested as services provided to customers around the clock. These AI-powered tools facilitate business transactions and enhance customer experiences. AI services can be such objects. In particular, customers or service providers represent organisms that perceive AI as an opportunity to attain added convenience (for customers) and can provide increased levels of customer engagement (for the provider). The affordance theoretical perspective suggests that AI tools have inherent meaning that users can understand and apply without necessarily understanding their sophisticated technological underpinning (Jones, 2003). It is plausible to posit that the spillover effect from "love me" (AI service) to "love my dog" (the service organisation) is only significant for customers who prefer AI service over interactions with service employees. The foregoing discussion leads to the following hypothesis:

AI preference has a significant moderation effect on the relationship between AI service quality and satisfaction, between satisfaction with AI and customer engagement.

The following sections present an empirical study to test these hypotheses. The method of the study is outlined first, followed by discussing the findings. The implications are highlighted to conclude this chapter.

7.6 The Empirical Study

7.6.1 Sample and Data Collection Procedure

A case study was undertaken at hotels in Australia to empirically test the proposed relationships. The data were collected from a sample of customers who had stayed in one of Australian hotels within last 12 months that used AI-powered tools to serve customers. The prospective respondents were those who understood and had used AI services in these hotels. The respondents were aged above 18 years. Screen questions were developed to ensure these criteria. Each AI service was explained in detail with examples and appropriate weblinks so that the prospective respondents had a better understanding of their AI service experience. The survey was conducted online through Qualtrics for flexibility, convenience and cost-efficiency. Virtual snowball sampling was employed to access hidden populations. Given AI service is manifested in various forms and some of which may not be perceived as AI, any relevant queries from respondents can be directed to their friends via social media for a speedy response rather than to the researchers.

A pilot study was conducted with Ph.D. students who had experienced AI services in hotels, to ensure appropriate response time and clarity of wording. Consequently, some wording of the questionnaire items was modified. The information enclosed with the survey stated that participation in the survey was voluntary and anonymous, and could be terminated at any time at the respondents' discretion; although the survey was designed to prevent skipping questions should they decide to participate. Respondents were requested to respond as truthfully and accurately as possible. The survey was closed after 3 weeks, with nearly 400 valid responses generated.

7.6.2 Instruments

The scale measurements of interest were adopted from the existing literature. AI-related variables including AI performance drivers, quality, and satisfaction were adopted from Wixom and Todd (2005). The *AI service performance drivers* scale contains 15 items pertaining to five aspects of AI performance, including *AI accuracy, currency, reliability, flexibility, and timeliness.* Accuracy and currency indicate the information provided by AI is correct and up to date. Reliability indicates the dependability of AI-powered systems. Flexibility represents adaptability and customisation that is provided for individual customers. Timeliness relates to the responsiveness of AI tools. Each driver contains three items, and it demonstrates adequate scale consistency with Cronbach's alpha (α) ≥ 0.80.

AI information quality and *AI system quality* both contain three items, and they demonstrate good scale consistency with $\alpha = 0.92$. Although *AI information satisfaction* and *AI system satisfaction* were assessed by two items, scale reliability remains adequate with $\alpha \geq 0.88$. AI preference was adopted based on the work of Cialdini et al. (1995). The scale contains three items, and it demonstrates good reliability with $\alpha = 0.93$.

A 25-item customer engagement measure was adopted from So et al.'s (2016) multidimensional scale. This measure was deemed to be suitable since it was developed in the tourism and hospitality context and reflects customers' affective, cognitive and psychological involvement with the brand or organisation. Five dimensions were included in this measure: (1) *identification*, representing customers' attachment to the brand; (2) *attention*, indicative of customers' attentiveness; (3) focus and connection with the brand, reflecting enthusiasm representing customers' excitement and interest; (4) *absorption*, indicating customers' pleasant state; and (5) *interaction*, indicating customers' participation.

7.6.3 Findings and Discussion

7.6.3.1 AI Service Quality and Customer Satisfaction

To test the proposed relationships, the demographic characteristics such as gender, age, education, and family income were controlled to minimise compounding effects. Five models are tested. Model 1 is focused on AI service and service quality; Model 2 on AI service quality and satisfaction; Models 3 and 5 on the moderating effects of AI preference; and Model 4 on AI satisfaction and engagement.

Results in Model 1 reveal that the five AI performance drivers are all significant predictors of AI information quality ($b_{Accuracy} = 0.14$, $p < 0.05$; $b_{Currency} = 0.19$, $p < 0.01$; $b_{Reliability} = 0.12$, $p < 0.10$; $b_{Flexibility} = 0.18$, $p < 0.01$; and $b_{Timeliness} = 0.49$, $p < 0.001$) and IA system quality ($b_{Accuracy} = 0.11$, $p < 0.10$; $b_{Currency} = 0.15$, $p < 0.05$; $b_{Reliability} = 0.29$, $p < 0.001$; $b_{Flexibility} = 0.17$, $p < 0.01$; and $b_{Timeliness} = 0.39$, $p < 0.001$). These findings are plausible. Although these services are offered by AI-powered tools, from the customer's perspective, they are part of the firm's service offering and influence customers' overall quality perception. These AI-powered service dimensions are consistent with traditional service quality assessment (see Parasuraman et al., 1991).

The findings shows that customers believe accurate and updated information is important in their decision-making. Necessity of information is both subjective and context-dependent. Presentation of the information appears irrelevant to customers' quality perceptions. Customers understand that the information from AI is computer-generated. Accordingly, they are more tolerant of the level of thoroughness and formatting. At a minimum, customers should expect correctness and currency from their provider, as computer-operated AI can be more advanced than humans in collecting and disseminating information.

The system characteristics represent internal operations, which inevitably affect user experience. For instance, customers may not fully understand the internal operative system of the concierge robot in hotels. Customers would expect the robot concierge to be capable of making restaurants reservations, provide sightseeing recommendations, and book transportation. Customers judge the quality of the robot service, as shown in in Tussyadiah and Parks (2018), based on whether the recommended tours are as anticipated and whether time and location of the restaurant are consistent with their booking (i.e., reliability); whether they could alter their reservation (i.e., flexibility); and whether the robot responds to their requests in a timely manner (i.e., timeliness).

Model 2 assesses the relationships between AI quality and AI satisfaction. Results indicate that both AI information quality and AI system quality are significant predictors for AI information satisfaction ($b_{AI\ information\ quality} = 0.63$, $p < 0.001$; $b_{AI\ system\ quality} = 0.31$, $p < 0.001$) and AI system satisfaction ($b_{AI\ information\ quality} = 0.52$, $p < 0.001$; $b_{AI\ system\ quality} = 0.43$, $p < 0.001$). Model 4 examines the relationship between AI satisfaction and customer engagement. Results indicate that AI information satisfaction ($b_{AI\,information\,satisfaction} = 0.38$, $p < 0.001$; $b_{AI\,system\,satisfaction} = 0.20$, $p < 0.001$) and AI system satisfaction are both significant predictors of customer engagement. The results are shown in Table 7.1.

The results indicate that information and system quality are equally important to customers, given that both simultaneously affect customer satisfaction, but that information quality has a larger effect. This finding suggests that customers tend to perceive AI as a tool for information generation and are less concerned with the system of operation. As AI service quality represents object-based beliefs, and customer satisfaction refers to object-related attitudes, the finding of this significant chain relationship conforms Ajzen's (1985) theory of planned behaviour. Customer engagement in this study indicates affective, cognitive and behavioural involvement with the service organisation (the hotel in this study). The result confirms that customers' positive attitudes (satisfaction) towards AI service quality permits them to engage with the hotel to the extent that they feel they are affiliated and connected with the hotel emotionally, intellectually and behaviourally.

Model 3 tests the moderating effect of AI preference on the quality–satisfaction relationship. Results show that the AI preference × information quality interaction ($b = -0.10, p < 0.01$) and AI preference × system quality interaction are significant only on AI information satisfaction. The direct effect of AI preference is also significant ($b \geq 0.09$, $p < 0.001$). Figure 7.1 depicts that the AI information quality—information satisfaction relationship is more salient for people who have a lower level of AI preference than for those who have higher preference; yet the effect of AI preference is only apparent for people who perceive a low AI information quality provided by a focal hotel. Figure 7.2 illustrates that the AI system quality—information satisfaction relationship is more acute for people who have high AI preference, and the effect of AI preference is only apparent for those who perceive a high AI system quality offered by a focal hotel. Model 5 tests the moderation of AI preference on the AI satisfaction – customer engagement relationship. Results show that only the AI preference × AI information satisfaction is significant ($b = 0.11$, $p < 0.05$). Figure 7.3 depicts that the AI information satisfaction – customer engagement relationship is more salient for high AI preference hotel guests.

These findings suggest that, amongst available services provided by the organization, those who prefer AI services generally hold positive attitudes toward AI service quality. Such preferences enhance their beliefs about AI information quality and satisfaction, which leads to enhanced satisfaction and improved engagement with the organization, in line with the significant and positive moderation effect of AI preference. Notably, the moderation effect is consistently significant in relation to information quality and satisfaction, lending support to the contention that customers perceive AI as information generation tools which provide convenience and flexibility.

Table 7.1 Results of parameter estimation

	Model 1		Model 2		Model 3		Model 4	Model 5
	AI information quality	AI system quality	AI information satisfaction	AI system satisfaction	AI information satisfaction	AI system satisfaction	Customer engagement	Customer engagement
Main effects								
AI accuracy	0.14*	0.11†						
AI currency	0.19**	0.15*						
AI reliability	0.12†	0.29***						
AI flexibility	0.18**	0.17**						
AI timeliness	0.49***	0.39***						
AI information quality (AIIQ)			0.63***	0.52***	0.60***	0.49***		
AI system quality (AISQ)			0.31***	0.43***	0.26***	0.35***		
AI information satisfaction (AIIS)							0.38***	0.28***
AI system satisfaction (AISS)							0.37***	0.20**
Moderating effect								
AI preference					0.09***	0.12***		0.02
AI Preference × AIIQ					−0.10**	−0.03		

(continued)

Table 7.1 (continued)

	Model 1		Model 2		Model 3		Model 4	Model 5
	AI information quality	AI system quality	AI information satisfaction	AI system satisfaction	AI information satisfaction	AI system satisfaction	Customer engagement	Customer engagement
AI preference × AISQ					0.08*	−0.02		
AI preference × AIIS								0.11*
AI preference × AISS								−0.04
R^2	0.61	0.60	0.79	0.75	0.81	0.76	0.42	0.54
ΔR^2					0.02	0.01		0.12

Note † $p < 0.10$, * $p < 0.05$, ** $p < 0.01$, *** $p < 0.001$

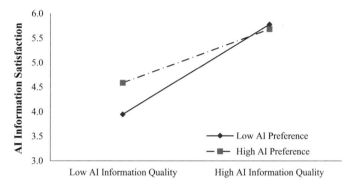

Fig. 7.1 AI information quality by AI preference interaction on AI information satisfaction

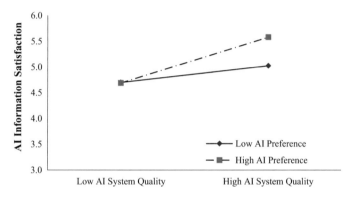

Fig. 7.2 AI system quality by AI preference interaction on AI information satisfaction

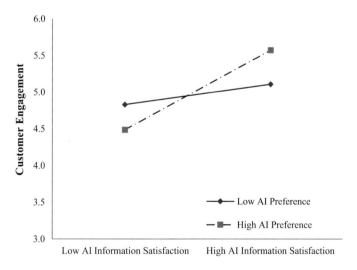

Fig. 7.3 AI information satisfaction by AI preference interaction on customer engagement

7.7 Implications and Conclusion

The chapter proposes AI as commercial service and adopts the affordance theoretical perspective to build understanding of how such services can be regarded as opportunities to influence customer engagement. This chapter discusses how service organisations can utilise AI-powered tools as service indicators that specifically cater to customers to create opportunities for customer actions and behaviours. AI technology-based services, object-based service quality (beliefs) and customer satisfaction (attitudes) are operationalised into information and system components. Given that AI service quality is an addition to traditional tangible and intangible service offerings, the chapter draws on the rational choice theory to propose preference as a moderator in the belief-attitude-engagement relationship chain.

From a services marketing perspective, this study introduces a new measure of service quality by adding the service performed by computers or machines to quality assessments. Such AI-empowered services now permeate service delivery in these organizations. Customers' perceptions of these services influence customer attitudes and behaviours, and these findings present an opportunity for academics to look beyond traditional service quality measures.

Furthermore, previous marketing research has tended to use TPB to explain the relationship between customer perceptions, satisfaction and loyalty indicators. This study models customer engagement as the outcome of customer perceptions and attitudes, as the engagement is reflected in affective, cognitive and behavioural connection with the service organization. The findings imply that customers' actual purchase and loyalty behaviours may be intervened by customer engagement. To better address customers' behavioural responses, it appears imperative to understand their involvement and connection with organizations. The empirical study for this chapter responds to Sniehotta et al.'s (2014) call for "time to retire the theory of planned behaviour"—demonstrating that it may not necessarily be prudent to retire TPB, but it may be worthwhile to modify the theory by looking into mediators and moderators as well as the study context, since customers' preferences show a significant moderation effect.

The study also contributes to customer engagement research by incorporating AI as an antecedent to customer engagement. Researchers have attempted to identify customer, organisation and context-based predictors or motivators of customer engagement. AI service quality can bridge these domains and be viewed as a service offered by the organisation, perceived by customers, and operated in a technological context. Technology-based AI can be considered a new means to manage customer relationships and engage with customers.

The practical implications from the findings of this study are threefold. For IT practitioners or consultants, this study shows that AI is more than a package of technology-centric tools and advanced computer programming. AI should be designed to be a commercial service that can improve customer relationships with the service organisation and enhance customer experiences. As all dimensions of AI service performance contribute to overall quality perception, IT technicians or experts should look into these aspects and ensure optimal performance to enhance customer satisfaction. Customers may not be aware of the difference between AI system and information quality. AI tools must be designed to be user friendly since both quality dimensions influence customer satisfaction and engagement.

For marketers, this study provides a fresh perspective to attract customer satisfaction and loyalty. It appears timely to look beyond traditional marketing offerings such as promotions, complimentary services, and/or loyalty programs. Offering quality service has been the key approach to customer satisfaction. Service quality primarily consists of tangible (e.g. facilities, pleasant atmospherics) and intangible offerings (e.g. employee empathy, reliability) manifested in each service encounter. This study shows that services provided by machines or robots can contribute to service quality perception, customer satisfaction and engagement. Customers are now more technologically equipped, and their demands extend beyond tangible and intangible services.

For service organisations such as hotels, this study provides a new means to engage customers and enhance customer experiences. In particular, the study provides an additional service quality measure for hotels or service organizations to improve overall service quality and service experiences. Given that AI preference has a significant moderation effect, we recommend that organizations identify those technology/AI inclined customers and provide appropriate technology-based services—particularly AI tools that provide information, as AI preference is closely related to information quality and satisfaction. In other words, customers generally use AI tools for information and decision-making.

In sum, this study contributes to AI research and extends the IT domain into marketing and customer relationship management. In particular, the study extends current understanding in the IT literature by including commercial customers rather than IT technicians as AI users.

References

Ajzen, I. (1980). Understanding attitudes and predicting social behavior.

Ajzen, I. (1985). From intentions to actions: A theory of planned behavior. In *Action control* (pp. 11–39). Springer.

Bagozzi, R. P. (1992). The self-regulation of attitudes, intentions, and behavior. *Social Psychology Quarterly*, 178–204.

Bitner, M. J., & Hubbert, A. R. (1994). Encounter satisfaction versus overall satisfaction versus quality. *Service Quality: New Directions in Theory and Practice, 34*(2), 72–94.

Blume, L. E., & Easley, D. (2016). Rationality. *The New Palgrave Dictionary of Economics*, 1–13.

Bowden, J. L. H. (2009). The process of customer engagement: A conceptual framework. *Journal of Marketing Theory and Practice, 17*(1), 63–74.

Bowen, J. T., & Chen, S. L. (2001). The relationship between customer loyalty and customer satisfaction. *International Journal of Contemporary Hospitality Management*.

Brodie, R. J., Hollebeek, L. D., & Smith, S. D. (2011). Engagement: An important bridging concept for the emerging SD logic lexicon. In *Proceedings*.

Burns, E., & Laskowski, N. (2018). Artificial intelligence in AI in IT tools promises better, faster and stronger ops. https://searchenterpriseai.techtarget.com/definition/AI-Artificial-Intelligence

Cabiddu, F., De Carlo, M., & Piccoli, G. (2014). Social media affordances: Enabling customer engagement. *Annals of Tourism Research, 48*, 175–192.

Carù, A., & Cova, B. (2003). Revisiting consumption experience: A more humble but complete view of the concept. *Marketing Theory, 3*(2), 267–286.

Chow, C. K. W. (2014). Customer satisfaction and service quality in the Chinese airline industry. *Journal of Air Transport Management, 35*, 102–107.

Cialdini, R. B., Trost, M. R., & Newsom, J. T. (1995). Preference for consistency: The development of a valid measure and the discovery of surprising behavioral implications. *Journal of Personality and Social Psychology, 69*(2), 318.

Cronin, J. J., Jr., Brady, M. K., & Hult, G. T. M. (2000). Assessing the effects of quality, value, and customer satisfaction on consumer behavioral intentions in service environments. *Journal of Retailing, 76*(2), 193–218.

Cronin, J. J., Jr., & Taylor, S. A. (1992). Measuring service quality: A reexamination and extension. *Journal of Marketing, 56*(3), 55–68.

de Kervenoael, R., Hasan, R., Schwob, A., & Goh, E. (2020). Leveraging human-robot interaction in hospitality services: Incorporating the role of perceived value, empathy, and information sharing into visitors' intentions to use social robots. *Tourism Management, 78*, 104042.

Delcourt, C., Gremler, D. D., Riel, A. C. R., & Birgelen, M. V. (2013). Effects of perceived employee emotional competence on customer satisfaction and loyalty the mediating role of rapport. *Journal of Service Management, 24*(1), 5–24.

Ganguli, S., & Roy, S. K. (2011). Generic technology-based service quality dimensions in banking: Impact on customer satisfaction and loyalty. *International Journal of Bank Marketing, 29*(2), 168–189.

García-Crespo, Á., López-Cuadrado, J. L., Colomo-Palacios, R., González-Carrasco, I., & Ruiz-Mezcua, B. (2011). Sem-Fit: A semantic based expert system to provide recommendations in the tourism domain. *Expert Systems with Applications, 38*(10), 13310–13319.

Garrido, P., Seron, F. J., Barrachina, J., & Martinez, F. J. (2017). *Smart tourist information points by combining agents, semantics and AI techniques* (No. ART-2017-99163).

Gibson, A. C., & Nobel, P. S. (1986). *The cactus primer*. Harvard University Press.

Gibson, E. J. (2000). Where is the information for affordances? *Ecological Psychology, 12*(1), 53–56.

Gustafsson, A., Johnson, M. D., & Roos, I. (2005). The effects of customer satisfaction, relationship commitment dimensions, and triggers on customer retention. *Journal of Marketing, 69*(4), 210–218.

Hayes, D., & MacLeod, N. (2007). Packaging places: Designing heritage trails using an experience economy perspective to maximize visitor engagement. *Journal of Vacation Marketing, 13*(1), 45–58.

Hollebeek, L. (2011). Exploring customer brand engagement: Definition and themes. *Journal of Strategic Marketing, 19*(7), 555–573.

Hong, W., Thong, J., Wong, W.-M., Tam, K.-Y. (2001/2002). Determinants of user acceptance of digital libraries: An empirical examination of individual differences and systems characteristics. *Journal of Management Information Systems, 18*(3) 97–124.

Hoyer, W. D., Chandy, R., Dorotic, M., Krafft, M., & Singh, S. S. (2010). Consumer cocreation in new product development. *Journal of Service Research, 13*(3), 283–296.

Hu, K. C., & Huang, M. C. (2011). Effects of service quality, innovation and corporate image on customer's satisfaction and loyalty of air cargo terminal. *International Journal of Operations Research, 8*(4), 36–47.

Jia, Y., Ye, Y., Feng, Y., Lai, Y., Yan, R., & Zhao, D. (2018, July). Modeling discourse cohesion for discourse parsing via memory network. In *Proceedings of the 56th Annual Meeting of the Association for Computational Linguistics (Volume 2: Short Papers)* (pp. 438–443).

Jones, K. S. (2003). What is affordance? *Ecological Psychology., 15*(2), 107–114.

Kandampully, J., & Suhartanto, D. (2000). Customer loyalty in the hotel industry: The role of customer satisfaction and image. *International Journal of Contemporary Hospitality Management, 12*(6), 346–351.

Kannan, P. V., & Bernoff. J. (2019). The future of customer service is AI-human collaboration. MITSloan. https://sloanreview.mit.edu/article/the-future-of-customer-service-is-ai-human-collaboration/. Published on 29 May 2019.

Kim, Y., Park, Y. J., Choi, J., & Yeon, J. (2016). The adoption of mobile payment services for "Fintech." *International Journal of Applied Engineering Research, 11*(2), 1058–1061.

Kivela, J., Inbakaran, R., & Reece, J. (2000). Consumer research in the restaurant environment. Part 3: Analysis, findings and conclusions. *International Journal of Contemporary Hospitality Management, 12*(1), 13–30.

Kumar, V., & Pansari, A. (2016). Competitive advantage through engagement. *Journal of Marketing Research, 53*(4), 497–514.

Lemon, K. N., & Verhoef, P. C. (2016). Understanding customer experience throughout the customer journey. *Journal of Marketing, 80*(6), 69–96.

Nambisan, S., & Nambisan, P. (2008). How to profit from a better 'virtual customer environment.' *MIT Sloan Management Review, 49*(3), 53.

Neal, W. D. (1999). Satisfaction is nice, but value drives loyalty. *Marketing Research, 11*(1), 20.

Oliver, R. L. (1980). A cognitive model of the antecedents and consequences of satisfaction decisions. *Journal of Marketing Research, 17*(4), 460–469.

Parasuraman, A. (1995). Measuring and monitoring service quality. *Understanding Services Management,* 143–177.

Parasuraman, A., Berry, L. L., & Zeithaml, V. A. (1991). Refinement and reassessment of the SERVQUAL scale. *Journal of Retailing, 67*(4), 420–450.

Prentice, C. (2013). Service quality perceptions and customer loyalty in casinos. *International Journal of Contemporary Hospitality Management, 25*(1), 49–64.

Prentice, C., Dominique Lopes, S., & Wang, X. (2019a). Emotional intelligence or artificial intelligence—An employee perspective. *Journal of Hospitality Marketing & Management,* 1–27.

Prentice, C., Han, X. Y., Hua, L. L., & Hu, L. (2019b). The influence of identity-driven customer engagement on purchase intention. *Journal of Retailing and Consumer Services, 47,* 339–347.

Prentice, C., Wang, X., & Loureiro, S. M. C. (2019c). The influence of brand experience and service quality on customer engagement. *Journal of Retailing and Consumer Services, 50,* 50–59.

Rodriguez-Lizundia, E., Marcos, S., Zalama, E., Gómez-García-Bermejo, J., & Gordaliza, A. (2015). A bellboy robot: Study of the effects of robot behaviour on user engagement and comfort. *International Journal of Human-Computer Studies, 82,* 83–95.

Russell Stuart, J., & Norvig, P. (2009). *Artificial intelligence: A modern approach.* Prentice Hall.

Rust, R. T., Zahorik, A. J., & Keiningham, T. L. (1995). Return on quality (ROQ): Making service quality financially accountable. *Journal of Marketing, 59*(2), 58–70.

Shi, Y., Prentice, C., & He, W. (2014). Linking service quality, customer satisfaction and loyalty in casinos, does membership matter? *International Journal of Hospitality Management, 40,* 81–91.

Sniehotta, F. F., Presseau, J., & Araújo-Soares, V. (2014). Time to retire the theory of planned behaviour. *Health Psychology Review, 8*(1), 1–7. https://doi.org/10.1080/17437199.2013.869710

So, K. K. F., King, C., Sparks, B. A., & Wang, Y. (2016). Enhancing customer relationships with retail service brands: The role of customer engagement. *Journal of Service Management, 27*(2), 170–193.

Tosun, C., Dedeoğlu, B. B., & Fyall, A. (2015). Destination service quality, affective image and revisit intention: The moderating role of past experience. *Journal of Destination Marketing & Management, 4*(4), 222–234.

Tussyadiah, I. P., & Park, S. (2018). Consumer evaluation of hotel service robots. In *Information and communication technologies in tourism 2018* (pp. 308–320). Springer.

Tversky, A., & Kahneman, D. (1986). Rational choice and the framing of decisions. *Journal of Business, 59*(4), S251–S278.

Tversky, A., & Thaler, R. H. (1990). Anomalies: preference reversals. *Journal of Economic Perspectives, 4*(2), 201–211.

Ullah, A., Aimin, W., & Ahmed, M. (2018). Smart automation, customer experience and customer engagement in electric vehicles. *Sustainability, 10*(5), 1350.

Van Doorn, J., Lemon, K. N., Mittal, V., Nass, S., Pick, D., Pirner, P., & Verhoef, P. C. (2010). Customer engagement behavior: Theoretical foundations and research directions. *Journal of Service Research, 13*(3), 253–266.

Veloutsou, C. (2015). Brand evaluation, satisfaction and trust as predictors of brand loyalty: The mediator-moderator effect of brand relationships. *Journal of Consumer Marketing, 32*(6), 405–421.

Verhoef, P. C., Reinartz, W. J., & Krafft, M. (2010). Customer engagement as a new perspective in customer management. *Journal of Service Research, 13*(3), 247–252.

Vivek, S. D., Beatty, S. E., Dalela, V., & Morgan, R. M. (2014). A generalized multidimensional scale for measuring customer engagement. *Journal of Marketing Theory and Practice, 22*(4), 401–420.

Walch, K. (2019). AI's increasing role in customer service. Cognitive World. https://www.forbes.com/sites/cognitiveworld/2019/07/02/ais-increasing-role-in-customer-service/#1fafeb2d73fc/. Published on 2 July 2019.

Walchuk, M. (2019). How to apply AI to your customer service. https://www.salesforce.com/blog/2019/06/customer-service-ai.html. Published on 21 July 2019.

Wixom, B. H., & Todd, P. A. (2005). A theoretical integration of user satisfaction and technology acceptance. *Information Systems Research, 16*(1), 85–102.

Woodside, A. G., Frey, L. L., & Daly, R. T. (1989). Linking sort/ice anility, customer satisfaction, and behavioral intention. *Journal of Health Care Marketing, 9*(4), 5–17.

Yoon, Y., & Uysal, M. (2005). An examination of the effects of motivation and satisfaction on destination loyalty: A structural model. *Tourism Management, 26*(1), 45–56.

Yuan, J., & Jang, S. C. (2008). The Effects of Quality and Satisfaction on Awareness and Behavioral Intentions: Exploring the Role of a Wine Festival. *Journal of Travel Research, 46*, 279.

Yuksel, A., Yuksel, F., & Bilim, Y. (2010). Destination attachment: Effects on customer satisfaction and cognitive, affective and conative loyalty. *Tourism Management, 31*(2), 274–284.

Zanker, M., Fuchs, M., Höpken, W., Tuta, M., & Müller, N. (2008). Evaluating recommender systems in tourism—A case study from Austria. In *Enter* (pp. 24–34).

Zeithaml, V. A., Berry, L. L., & Parasuraman, A. (1996). The behavioral consequences of service quality. *Journal of Marketing, 60*(2), 31–46.

Chapter 8
Developing a Scale to Measure Artificial Intelligence Service Quality

Abstract Given the service nature and wide applications of AI in service organisations, consistent with the discussion of the preceding chapters, the current chapter develops a scale to measure AI service quality and proposes AI applications as a service product that can be offered by a service firm to customers for creating values. This initiative provides a better understanding of AI service and its impact on organisational outcomes since service quality has been widely acknowledged as an antecedent of customer satisfaction and loyalty. The scale development undertakes several stages including item generation, domain specification, scale refinement, validity testing as well as internal and external cross validation. A range of methods were used in this process. Data were collected from Country 1, Country 3 and Country 2 for testing external validity. Establishment of this scale extends AI research and applications to a new domain. This scale has implications for services and relationship marketing literature, as well as providing a fresh approach for practitioners to enhancing customer experience and generating positive response from customers. The chapter begins with proving the rationale for assessing AI service quality. The methods for the scale development process is elaborated subsequently, followed by presenting the findings and implications.

8.1 AI Applications

Artificial intelligence (AI) is used in organisations to facilitate business operations and customer service. These applications exist in various forms such as digital assistants, chatbots, service robots, or some invisible software applications. These AI-powered applications are integrated into organisational service provision. In the academic community, a growing body of literature has discussed AI service in various industries, especially in hospitality and tourism sectors (e.g. Ivanov & Webster, 2019; Tussyadiah & Park, 2018).

To a large degree, AI in service organisations become part of service provided to customers to enhance their service experience (Prentice et al., 2020). For example, AI-powered chabots can enhance customer interaction by enabling self-service procedures (Kumar & Balaramachandran, 2018). A concierge robot Connie (e.g.

© The Author(s), under exclusive license to Springer Nature Singapore Pte Ltd. 2023   105
C. Prentice, *Leveraging Emotional and Artificial Intelligence for Organisational Performance*, https://doi.org/10.1007/978-981-99-1865-2_8

Hilton Worldwide) can interact with guests and respond to their tailored questions. Hennna Hotel in Japan was the first hotel to deploy robots to provide information, frontline and concierge services, as well as assisting check-in and check-out. These AI services can minimise cost by reducing human employees' workload as well as acquiring new customers and retaining existing ones by providing service to increase operational efficiency and effectiveness (Cobos et al., 2016; Marinova et al., 2017; West et al., 2018). Adoption of AI in the service delivery process is not only a fad but also a rising trend because of its advantages over human employees to some degree (Gursoy et al., 2019).

8.2   AI Service

Services in the marketing literature are defined as acts, deeds, performances and efforts that are offered as value-added activities for exchange to benefit the stakeholders (see Wirtz & Lovelock, 2018a, 2018b). Services are generally categorised into four domains: people processing, possession processing, mental stimulus processing and information processing, and characterised as being intangible, perishable, heterogenous and simultaneous (Wirtz & Lovelock, 2018a, 2018b). People processing services refer to those that directly serve customers, such as medical centres providing medical service and examination on patients requiring simultaneous participation from both service provider and customers. Possession processing services refer to those directed at customers' tangible possessions such as house cleaning. Mental stimulus processing services refer to offerings that are aimed at serving mental capacity such as education. Information processing services refer to those that the core component of the service offering is information based, such as banking, accounting and legal services. Based on the conceptualisation of service in general, AI applications can be classified as an element of service that is offered to customers for value creation.

AI can refer to (1) information system's ability to interpret and learn from external data for predefined goals and tasks from a technical perspective (Kaplan & Haenlein, 2019); (2) intelligent machines which can act like humans to perceive, learn, memorise, reason and solve problems through machine learning, deep learning or natural language processing (Russell et al., 2016); (3) intelligent physical devices with programmed autonomy, mobility and sensor ability to perform certain human tasks (Murphy et al., 2017); and (4) service agents (e.g., concierge robots) to deliver customer service.

Consistent with Wirtz and Lovelock's (2018a, 2018b) conceptualisation, AI can be categorised as people process service. For instance, AI-powered robots provide such services. Robotic medical assistants have been used to monitor patients and alert the medical staff when in need. AI-powered vacuum cleaner is such an example. AI can be process possession service, such as AI-powered vacuum cleaner. AI can be mental stimulus processing. For instance, AI with big data analytics is used to create personalized learning experience tailoring to students' individual abilities and needs

(Rouhiainen, 2019). Social robots are used to create personalized learning experience tailoring to individual students' abilities and needs (Belpaeme et al., 2018). AI can be information process service. AI-powered applications have been largely information-based services, using advanced data analytics for fraudulent transactions and improvement of compliance. AI-powered chatbots provide round-the-clock information-based services.

8.3 Technical or Functional Service

Although AI service is functioned through machine learning from the environment and past experience to improve decision making (Wu & Tegmark, 2019), or deep learning by mimicking the human brain to analyse data and draw conclusions manifested in image recognition, sound recognition, recommender systems, natural language processing etc. (Wu & Tegmark, 2019), the level of AI functional quality is manifested in technical outcomes by providing consistent and timely service (West et al., 2018). For instance, AI-powered robots in hotels are deployed to carry out concierge and room services and provide information to guests, assist check-in and check-out, order taxi, answer customers' queries, refining responses based on customers' behaviours (Solomon, 2016). Hilton Worldwide employs a robotic concierge named "Connie" to interact with customers like regular frontline employees. Connie could personalise customers' experience, provide information, and address customers' general needs (Tavakoli & Mura, 2018). In the airline industry, AI-powered "Spencer" adopted by KLM Airlines can answer travellers' queries and enhance their travel experiences (West et al., 2018). 1A-TA robot is used by travel agencies to identify travellers' needs and preferences for tailored service provision.

In the retail industry, AI-powered Watson is used by the North Face to support customers in choosing the most suitable jackets through providing personalized recommendations to customers based on an analysis of a huge multi-variance dataset. These AI services provide quick and accurate personalised suggestions to enhance customer-brand interaction and also saves a considerable amount of human labour cost for the organisation (Gursoy et al., 2019). These technical outcomes are reflective of service performance, acts or efforts that are intentionally developed to value creation.

8.4 AI Service Quality

Any service that is offered for exchange manifests its value in creating positive business outcomes (e.g. brand reputation, financial performance). In the marketing literature, the value of service is assessed on the quality level and its impact on customers since service of any category is aimed for generating customers' positive responses (e.g. customer satisfaction, repurchase and loyalty) and business profitability (Prentice, 2019; Zeithaml, 2000). In the services marketing literature, service quality is defined as a customer's perception or evaluations of a service organisation's overall excellence or superiority (Parasuraman et al., 1988). Overwhelming empirical research has examined and confirmed to certain degree the link between service quality, customer satisfaction and loyalty over last few decades (Helgesen, 2006; Kim, 2011; Woodside et al., 1989; Zeithaml, 2000). A high level of service quality and customer satisfaction leads to revisit, reuse, or purchase with the firm (Prentice, 2013; Shi et al., 2014). Hence, assessing and evaluating service quality is imperative to understand its impact on organisational outcomes.

Viewing AI service as one type of customer service, this chapter argues that the commercial value must be reflective of the level of quality assessed on users' perceptions and evaluations. There are numerous measures that have been developed to assess service quality, from various context and industry perspectives, for instance, retails (Dabholkar et al., 1996; Siu & Tak-Hing Cheung, 2001), education (Brochado, 2009), health (Akter et al., 2013), casino (Wong & Fong, 2012), online services (Boshoff, 2007; Ding et al., 2011; Yang et al., 2004). None of existing service quality measures captured AI service. This chapter approaches AI service from technical perspective and develops a scale to measure AI service quality. This initiative provides a better understanding of AI service and its impact on organisational outcomes since service quality has been widely acknowledged as an antecedent of customer satisfaction and loyalty.

8.5   Service Quality Measurement

Service quality in marketing literature refers to customers' perceptions and value-judgment of a product or service and has been recognised as an imperative factor of a firm's competitive advantages and organisational profitability (Prentice, 2014; Shi et al., 2014). These outcomes result from positive customer responses manifested in market share expansions, customer satisfaction and loyalty (Ozment & Morash, 1994). The underlying logic is that improving service quality leads to customer satisfaction and customer loyalty which relates to business profitability (Heskett et al., 1994). Consequently, measuring a firm's service quality becomes imperative to understand its impact on organisational outcomes.

Various service quality measures and models have emerged in the relevant literature over last three decades. Among those, although none without being criticised, the models proposed by Gronroos (1982), Parasuraman et al. (1988), Parasuraman et al. (1985), and Brady and Cronin (2001) have attracted most attention and been extensively cited. Gronroos assessed service quality from technical and functional perspective. The former refers to the outcome of the service performance or what the customer receives in the service encounter; whereas the latter indicates the subjective perception of service delivery. Parasuraman et al.'s (1988) SERVQUAL describes service quality as the discrepancy between a customer's expectations and perceptions of a service. Later on, Cronin and Taylor (1992) argued that adding customer expectation can be inefficient and unnecessary, and customers' perceptions alone are adequate to capture service quality assessment (McDougall & Levesque, 1995). Despite discrepancies in these measurements, these models consist of tangible and intangible services delivered through personal and impersonal encounters. Personal encounters generally refer to interpersonal interactions between service employees who deliver the service and customers who receive the service (Prentice, 2019). Impersonal encounters indicate, in the absence of employee service, customers' interaction with physical or cyber settings of the service organisation (Prentice, 2019; Yang et al., 2004). These measurements fail to capture AI services (e.g. service automation, robotic service).

Existing service quality measures are focused on customers' perceptions and evaluations of their service counters with service providers. A service encounter is dyadic with limited or narrow relational contact and communication (Gronroos, 1994). The dyadic encounter can be interpersonal and impersonal. The former indicates personal interactions between one employee and the other (internal service encounter), a service employee and a customer, and an employee and customers' possessions; the latter broadly refers to contact between personnel and physical or online settings (Prentice, 2019). The physical settings include any tangible offerings, servicescape, ambience, or atmosphere. The online settings can be any virtual encounters. The foregoing discussion shows that AI service quality should be approached from the encounter with customers; hence, the assessment must be drawn from perceptions and evaluations of customers. The technology acceptance literature indicates that technology quality must be assessed from information and system perspectives and how these affect users' beliefs, attitudes and behaviours (Wixom & Todd, 2005; Xu et al., 2017). This view is taken into account in developing AI service quality. The following section describes the procedure of developing a scale to measure AI service quality.

8.6 Developing AI Service Quality Scale

Both qualitative and quantitative methods were employed to determine the dimensionality of AI service. In accordance with conventional scale development protocol discussed in the literature, three stages were undertaken in this process across three countries (named as Country 1, Country 2 and Country 3 hereafter) (1) item generation, (2) scale refinement and validation, and (3) scale cross-validation. Details of three stages are as follows.

8.6.1 Stage 1: Item Generation and Initial Purification

8.6.1.1 Domain Specification

Prior to identifying the dimensions and items for developing AI service quality. The domain of AI service was specified (Churchill, 1979). In this process, we reviewed all relevant literature and other sources (e.g. blogs, magazines, news, industry reports) on artificial intelligence. We adopted Huang and Rust's (2018) four intelligences approach to classify AI service: mechanic, analytical, intuitive, and empathetic AI, which were further categorised into physical and virtual forms of AI. Physical form of AI includes both humanoid and non-humanoid robots, and can be symbolised as frontline service employees; whereas virtual AI as employees offering online service. After reviewing all existing service quality measures, we focused on Parasuraman et al.'s (1991) service quality measure SERVQUAL and Zeithaml et al.'s (2002) e-SERVQUAL. The SERVQUAL model with five core dimensions: reliability, assurance, empathy, responsiveness, and tangible, the first four dimensions correspond to the service delivery performed by the employees with emphasis on service promptness, accuracy, consistency, and employee friendliness and caring. The last dimension corresponds to the physical setting of the service premises including employees' appearance. This model was drawn upon to understand the encounter between humanoid AI-powered robots and customers. Zeithaml et al.'s e-SERVQUAL with its four core dimensions (i.e. efficiency, reliability, fulfillment and privacy) was drawn upon to understand virtual AI service. Since AI service is information-based technology, Wixom and Todd's (2005) integrated user satisfaction and technology acceptance scale was analysed to understand the informational and technological aspects of AI service. After scrutinising these scales and perusing web information relating to AI, three domains were determined to represent AI service quality: automated service, robotic service, and informational service. Automated service represents mechanical AI service such as hotel mobile check-in/out. Robotic service represents intuitive and empathetic AI services delivered by humanoid and non-humanoid robots, for instance, concierge robots, robot bartenders, robot chefs, porter robots, vacuum cleaning robots. Informational service represents analytical AI that provides accurate and updated information (e.g. chatbots).

8.6.1.2 Item Generation

To ensure appropriateness of items, a panel of IT experts who had been involved in AI research and design and operation managers from five service organisations that have used AI service to assess the domains and proposed items. The items were drawn from the aforementioned three models and various blogs relating to service robots. We asked the panel to assess representativeness and appropriateness of these items. 32 items were remained as a result of this assessment. Since service quality is formed on customers' perceptions and evaluation, subsequently we invited 30 people who had used AI service to evaluate these items and assess the importance and relevance to robotic service using a seven-point scale ranging from 1 as "not important" to 7 as "very important". Any item with an average score less than 5 as "somewhat important" was removed from consideration following the suggestion by Brakus et al. (2009). Only 18 items were remained for scale refinement and validation.

8.6.2 Stage 2: Scale Refinement and Validation

8.6.2.1 Sample and Data Collection

To refine these items, we conducted online survey using Qualtrics platform on Country 1 consumers who had experience with AI service. The target respondents must have used robotic services within last 12 months. To ensure appropriateness of the sample, we developed a few screen questions to help the prospective respondents understand the research purpose and filter those who did not fulfil the study criteria. A total of 380 usable questionnaires were obtained from those who use AI service in the last 12 months. Of the respondents, 49.2% were male, 48.2% were between the ages of 26–45; and 59.7% hold bachelor's degree or higher.

8.6.2.2 Findings

Following the suggestion of Hair et al. (2014) and Schumacker and Lomax (2004), the dataset was split up into two sub-samples to compare results, with one sub-sample (Sample 1) being used for principal component analysis and another sub-sample (Sample 2) for confirmatory factor analysis (see Table 8.1). The principal component analysis with Promax oblique rotation was conducted with remained items, revealing four factors after removing 6 item due to low factor or cross loadings. The four-factor solution accounted for 85.16 of variation. The Kaiser-Mayer-Olkin value were 0.90, revealing satisfactory sampling adequacy. The primary loading of all the remaining items was above 0.5 and the secondary loading of them was less than 0.3. Coefficient alpha for each factor is above 0.7, indicating adequate internal consistency (Nunnally, 1994).

Four factors were labelled as automisation, personalisation, precision, and efficiency. automisation the highest eigenvalue (7.40) and explain 61.69% of the variance respectively in AI service quality, whereas precision has the lowest eigenvalue (0.66) with 5.53% variance explained. These results suggest that automisation is the most important component of AI service quality evaluation while precision is probably expected and presumed. The average variance extracted of all factors was beyond the 0.50 threshold, indicating adequate convergence (Fornell & Larcker, 1981). The composite reliability for each factor was higher than the cut-off level of 0.70.

Next, the aforementioned four-factor solution was identified through confirmatory factor analysis. This analysis was performed using maximum likelihood method in

Table 8.1 Item descriptions and measurement model results for robotic service quality

Scale items	Pattern coefficient	Variance explained	Cronbach's alpha	CR	AVE
Automation	β = 7.40	61.69%	0.92	0.92	0.79
AI-powered automation operates reliably	0.78				
AI-powered automation performs effectively	0.87				
AI-powered automation functions dependably	0.78				
CFI = 1.00; IFI = 1.00; SRMR = 0.00					
Personalisation	β = 0.76	6.33%	0.88	0.88	0.71
AI-powered service is adaptive to meet a variety of my needs	0.87				
AI-powered service is flexibly adjusted to meet my new demands	0.88				
AI-powered service is versatile in addressing my needs	0.68				
CFI = 1.00; IFI = 1.00; SRMR = 0.00					
Efficiency	β = 1.39	11.62%	0.93	0.92	0.80
AI-powered tools are very responsive to my requests	0.96				
AI-powered tools provide service in a timely manner	0.85				
AI-powered tools solve my problems effectively	0.96				
CFI = 1.00; IFI = 1.00; SRMR = 0.00					
Precision	β = 0.66	5.53%	0.90	0.90	0.76
Information from AI system is accurate	0.85				

(continued)

Table 8.1 (continued)

Scale items	Pattern coefficient	Variance explained	Cronbach's alpha	CR	AVE
Information from AI system is reliable	0.87				
Information from AI system is always up to date	0.67				
CFI = 1.00; IFI = 1.00; SRMR = 0.00					

β Eigenvalues; *CR* Composite reliability; *AVE* Average variance extracted

AMOS 25. The measurement fit for each construct was excellent with comparative fit index (CFI) = 1.00, IFI = 1.00 and SRMR = 0.00. As suggested by Brakus et al. (2009), three competing models were analysed to examine whether the measurement model fits the data best: (1) the one-factor model with all items loading on a single AI service quality; (2) the four-factor model; and (3) the second-order model with AI service as the second order and the four aforementioned first-order factors as sub-dimensions. The results in Table 8.2 show that the second-order model is the most desirable since it produced the best fit statistics for both sample groups: χ^2/df = 1.87, CFI = 0.99, RMSEA = 0.05, SRMR = 0.02. The Akaike's information criterion (AIC) was used to select the most competing models (Hu & Bentler, 1995). As shown in Table 8.2, Model 3 was the most accurate and most parsimonious as it had the lowest value of AIC.

The nomological validity of AI service quality was examined by assessing the inter-factor correlations among the four factors. The results show significant correlations among the four dimensions ranging from 0.51 to 0.76 (see Table 8.3). The criterion validity was further tested by examining the relationship between AI service quality as the second-order construct and customer satisfaction through structural equation modelling since these two are related as shown in the relevant literature (Prentice, 2013, 2014, 2019). Customer satisfaction measure was adopted from Wixom and Todd (2005). The model fit indices were acceptable: χ^2/df = 1.73, CFI = 0.99, IFI = 0.99 SRMR = 0.04. The standardised path coefficient between AI service quality and customer satisfaction is 0.69 ($p < 0.001$).

Table 8.2 Confirmatory factor analysis model fit comparisons

Model	Description	χ^2	df	χ^2/df	p	CFI	RMSEA	SRMR	AIC
1	One factor	550.77	54	10.20	0.00	0.86	0.16	0.05	598.77
2	First-order factor	125.79	38	3.31	0.00	0.98	0.08	0.03	181.79
3	Second-order factor	86.19	46	1.87	0.00	0.99	0.05	0.02	150.19

Table 8.3 Correlation coefficients, means, and standard deviations of AI service quality and customer satisfaction

	Means	SD	1	2	3	4
1. Automisation	4.93	1.10				
2. Personalisation	4.94	1.12	0.72**			
3. Efficiency	4.10	1.53	0.59**	0.51**		
4. Precision	4.95	1.12	0.76**	0.69**	0.57**	
5. Cust. satisfaction	4.81	1.27	0.66**	0.60**	0.61**	0.60**

** $p < 0.01$

8.6.3 Internal Cross-validation

The forgoing analyses show content validity, convergent validity, discriminant validity, nomological validity, and criterion validity (Hair et al., 2014). To cross-validate the scale, full metric and scalar invariance was assessed. Following Hair et al.'s (2014) suggestion, Samples 1 and 2 of Country 1dataset were used. With AI service quality as a second-order construct, the factor loadings were freely estimated for both groups in Model 1 and then constrained to be equal between the two groups in Model 2. The results in Table 8.4 show that the measurement model is invariant ($\Delta\chi^2$ (11) = 12.03, p = 0.36; ΔCFI = 0.00); thus, full metric invariance is established.

For full scalar invariance, following the suggestion of Wong and Fong (2012), the dataset was divided into two groups by gender. The full metric invariance by gender was examined. The results in Model 3 and 4 in Table 8.4 reveal that the factor loadings of the two groups are invariant ($\Delta\chi^2$ (11) = 18.92, p = 0.06; ΔCFI = 0.00). Latent mean analysis was then performed by constraining the intercepts of the structural equation of the observed variables on the latent factors to be equivalent across these two groups. The results in Model 5 suggest that the model fit of the latent mean

Table 8.4 Test of measurement model invariance

Model	Compare with	χ^2	df	$\Delta\chi^2$ (Δdf)	p	CFI	ΔCFI	RMSEA	SRMR
1	–	154.20	90	–	–	0.98	–	0.05	0.03
2	Model 1	169.66	101	12.03 (11)	0.36	0.98	0.00	0.04	0.04
3	–	157.19	90	–	–	0.98	–	0.04	0.03
4	Model 3	176.11	101	18.92 (11)	0.06	0.98	0.00	0.04	0.03
5	Model 4	188.61	111	12.50 (10)	0.25	0.98	0.00	0.04	0.04
6	–	300.50	90	–	–	0.96	–	0.06	0.04
7	Model 6	314.05	101	13.55(11)	0.26	0.96	0.00	0.04	0.04
8	–	240.12	90	–	–	0.97	–	0.05	0.04
9	Model 8	255.83	101	15.71 (11)	0.15	0.97	0.00	0.04	0.05

model is not significantly different from the full metric invariant model ($\Delta\chi^2$ (10) = 12.50, p = 0.25; ΔCFI = 0.00); thus, full scalar invariance is achieved. Results of the two invariances tests confirm a strong factorial invariance of the robotic service quality scale.

8.6.4 External Cross-validation

The literature contends that a new scale should be cross-validated to be replicable and generalisable. Additional data was collected from Country 2 (350 usable responses) and Country 3 (423 usable responses). Confirmatory factor analysis was tested the fit of the hypothesised AI service quality measurement model. The results indicate good model fit (Country 2: χ^2/df = 1.80, CFI = 0.97, RMSEA = 0.07, SRMR = 0.03; Country 3: χ^2/df = 3.39, CFI = 0.95, RMSEA = 0.08, SRMR = 0.04). To assess full metric invariance, datasets from Country 1 and Country 2 and from Country 1 and Country 3 were used to perform a group invariances test by constraining the factor-loading estimates to be equal between both samples. The results in Model 6 and 7 in Table 8.4 reveal that the model is invariant across different samples between Country 1 and Country 2 ($\Delta\chi^2$ (11) = 13.55, p = 0.26; ΔCFI = 0.00); the results in Model 8 and 9 reveal that the model is invariant across different samples between Country 1 and Country 3 ($\Delta\chi^2$ (11) = 15.71, p = 0.15; ΔCFI = 0.00); thus, external replicability of the scale is warranted.

Cross validation among the three datasets was conducted. 350 respondents were randomly selected from three countries to validate AI service quality scale across countries. The relationship between AI service quality as the second-order construct and user satisfaction through structural equation modelling were further tested across the three datasets (see Table 8.5). The standardised path coefficient between AI service quality and customer satisfaction is significant across the three datasets; thus, external validity of AI service quality is supported.

Table 8.5 External cross-validation

		Customer satisfaction		
		Country 1	Country 2	Country 3
AI service quality	Country 1	0.78***	0.31*	0.85***
	Country 2	0.50***	0.57***	0.44***
	Country 3	0.70***	0.15*	0.68***

*$p < 0.05$, ** $p < 0.01$, *** $p < 0.001$

8.7   Conclusion and Implications

This study draws upon service quality conceptualisation and develops a scale to measure AI service quality. Service quality is formed on customers' service encounter experience with the service provider. The service encounter in the service quality literature primarily refers to customers' interaction with service employees and impersonal service provision such as online and physical settings associated with the service organisation. Existing service quality measures fail to capture the services provided by AI-powered tools (hereafter AI) that have been widely used in service industries. AI can be manifested in physical and virtual forms. The former includes humanoid robots that look and behave like humans (e.g. Connie), and non-humanoid robots (e.g. mobile robots). The latter refers to online automated service. Service organisations utilise AI service to improve customer experience and generate positive customer response. This study views it as one type of commercial service that is offered to customers for value creation and develops AI service quality scale. The interaction between customers and humanoid AI is referred to as personal encounter, between customers and other forms of AI as impersonal encounter. Given the service provided by AI is largely information and technology based, the items that are generated to develop the scale are drawn from service quality and technology acceptance literature to reflect customers' perception and evaluation of AI service quality.

8.7.1   The Four Dimensions

The scale development processes generated four dimensions to represent AI service quality: automisation, personalisation, precision, and efficiency. These dimensions are indicative of mechanical, analytical, intuitive and empathetic AI proposed in Huang and Rust (2018).

Automisation refers to the level of automation and performance by AI. This dimension mainly captures customers' experience with AI system quality. Sluggish operating system underlying AI services evokes negative customer response. Advanced technology today has changed customers' expectation on any technology-related services. *Personalisation* indicates how AI, particularly robots, can be flexible like service employees to meet individual customer's requests and demands. Service robots are designed to represent and behave like humans. Customers expect their interactions with these robots to be similar to those with service employees. Robots could represent these employees to provide the requested information and function like employees. Customers may have different needs and wants from the service provider. Whilst employees' adaptability is expected, they are nevertheless limited to fixed working hours and inadequate training. Human physical and emotional constraints are not applicable to machine operated robots. These robots are not only available around the clock service, but also capable of storing infinite information from various sources that can be adapted to meet customers' requests.

Precision is reflective of accuracy and exactness of the information provided by AI. Such information is programmed through big data analytics and machine learning without unintended human intervention. The information from AI must be in a timely manner. Outdated information can be misleading. Customers expect information from AI to be updated, objective, thorough and accurate. Precise information can guide customers to make informative decisions on their consumption and purchase. *Efficiency* indicates timely and responsive service from AI. The ability to respond to customer requests dependably and reliably affects customer experience, attitudes and subsequent behaviours.

8.7.2 Applications of AI Service Quality

Establishment of this scale enriches the service quality and marketing literature. Numerous scales have been developed to measure service quality. Some are modelled to measure generic service quality (e.g. SERVQUAL, SERVPERF), others are more context based, for instance, e-travel service quality (Ho & Lee, 2007), retail service quality (Dabholkar et al., 1996); bank service quality (Karatepe et al., 2005), e-service quality (Li & Suomi, 2009), web information service quality (Yang et al., 2005) and healthcare service quality (Dagger et al., 2007). Given extensive use of AI service in various service industries, such service is intended for customer service, it is imperative to understand how AI service quality is measured and affects customer attitudes and behaviours.

AI-powered tools such as service robots can deliver service like or beyond service employees. Therefore, AI service quality can complement the aforementioned service quality scales for industries where AI is applied. For instance, AI-powered robots in HSBC can greet customers, guide them on selecting appropriate banking service, and summon an employee to help with transaction. The robot Pepper (Fig. 8.1) can also pose selfies and tell jokes. AI service quality can be used in conjunction with Karetepe et al.'s (2005) service quality of retail banks to measure bank service quality and understand its impact on customer satisfaction and behaviours.

AI service quality can also be integrated with Parasuraman et al.'s SERVQUAL which consists of 5 dimensions (tangibility, reliability, assurance, responsiveness and empathy). Each of them has relevance to service employees (Prentice, 2013). This scale has been widely used in hospitality industry (Gabbie & O'Neill, 1996; Raspor, 2010; Saleh & Ryan, 1991; Shi et al., 2014). AI-powered robots in hotels (see Fig. 8.2) are able to interact with guests and provide requested information. In addition to measuring customer perception of hotel service quality on the five SERVQUAL dimensions, AI service quality can be assessed to understand a wholistic picture of hotel service quality and its influence on customer experience.

Given that some AI service is online information based, AI service quality can also be integrated to e-service quality to have a broader perspective on qualtiy of web service. Exisitng e-service qualty scales (Dabholkar et al., 1996; Madu & Madu, 2002; Zeithaml et al., 2002) fail to capture the service provided by chatbots that are

Fig. 8.1 Meeting Pepper. *Source* http://us.softbankrobotics.com/pepper

Fig. 8.2 Connie in Hilton interacting with hotel guests. *Source* Muoio (2016). https://www.busine ssinsider.com/meet-connie-the-robot-hilton-hotels-newest-concierge-2016-3

available to answer queries and offer requested information around the clock. Chatbot service is ubiquitous and the topic is popularing in the relevant literature (Dale, 2016; Feine et al., 2019; Jones & Jones, 2019; Lasek & Jessa, 2013). Understanding its service qualty is conducive to improving customer experience. AI service quality addresses the void in chatbot literature.

The study also adds a new measure to services and relationship marketing to manage customer relationships. Traditional service marketing strategies are primarily focused on 7Ps (product, promotion, price, place, people, process and physical evidence) and manifested in defensive (or relationship marketing) and aggressive approaches (Prentice, 2019). Service quality is considered a relationship marketing technique to elicit customer satisfaction and loyalty. AI sevice quality can be incorporated into services and relationship marketing literature to understand customer atttiudes and behaviours.

AI service quality developed in this study can be applied to the relevant industries and organisations that extensively use AI (e.g. service robots) to provide customer service. AI-powered tools are mostly designed and developed by IT experts. Most users may be layman and not understand the underlying principles and operating system. This scale helps service providers and customers appreciate the importance of AI service without understanding the complex IT construction. Service providers can use this scale to assess the return on investment in purchasing AI tools (robots can be expensive). They are also able to get a better understanding of quality of those tools and its impact on customer response. AI service quality can help them address advantages and flaws of AI service. From customer perspective, AI service quality can be a useful tool for them to communicate with service providers to address their appreciation and concerns. This scale can also assist customers providing feedback to the service provider. For example, some information provided by chatbots can be limited and unhelpful. Without a proper measure, customers are unable to raise the issue to the service provider. This scale serves this purpose so that providers can be guided to improve AI service quality to enhance customer experience and positive response.

8.8 Acknowledgement of Limitations

Despite every endeavour attempted in this study, a few limitations must be acknowledged. First, the sample frame is not representative of every service industry. Generalisability of this scale is not optimal. The sample frame could be extended to have a better represenation of the targeted population. Second, AI service varies across different service contexts and industries. Development of this scale should differentiate such service to be more insightful and wholistic. Third, cross-validation in different countries should have taken the cultural effect into account. Future research should address these limitations.

References

Akter, S., D'Ambra, J., & Ray, P. (2013). Development and validation of an instrument to measure user perceived service quality of mHealth. *Information & Management, 50*(4), 181–195. https://doi.org/10.1016/j.im.2013.03.001

Belpaeme, T., Kennedy, J., Ramachandran, A., Scassellati, B., & Tanaka, F. (2018). Social robots for education: A review. *Science Robotics, 3*(21), 1–9.

Boshoff, C. (2007). A psychometric assessment of E-S-QUAL: A scale to measure electronic service quality. *Journal of Electronic Commerce Research, 8*(1), 101.

Brady, M. K., & Cronin, J. J. (2001). Some new thoughts on conceptualizing perceived service quality: A hierarchical approach. *Journal of Marketing, 65*(3), 34–49. https://doi.org/10.1509/jmkg.65.3.34.18334

Brakus, J. J., Schmitt, B. H., & Zarantonello, L. (2009). Brand experience: What is it? How is it measured? Does it affect loyalty? *Journal of Marketing, 73*(3), 52–68. https://doi.org/10.1509/jmkg.73.3.52

Brochado, A. (2009). Comparing alternative instruments to measure service quality in higher education. *Quality Assurance in Education, 17*(2), 174–190. https://doi.org/10.1108/09684880910951381

Churchill, G. A. (1979). A Paradigm for developing better measures of marketing constructs. *Journal of Marketing Research, 16*(1), 64–73. https://doi.org/10.2307/3150876

Cobos, L. M., Mejia, C., Ozturk, A. B., & Wang, Y. (2016). A technology adoption and implementation process in an independent hotel chain. *International Journal of Hospitality Management, 57*, 93–105. https://doi.org/10.1016/j.ijhm.2016.06.005

Cronin, J. J., & Taylor, S. A. (1992). Measuring service quality: A reexamination and extension. *Journal of Marketing, 56*(3), 55–68. https://doi.org/10.1177/002224299205600304

Dabholkar, P. A., Thorpe, D. I., & Rentz, J. O. (1996). A measure of service quality for retail stores: Scale development and validation. *Journal of the Academy of Marketing Science, 24*(1), 3–16. https://doi.org/10.1007/BF02893933

Dagger, T. S., Sweeney, J. C., & Johnson, L. W. (2007). A hierarchical model of health service quality: Scale development and investigation of an integrated model. *Journal of Service Research, 10*(2), 123–142. https://doi.org/10.1177/1094670507309594

Dale, R. (2016). The return of the chatbots. *Natural Language Engineering, 22*(5), 811–817. https://doi.org/10.1017/S1351324916000243

Ding, D. X., Hu, P.J.-H., & Sheng, O. R. L. (2011). e-SELFQUAL: A scale for measuring online self-service quality. *Journal of Business Research, 64*(5), 508–515. https://doi.org/10.1016/j.jbusres.2010.04.007

Feine, J., Morana, S., & Gnewuch, U. (2019). *Measuring service encounter satisfaction with customer service chatbots using sentiment analysis.* Paper presented at the in Proceedings of the 14th International Conference on Wirtschaftsinformatik (WI2019), Siegen, Germany.

Fornell, C., & Larcker, D. F. (1981). Evaluating structural equation models with unobservable variables and measurement error. *Journal of Marketing Research, 18*(1), 39–50. https://doi.org/10.2307/3151312

Gabbie, O., & O'Neill, M. A. (1996). SERVQUAL and the Northern Ireland hotel sector: A comparative analysis - part 1. *Managing Service Quality: An International Journal, 6*(6), 25–32. https://doi.org/10.1108/09604529610149194

Gronroos, C. (1982). *Strategic management and marketing in the service sector.* Chartwell-Bratt.

Gronroos, C. (1994). From marketing mix to relationship marketing: Towards a paradigm shift in marketing. *Asia-Country 1 Marketing Journal, 2*(1), 9–29.

Gursoy, D., Chi, O. H., Lu, L., & Nunkoo, R. (2019). Consumers acceptance of artificially intelligent (AI) device use in service delivery. *International Journal of Information Management, 49*, 157–169. https://doi.org/10.1016/j.ijinfomgt.2019.03.008

Hair, J. F., Black, W. C., Babin, B. J., & Anderson, R. E. (2014). *Multivariate data analysis* (Seventh, Pearson New International ed.). Pearson Education Limited.

Helgesen, Ø. (2006). Are loyal customers profitable? Customer satisfaction, customer (action) loyalty and customer profitability at the individual level. *Journal of Marketing Management, 22*(3–4), 245–266. https://doi.org/10.1362/026725706776861226

Heskett, J. L., Jones, T. O., Loveman, G. W., Sasser, W. E., & Schlesinger, L. A. (1994). Putting the service-profit chain to work. *Harvard Business Review, 72*(2), 164–174. Retrieved from https://hbr.org/2008/07/putting-the-service-profit-chain-to-work

Ho, C.-I., & Lee, Y.-L. (2007). The development of an e-travel service quality scale. *Tourism Management, 28*(6), 1434–1449. https://doi.org/10.1016/j.tourman.2006.12.002

Hu, L.-T., & Bentler, P. M. (1995). Evaluating model fit. In R. H. Hoyle (Ed.), *Structural equation modeling: Concepts, issues, and applications.* Sage.

Huang, M.-H., & Rust, R. T. (2018). Artificial intelligence in service. *Journal of Service Research, 21*(2), 155–172.

Ivanov, S., & Webster, C. (2019). Conceptual framework of the use of robots, artificial intelligence and service automation in travel, tourism, and hospitality companies. In *Robots, artificial intelligence, and service automation in travel, tourism and hospitality* (pp. 7–37). Emerald Publishing Limited.

Jones, B., & Jones, R. (2019). Public service chatbots: Automating conversation with BBC news. *Digital Journalism, 7*(8), 1032–1053. https://doi.org/10.1080/21670811.2019.1609371

Kaplan, A., & Haenlein, M. (2019). Siri, Siri, in my hand: Who's the fairest in the land? On the interpretations, illustrations, and implications of artificial intelligence. *Business Horizons, 62*(1), 15–25. https://doi.org/10.1016/j.bushor.2018.08.004

Karatepe, O. M., Yavas, U., & Babakus, E. (2005). Measuring service quality of banks: Scale development and validation. *Journal of Retailing and Consumer Services, 12*(5), 373–383. https://doi.org/10.1016/j.jretconser.2005.01.001

Kim, H. J. (2011). Service orientation, service quality, customer satisfaction, and customer loyalty: Testing a structural model. *Journal of Hospitality Marketing & Management, 20*(6), 619–637. https://doi.org/10.1080/19368623.2011.577698

Kumar, K. N., & Balaramachandran, P. R. (2018). Robotic process automation—A study of the impact on customer experience in retail banking industry. *Journal of Internet Banking and Commerce, 23*(3), 1–27.

Lasek, M., & Jessa, S. (2013). Chatbots for customer service on hotels' websites. *Information Systems in Management, 2*(2), 146–158.

Li, H., & Suomi, R. (2009). A proposed scale for measuring e-service quality. *International Journal of u-and e-Service, Science and Technology, 2*(1), 1–10.

Madu, C. N., & Madu, A. A. (2002). Dimensions of e-quality. *International Journal of Quality & Reliability Management.*

Marinova, D., de Ruyter, K., Huang, M.-H., Meuter, M. L., & Challagalla, G. (2017). Getting smart: Learning from technology-Empowered frontline interactions. *Journal of Service Research, 20*(1), 29–42. https://doi.org/10.1177/1094670516679273

McDougall, G. H. G., & Levesque, T. J. (1995). A revised view of service quality dimensions: An empirical investigation. *Journal of Professional Services Marketing, 11*(1), 189–210. https://doi.org/10.1300/J090v11n01_13

Muoio, D. (2016). *Why Go is so much harder for AI to beat than chess.* Business Insider.

Murphy, J., Hofacker, C., & Gretzel, U. (2017). Dawning of the age of robots in hospitality and tourism: Challenges for teaching and research. *European Journal of Tourism Research, 15*(2017), 104–111.

Nunnally, J. C. (1994). *Psychometric theory* (3rd ed.). McGraw-Hill.

Ozment, J., & Morash, E. A. (1994). The augmented service offering for perceived and actual service quality. *Journal of the Academy of Marketing Science, 22*(4), 352–363. https://doi.org/10.1177/0092070394224004

Parasuraman, A., Berry, L. L., & Zeithaml, V. A. (1991). Refinement and reassessment of the SERVQUAL scale. *Journal of Retailing, 67*(4), 420–450.

Parasuraman, A., Zeithaml, V. A., & Berry, L. L. (1985). A conceptual model of service quality and its implications for future research. *Journal of Marketing, 49*(4), 41–50. https://doi.org/10.1177/002224298504900403

Parasuraman, A., Zeithaml, V. A., & Berry, L. L. (1988). SERVQUAL: A multiple-item scale for measuring consumer perc. *Journal of Retailing, 64*(1), 12.

Prentice, C. (2013). Service quality perceptions and customer loyalty in casinos. *International Journal of Contemporary Hospitality Management., 25*(1), 49–64.

Prentice, C. (2014). Who stays, who walks, and why in high-intensity service contexts. *Journal of Business Research, 67*(4), 608–614.

Prentice, C. (2019). *Emotional intelligence and marketing*. World Scientific.

Prentice, C., Dominique Lopes, S., & Wang, X. (2020). The impact of artificial intelligence and employee service quality on customer satisfaction and loyalty. *Journal of Hospitality Marketing & Management, 29*(7), 739–756.

Raspor, S. (2010). Measuring perceived service quality using SERVQUAL: A case study of the Croatian hotel industry. *Management (18544223), 5*(3).

Rouhiainen, L. (2019). How AI and data could personalize higher education. Retrieved from https://hbr.org/2019/10/how-ai-and-data-could-personalize-higher-education

Russell, S. J., Norvig, P., & ProQuest. (2016). *Artificial intelligence: A modern approach* (Global; 3rd ed.). Pearson Education Limited.

Saleh, F., & Ryan, C. (1991). Analysing service quality in the hospitality Industry using the SERVQUAL model. *The Service Industries Journal, 11*(3), 324–345. https://doi.org/10.1080/02642069100000049

Schumacker, R. E., & Lomax, R. G. (2004). *A beginner's guide to structural equation modeling* (2nd ed.). Lawrence Erlbaum Associates.

Shi, Y., Prentice, C., & He, W. (2014). Linking service quality, customer satisfaction and loyalty in casinos, does membership matter? *International Journal of Hospitality Management, 40*, 81–91. https://doi.org/10.1016/j.ijhm.2014.03.013

Siu, N. Y. M., & Tak-Hing Cheung, J. (2001). A measure of retail service quality. *Marketing Intelligence & Planning, 19*(2), 88–96. https://doi.org/10.1108/02634500110385327

Solomon, M. (2016). Technology invades the hospitality industry: Hilton Robot, Domino Delivery, Droid, Ritz-Carlton Mystique. *Forbes*. Retrieved 22 August 2017. https://www.forbes.com/sites/micahsolomon/2016/03/18/high-tech-hospitality-hiltonrobot-concierge-dominosdelivery-droid-ritz-carltonmystique/#3c8f92e3120b

Tavakoli, R., & Mura, P. (2018). Netnography in tourism—Beyond Web 2.0. *Annals of Tourism Research, 73*, 190–192. https://doi.org/10.1016/j.annals.2018.06.002

Tussyadiah, I. P., & Park, S. (2018). When guests trust hosts for their words: Host description and trust in sharing economy. *Tourism Management, 67*, 261–272.

West, A., Clifford, J., & Atkinson, D. (2018). *Alexa, build me a brand*. An investigation into the impact of artificial intelligence on branding.

Wirtz, J., & Lovelock, C. (2018a). *Developing service products and brands*. WS Professional.

Wirtz, J., & Lovelock, C. (2018b). *Crafting the service environment*. World Scientific.

Wixom, B. H., & Todd, P. A. (2005). A theoretical integration of user satisfaction and technology acceptance. *Information Systems Research, 16*(1), 85–102. https://doi.org/10.1287/isre.1050.0042

Wong, I. A., & Fong, V. H. I. (2012). Development and validation of the casino service quality scale: CASERV. *International Journal of Hospitality Management, 31*(1), 209–217. https://doi.org/10.1016/j.ijhm.2011.04.005

Woodside, A. G., Frey, L. L., & Daly, R. T. (1989). Linking sort/ice anility, customer satisfaction, and behavioral intention. *Journal of Health Care Marketing, 9*(4), 5–17.

Wu, T., & Tegmark, M. (2019). Toward an artificial intelligence physicist for unsupervised learning. *Physical Review E, 100*(3), 033311.

Xu, X., Wang, X., Li, Y., & Haghighi, M. (2017). Business intelligence in online customer textual reviews: Understanding consumer perceptions and influential factors. *International Journal of Information Management, 37*(6), 673–683.

Yang, Z., Cai, S., Zhou, Z., & Zhou, N. (2005). Development and validation of an instrument to measure user perceived service quality of information presenting Web portals. *Information and Management, 42*(4), 575–589. https://doi.org/10.1016/S0378-7206(04)00073-4

Yang, Z., Jun, M., & Peterson, R. T. (2004). Measuring customer perceived online service quality. *International Journal of Operations & Production Management, 24*(11), 1149–1174. https://doi.org/10.1108/01443570410563278

Zeithaml, V. A. (2000). Service quality, profitability, and the economic worth of customers: What we know and what we need to learn. *Journal of the Academy of Marketing Science, 28*(1), 67–85. https://doi.org/10.1177/0092070300281007

Zeithaml, V. A., Parasuraman, A., & Malhotra, A. (2002). Service quality delivery through web sites: A critical review of extant knowledge. *Journal of the Academy of Marketing Science, 30*(4), 362–375. https://doi.org/10.1177/009207002236911

Chapter 9
Leverage Emotional and Artificial Intelligences for Employees

Abstract Emotional intelligence has been popularising in both scientific and no-scientific communities as a new domain of human intelligence to predict individual and organizational success. Artificial intelligence has permeated the business world as a transformational evolution of utilising machines for human jobs. In view of the controversies over the role of artificial intelligence in replacing human jobs, this chapter discusses how emotional intelligence as human intelligence trumps artificial intelligence as machine intelligence over employee loyalty and performance and how artificial intelligence facilitates the latter. Employee performance is operationalised into internal and external dimensions that capture employees' task efficiency over both internal and external service encounter with co-workers and customers respectively. A case study with service employees working in the hotel was conducted to verify these claims.

9.1 Popularity of Artificial Intelligence

AI permeates in various industries and has potential to generate substantial financial profitability for businesses, particularly in the service sector such as banking, human recourses recruitment, healthcare transit, tourism and hotel industry (e.g., Buahlis & Leung, 2018; Kim, 2011; Yu & Schwartz, 2006). AI is predicted to add 1.2 trillion dollars to financial services by 2035 (Vochozka et al., 2018). Surveying more than 3,000 Japanese firms, Morikawa (2017a) found that firms with highly educated employees expect more positive impacts of AI-related technologies in their business.

In the service industry, Wirtz et al. (2018) analysed how service robots in conjunction with AI would impact the service organisations and employees across micro, meso and macro levels. AI not only improves operational efficiency by automating mundane tasks but also enhances customer experience (Bolton et al., 2018). For instance, large hotels rely on sophisticated computer programs that use AI to scan historical data and track patterns, resetting overbooking levels every 15 min, based on their goal reservation systems (Ma et al., 2018). Using Chatbots and messaging, AI allows service organizations to improve service quality in both functional and technical processes (Chung et al., 2018; Ivanov & Webster, 2017; Larivière et al., 2017) and to automate tasks that are traditionally performed by service employees. Restaurant managers use robotic servers and AI to assist self-service ordering. AI can also be used to improve energy consumption in hotel building (Wang et al., 2015). Hilton Hotels & Resorts has adopted Connie as their first AI robot to provide information to tourists and improve interactions with customers (Solomon, 2016). AI plays different roles in the service encounter, such as augmentation and substitution of service employees, and network facilitation (Larivière et al., 2017).

9.2 Concerns About Artificial Intelligence

Whilst acknowledging its prevalence and impact on improving the business efficiency, AI also sparks growing concern on its replacement of human jobs (Larivière et al., 2017). Robinson (2017) refers to the "Momentum Machines Project" as a one step closer to reduce fast-food jobs. In the case of hotels and restaurants, around 25% activities can be automated by the existing technology (Chui, Manyika & Miremadi, 2016). A report by Organization for Economic Co-operation and Development (OECD, 2016) shows that 9% of jobs could become automated in 21 countries. 2017 McKinsey report predicts a loss of 5% of jobs caused by AI (Manyika et al., 2017). An Oxford University research predicted that 47% of jobs could be automated by 2033 (Ramaswamy, 2017). About 50% of financial services and insurance jobs that are related to activities such as collecting and processing data are very likely to be replaced by AI (He & Guo, 2018). Reports from Pew Research Internet (Smith & Anderson, 2017) show that about 72 percent Americans express concern about replacement of human jobs by AI, only about 33 percent are enthusiastic about capabilities of AI.

9.3 Popularisation of Emotional Intelligence

However, research (Morikawa, 2017b; Smith & Anderson, 2017) also shows that AI can only play a dominant role in low-level mundane jobs, but very minor role in high level jobs that require occupation-specific skills. In this service dominant era, human intelligence and skills are imperative for business growth and sustainability. In the case of people-intensive industries (e.g., tourism, hospitality), employees' empathy and social skills that are derived from their emotional intelligence (EI) are critical for customer experience and loyalty. EI exhibited in employees affects customers' attitudes and behaviours through its influence on employee service behaviours and performance over the service encounter with customers. In these personal service encounters, AI may play a role facilitating employees' service encounter performance.

Emotional intelligence has been extensively discussed as a valid predictor of job performance (Carmeli & Josman, 2006; Cote & Miners, 2006). The efficiency of emotional intelligence in predicting job behaviours depends on the type of job and the nature of the business. For jobs that require teamwork, research (Clarke, 2010; Mayer & Salovey, 1997) shows that emotional intelligence significantly impacts employee job efficiency with co-workers (hereafter internal service performance) because emotionally intelligence people have better personal skills which are needed for group work. Emotional intelligence is particularly important for jobs that require social skills and interpersonal interactions, such as the frontline positions that involve interactions between service employees and customers (Ashkanasy & Daus, 2005; Caruso, Mayer & Salovey, 2002; Darvishmotevali et al., 2018). Employees with a high level of EI are better at dealing with the service encounter with customers and achieve better service performance (refer to external service performance herein).

In addition to its influence on job performance, EI has been found to affect a wide variety of job attitudes and behaviours. For instance, EI has a positive influence on job satisfaction because it affects one's ability to succeed in coping with environmental demands and pressures, thus managing stressful work conditions (Bar-On, 1997; Shi et al., 2014), and on employee commitment because EI facilitates communication, and emotionally intelligent people make others feel better suited to the occupational environment (Goleman, 1998; Nikolaou & Tsaousis, 2002; Rozell et al., 2004). Job satisfaction and commitment are common precursors of employee loyalty (e.g., Brown & Yoshioka, 2003; D'Amato & Herzfeldt, 2008; Saari & Judge, 2004).

9.4 Artificial Intelligence Facilitates Emotional Intelligence

AI-powered tools and applications have been used in different industries. For example, in retailing, Amazon has used analytical AI to support inventory management. In entertainment, newspapers such as The Los Angeles Times have used analytical AI to write articles. In museum, AI tour-guide robot has been used to increase the attendance (Burgard et al., 1999). Analytical AI in human resource management can help screen and select candidates. In marketing, AI is widely used to improve customer service (Bolton et al, 2013, 2018; Chung et al., 2018). For example, chatbots applying analytical AI can generate automatic responses to customer inquiries (Chung et al., 2018). AI has also been deployed in contact centres to improve the customer service experience (Kirkpatrick, 2017).

Despite its widespread use in businesses, however, the role of AI in organisations is dependent upon the type of jobs and the level of complexity. In general, AI is used to automate mundane and low-level tasks. Based on the four taxonomies of analytical intelligence (mechanical, analytical, intuitive, and empathetic intelligence) proposed by Huang and Rust (2018), Wirtz et al. (2018) propose an intuitive understanding of service delivery based on the complexity of emotional and cognitive tasks (see Fig. 2). The authors indicate that complex emotional-social task will tend to be performed by humans, and complex cognitive-analytical task will tend to be executed by robots.

The job of service employees is deemed to be complex emotional-social tasks as it involves interpersonal interactions with customers (Prentice et al., 2013), and this type of job requires emotional intelligence to manage the interactions (Ashkanasy & Daus, 2005; Caruso, Mayer & Salovey, 2002; Sjöberg et al., 2005). Although it may not play a dominant role in these tasks, AI can enhance these social tasks. For example, AI can facilitate the job of human agents from contact centres by interpreting customers' questions (e.g., language translation), searching business knowledge system, and preparing human-friendly responses (Kirkpatrick, 2017). AI can also provide information including change fees and scheduling issues when customers request to change their tickets, facilitating employee task efficiency. In the travel industry, Serbanescu and Necsulescu (2013) show that analytical AI can enhance the task performance and efficiency. Consequently, employees would get their work done more effectively which likely affects their job retention.

The foregoing discussion indicates that (1) emotional intelligence has a significant influence on employee service performance and retention; (2) AI enhances the relationship between EI and employee loyalty, and between EI and employee service performance. A study was conducted in the hotel sector to confirm these claims. The following section outlines the method of this study including sampling, data collection procedure and instruments. Findings of the study will be discussed.

9.5   The Empirical Study

9.5.1   Sample and Data Collection Procedure

To confirm how EI and AI affect service employees' performance and retention respectively, the study was undertaken at 60 hotels of different types (based on star rankings, namely, five, four, three and 2 stars hotels) in Portugal. Data were collected from service representatives who have direct contact with customers and work with some kind of artificial intelligent tools. About 12 percent of the employees were from 5-star hotel, 56% of 4-star hotels, 28% of 3-star hotels and 4% of 2-star hotels.

The survey was conducted online through SurveyMonkey. The researchers had a thorough discussion with AI experts from various hotels on the original questionnaire relating to AI dimensionality prior to the survey. To confirm the validity of the questionnaire (Tabachnick et al., 2007) and ensure the survey completion time less than 15 min to minimise respondents' fatigue, a pilot test was conducted with 20 randomly selected employees who have experience with AI tools working in the hotels. After this testing, the questionnaire was modified on the basis of inputs provided by these participants. Modifications were applied with a view to improving face validity and readability.

Of the total responses, 51.8% of respondents were male, and 48.2% were female. The age of participants ranged from 18 to 55 years old and above. About 33 percent of respondents fell in the age group of 18–24, 30 percent from the age group of 25–34, 20% in the 35–44 group, 13% in the 45–54 group, and only 5% in the 55 or above group. The majority (90%) had university degrees. About 46% had bachelor degree or above. Table 2 shows the demographic characteristics of the respondents.

9.5.2 Instruments

All items that were used to measure the study variables on a seven-point Likert scale, with 1 indicating strongly disagree, and 7 strongly agree. *Emotional intelligence* was measured by Law et al. (2004) self-report emotional intelligence scale (WEIS). Several measures are available in the literature for assessing emotional intelligence.

Employee performance was measured on the internal service performance that is focused on work behaviours with co-workers over the internal encounters and mandatory tasks within the organization, as well as external service performance that is based on customer-oriented behaviours over the service encounter with customers that is reflective of customer service performance. The items that were used to measure internal service performance were adapted from O'Reilly and Chatman (1986) to reflect each employee's general job performance within the organisation. To ensure item appropriateness and consistency with general job descriptions for employees working in different hotels, four items that reflect employee performance over internal encounters and are associated with the systems of the hotel organizations were retained for further analysis. The items measuring external service performance were adapted from Hallowell (1996) with regards to employee service that is specifically aimed for satisfying customers. These items are indicative of employees' consistent, reliable, prompt and individualised service.

Employee retention was measured by indicating their willingness to stay with the company, and by asking the respondents to indicate their intention to leave the job and explore other career opportunities within next 12 months. The items assessing this variable were adapted from Kelloway et al., (1999). For example, "How likely do you think you would get out of your current job within next 12 months;" and "How likely it is that you would explore other career opportunities within next 12 months." The reliability value for this scale was 0.91.

The measure that assessed employees' perception of AI was adapted from Wixom and Todd (2005). This measure has multiple dimensions including comprehensiveness, format, accuracy, currency, reliability, accessibility, flexibility, integrity, and timeliness. Each dimension has 3 items. The items that were used to measure comprehensiveness include "AI tools provide me with a complete set of information". The dimension format includes items such as "The information provided by AI tools is well formatted". Items such as "AI tools produce correct information" are included in the dimension accuracy. The items used to measure currency include "AI tools provide me with the most recent information". The reliability was measured by items such as "AI tools operate reliably". Items such as "AI tools allow information to be readily accessible to me" are included in the measurement of accessibility. The items measuring flexibly include "AI tools can be adapted to meet a variety of needs". The integrity was measured by items such as "AI tools effectively integrate data from different areas of the company". Items such as "AI tools provide information in a timely fashion" are included in measuring timeliness. The reliabilities for each dimension were all above 0.70.

9.5.3 Findings

9.5.3.1 Emotional Intelligence, Employee Performance and Retention

The empirical study shows that emotional intelligence has a significant effect on employee retention ($\beta = -0.28, p < 0.001$), internal service performance ($\beta = 0.47$, $p < 0.0005$), external service performance $\beta = 0.43, p < 0.0005$). Further analysis was performed to examine whether AI has direct effects on employee performance and retention. The results show that AI only has a significant effect on internal service performance ($\beta = 0.23, p < 0.001$), and external service performance ($\beta = 0.30, p < 0.001$). Those results are summarized in Table 9.1.

To gain more insights into the influence of AI and EI on the outcome variables, further analyses were performed to understand the unique variance explained by each dimension of AI and EI. Interestingly, none of AI and EI dimensions had a significant effect on employee loyalty. In the case of internal service performance, only the effect of self-emotional appraisal ($\beta = 0.49, p < 0.001$) and use of emotion ($\beta = 0.19, p < 0.05$) were significant. For external service performance, accuracy ($\beta = 0.19, p < 0.05$) exerted a significant effect' whereas the effects of self-emotion appraisal ($\beta = 0.17, p < 0.05$), others' emotion appraisal ($\beta = 0.15, p < 0.05$), and regulation of emotion ($\beta = 0.17, p < 0.05$) were also significant. The results are shown in Table 9.2.

This study provides evidence that employee loyalty to the hotel organization is largely attributed to their emotional abilities. Despite the prevalent use of advanced technologies, service employees in most hotels still play a significant role in serving and interacting with customers (e.g.: Larivière et al., 2017). These interpersonal encounters with customers can be emotionally charged (Prentice & Thaichon, 2019; Prentice, 2014, 2016) and they play an important role in the customer experience

Table 9.1 The direct effect of EI and AI

Variables	Employee retention	Internal service performance	External service performance
Artificial intelligence	−0.08	0.23**	0.30**
Emotional intelligence	0.28***	0.47***	0.43***
R^2	0.06	0.37	0.39

$^*p < .05; \ ^{**}p < .01; \ ^{***}p < .0005$

Table 9.2 The influence of AI and EI dimensions on the proposed outcome variables

Variables	Employee retention	Internal service performance	External service performance
Artificial intelligence			
Comprehensiveness	−0.02	−0.12	−0.03
Format	−0.11	−0.06	0.04
Accuracy	0.00	0.13	0.19*
Currency	0.11	0.10	0.10
Reliability	−0.00	0.11	0.05
Accessibility	−0.15	0.07	0.11
Flexibility	0.19	0.11	−0.02
Integrity	0.02	0.05	0.08
Timeliness	0.03	−0.08	0.04
Emotional intelligence			
Self-emotion appraisal	−0.05	0.49***	0.17*
Others' emotion appraisal	0.12	−0.03	0.15*
Use of emotion	0.14	0.19*	0.15
Regulation of emotion	0.07	−0.01	0.17*
R^2	0.06*	0.39***	0.31***

$^* p < .05;\ ^{**} p < .01;\ ^{***} p < .0005$

(Yachin, 2018). Employees with a high level of emotional intelligence are able to manage the encounter with customers and create positive customer service experience which affects their evaluation of employee service performance and their satisfaction with the employees then with the hotel. Numerous studies (e.g. Nasution & Mavondo, 2008; Wu & Liang, 2009; Xiang et al., 2015) have shown that customer experience is mostly attributed to employee service performance over the service encounter. Each encounter experience forms cumulative impression of the hotel service. A negative experience with a hotel employees (e.g. a receptionist, a bellboy, a housekeeping employee) would affect the customer's perception of the hotel. Therefore, employees are required to perform emotional labour that requires appropriate acting strategies to ensure positive customer experience. Emotional labour strategies generate positive organizational outcomes, however also have detrimental effects on service employees given the acting requires emotional management skills. Employees with a high level of emotional intelligence suffer less negative consequences from performing emotional labour, hence, have more positive attitude toward working at the hotel. Consequently, they are more likely to stay with the hotel.

The study shows that only self-emotion appraisal and utilisation of emotions explain significant variance in internal encounter performance. This is plausible. Service employees must be able to understand their own emotions and have their ability to utilise their emotions to manage the internal encounter that involves interactions with co-workers. Appropriately managing the internal encounter has implication for external service performance that is aimed at satisfying customers. Knowingly customer satisfaction with the hotel has implications for their subsequent behaviours such as being referrals, spreading word of mouth communications, and revisiting the hotel. Customers can be emotional when their requests and demands are not fulfilled. Employees bear the onus of managing their emotions and demands so that an optimal outcome can be reached for benefiting both the organization and the customers. This onus entails employees understanding their own emotions before they are able to assess others' emotions as indicated in self-emotion appraisal, and using their own emotions to guide their behaviours as indicated in utilisation of emotions. This ability would facilitate their service performance.

On the other hand, customer satisfaction is affected by employee external service performance which entails employees' ability to appraise the emotions of oneself and others, as well as regulating emotions. To be able to perform well over each service encounter with customers, it is important to understand their emotions, either positive or negative, this understanding helps them manage emotions, turning negative emotions to be positive and to reinforce their positive emotions. For instance, an effective service recovery strategy by offering better service (more than expected) to a complaining customer, or by addressing the issues in a timely manner often leads to better customer-related outcomes (loyalty behaviours). This is in line with Ogbeide et al. (2015), Wu et al. (2018), Xu and Li (2016). Based on the different roles played by employees presented by Larivière et al. (2017), emotional intelligence can lead employees to play the role of differentiator, i.e., employees become a differentiating attribute in service encounter situations (e.g.: Bowen, 2016; Larivière et al., 2017).

9.6   Artificial Intelligence as a Facilitator

To test the moderation of AI between EI and the outcome variables. The results show that AI significantly moderates the effect of EI on Internal service performance (β = 0.15, $p < 0.05$), and external service performance ($\beta = 0.32$, $p < 0.001$). The moderation effect exerted are graphed below (Figs. 9.1 and 9.2).

Although it has a significant effect on employee performance, artificial intelligence is not related to employee retention. The effects are less weighted compared to those exerted by emotional intelligence. Nevertheless, AI plays a moderating role in facilitating employee efficiency in performing their internal job tasks (internal service performance) and improving customer satisfaction (external service performance). These findings are consistent with claims and reports that artificial intelligence will not replace human tasks, but facilitate them (Bowen, 2016; Larivière, 2017; McKendrick, 2018; Mohanty, 2018). The Gartner reports show that artificial intelligence creates more jobs than it destroys. The level of replacement or facilitation is dependent upon the nature of the jobs. Reports from Smith and Anderson (2017) show that only low-level human jobs may be replaced by robots or artificial intelligence.

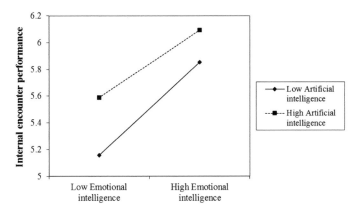

Fig. 9.1   The moderation effect of artificial intelligence on EI and internal service performance

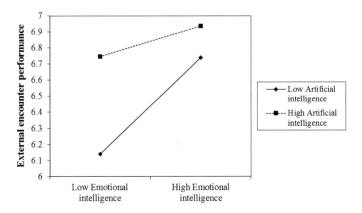

Fig. 9.2   The moderation effect of artificial intelligence on EI and external service performance

9.7   Implications and Conclusion

This chapter discusses how emotional intelligence as a human intelligence and artificial intelligence as a machine intelligence affect employee retention and performance.

The case study confirms that human intelligence, compared to machine intelligence, has a dominant influence on employees, particularly in the people-intensive industry. Artificial intelligence plays a facilitating role in enhancing the influence.

Emotional intelligence has been acknowledged as a valid predictor of employee attitudes and behaviours (e.g. job performance, organizational commitment, employee retention). The findings of the case study confirm these relationships in the hotel industry. In particular, this study extends this scope into customer loyalty research domain by linking emotional intelligence and customer service which has impact on customers' attitudes and behaviours.

This study also extends artificial intelligence research that has been primarily focused on its technical and functional efficiency in the relevant literature into human intelligence research in the organizational context to understand its impact on employee and organizational performance. The findings provide insights into the role of machine intelligence in employee behaviours and business efficiency.

The research has particular implications for practitioners. The findings provide management and the relevant EI and AI consultants with a guideline on what should be focused on in order to optimise organizational performance through managing the behaviours of employees and customers. Although artificial intelligence has become a buzz word to improve business operations, it is human intelligence with regards to emotional abilities that plays a dominant role in managing employees and customers. In comparison customers today still prefer to interact with employees rather than machines or robots which can be an instantaneous novelty. The study confirms that artificial intelligence can facilitate human tasks but not replacing human jobs. The significant impact on employees and customers exerted by emotional intelligence indicates that the organizational resources should be allocated for the relevant training to enhance employee emotional competence. This finding is in line with that in Hewagama et al. (2019) and in Yao et al. (2019). The management should identify the tasks that artificial intelligence is able to perform or better at so that human resources can be optimised for other tasks.

In sum, emotional intelligence has a significant and larger impact on employee performance and retention, whereas artificial intelligence is significantly related to employee performance. Additionally, artificial intelligence enhances the predicting effect of employee's emotional intelligence on job performance and retention.

References

Ashkanasy, N. M., & Daus, C. S. (2005). Rumors of the death of emotional intelligence in organizational behavior are vastly exaggerated. *Journal of Organizational Behavior, 26*(4), 441–452.

Bar-On, R. (1997). *The emotional intelligence inventory (EQI): Technical manual*. Multi-Health Systems.

Bolton, C., Machova, V., Kovacova, M., & Valaskova, K. (2018). The power of human-machine collaboration: Artificial intelligence, business automation, and the smart economy. *Economics, Management, and Financial Markets, 13*(4), 51–56.

Bolton, R. N., Parasuraman, A., Hoefnagels, A., Migchels, N., Kabadayi, S., Gruber, T., Komarova, Y., & Solnet, D. (2013). Understanding generation Y and their use of social media: A review and research agenda. *Journal of Service Management, 24*(3), 245–267.

Bowen, D. E. (2016). The changing role of employees in service theory and practice: An interdisciplinary view. *Human Resource Management Review, 26*(1), 4–13.

Brown, W. A., & Yoshioka, C. F. (2003). Mission attachment and satisfaction as factors in employee retention. *Nonprofit Management and Leadership, 14*(1), 5–18.

Buahlis, D., & Leung, R. (2018). Smart hospitality—Interconnectivity and interoperability towards an ecosystem. *International Journal of Hospitality Management, 71*, 41–50.

Burgard, W., Cremers, A. B., Fox, D., Hahnel, D., Lakemeyer, G., Schulz, D., Steiner, W., & Thrun, S. (1999). Experiences with an interactive museum tour-guide robot. *Artificial Intelligence, 114*, 3–55.

Carmeli, A., & Josman, Z. E. (2006). The relationship among emotional intelligence, task performance, and organizational citizenship behaviors. *Human Performance, 19*(4), 403–419.

Caruso, D. R., Mayer, J. D., & Salovey, P. (2002). *Emotional intelligence and emotional leadership*. In Kravis-de Roulet Leadership Conference, 9th, Apr, 1999, Claremont McKenna Coll, Claremont, CA, US. Lawrence Erlbaum Associates Publishers.

Chui, M., Manyika, J., & Miremadi, M. (2016). *Where machines could replace humans—and where they can't (yet)*. https://www.mckinsey.com/business-functions/digital-mckinsey/our-insights/where-machines-could-replace-humans-and-where-they-cant-yet

Chung, M., Ko, E., Joung, H., & Kim, S. J. (2018, in press). Chatbot e-service and customer satisfaction regarding luxury brands. *Journal of Business Research.*

Clarke, N. (2010). Emotional Intelligence and learning in teams. *Journal of Workplace Learning, 22*(3), 125–145.

Cote, S., & Miners, C. T. (2006). Emotional intelligence, cognitive intelligence, and job performance. *Administrative Science Quarterly, 51*(1), 1–28.

D'Amato, A., & Herzfeldt, R. (2008). Learning orientation, organizational commitment and talent retention across generations: A study of European managers. *Journal of Managerial Psychology, 23*(8), 929–953.

Darvishmotevali, M., Altinay, L., & De Vita, G. (2018). Emotional intelligence and creative performance: Looking through the lens of environmental uncertainty and cultural intelligence. *International Journal of Hospitality Management, 73*, 44–54.

Goleman, D. (1998). *Working with emotional intelligence*. Bantam Books.

Hallowell, R. (1996). The relationships of customer satisfaction, customer loyalty, and profitability: An empirical study. *International Journal of Service Industry Management, 7*(4), 27–42.

He, D., & Guo, V. (2018). 4 ways AI will impact the financial job market. *World Economic Forum*. https://www.weforum.org/agenda/2018/09/4-ways-ai-artificial-intelligence-impact-financial-job-market/. Published 14 September 2018.

Hewagama, G., Boxall, P., Cheung, G., & Hutchison, A. (2019). Service recovery through empowerment? HRM, employee performance and job satisfaction in hotels. *International Journal of Hospitality Management, 81*, 73–82.

Huang, M.-H., & Rust, R. T. (2018). Artificial intelligence in service. *Journal of Service Research, 21*(2), 155–172.

Ivanov, S. H., & Webster, C. (2017). *Adoption of robots, artificial intelligence and service automation by travel, tourism and hospitality companies—A cost-benefit analysis*. International Scientific Conference Contemporary Tourism–Traditions and Innovations. Sofia University, Sofia.

Kelloway, E. K., Gottlieb, B. H., & Barham, L. (1999). The source, nature, and direction of work and family conflict: A longitudinal investigation. *Journal of Occupational Health Psychology, 4*(4), 337–346.

Kim, S. Y. (2011). Prediction of hotel bankruptcy using support vector machine, artificial neural network, logistic regression, and multivariate discriminant analysis. *The Service Industries Journal, 31*(3), 441–468.

Kirkpatrick, K. (2017). AI in contact centers. *Communications of the ACM, 60*(8), 18–19.

Larivière, B., Bowen, D., Andreassen, T. W., Kunz, W., Sirianni, N. J., Voss, C., Wunderlich, N. V., & De Keyser, A. (2017). "Service Encounter 2.0": An investigation into the roles of technology, employees and customers. *Journal of Business Research, 79*, 238–246.

Law, K. S., Wong, C.-S., & Song, L. J. (2004). The construct and criterion validity of emotional intelligence and its potential utility for management studies. *Journal of Applied Psychology, 89*(3), 483–496.

Ma, Y., Xiang, Z., Du, Q., & Fan, W. (2018). Effects of user-provided photos on hotel review helpfulness: An analytical approach with deep leaning. *International Journal of Hospitality Management, 71*, 120–131.

Manyika, J., Lund, S., Chui, M., Bughin, J., Woetzel, J., Batra, P., Ko, R., Sanghvi, S. (2017). *Jobs lost, jobs gained: What the future of work will mean for jobs, skills, and wages.* https://www.mckinsey.com/featured-insights/future-of-work/jobs-lost-jobs-gained-what-the-future-of-work-will-mean-for-jobs-skills-and-wages

Mayer, J. D., & Salovey, P. (1997). What is emotional intelligence. *Emotional Development and Emotional Intelligence: Educational Implications, 3*, 31.

McKendrick, J. (2018, August 14). Artificial intelligence will replace tasks, not jobs. *Forbes.* https://www.forbes.com/sites/joemckendrick/2018/08/14/artificial-intelligence-will-replace-tasks-not-jobs/#2b2fda7ba7fa

Mohanty, P. (2018, July 6). Do you fear artificial intelligence will take your job? *Forbes.* https://www.forbes.com/sites/theyec/2018/07/06/do-you-fear-artificial-intelligence-will-take-your-job/#7b4fda0c11aa

Morikawa, M. (2017a). Firms' expectations about the impact of AI and Robotics: Evidence from a survey. *Economic Inquiry, 55*(2), 1054–1063.

Morikawa, M. (2017b). *Who are afraid of losing their jobs to artificial intelligence and robots? Evidence from a survey.* Research Institute of Economy, Trade and Industry (RIETI).

Nasution, H. N., & Mavondo, F. T. (2008). Customer value in the hotel industry: What managers believe they deliver and what customer experience. *International Journal of Hospitality Management, 27*(2), 204–213.

Nikolaou, I., & Tsaousis, I. (2002). Emotional intelligence in the workplace: Exploring its effects on occupational stress and organizational commitment. *The International Journal of Organizational Analysis, 10*(4), 327–342.

OECD (2016). *Automation and independent work in a digital economy.* https://www.oecd.org/employment/Policy%20brief%20-%20Automation%20and%20Independent%20Work%20in%20a%20Digital%20Economy.pdf

Ogbeide, G., Boser, S., Harrinton, R., & Ottenbacher, M. (2015). Complaint management in hospitality organizations: The role empowerment and other service recovery attributes impacting loyalty and satisfaction. *Tourism and Hospitality Research, 17*, 204–216.

O'Reilly, C. A., & Chatman, J. (1986). Organizational commitment and psychological attachment: The effects of compliance, identification, and internalization on prosocial behavior. *Journal of Applied Psychology, 71*(3), 492–499.

Prentice, C. (2014). Who stays, who walks, and why in high-intensity service contexts. *Journal of Business Research, 67*(4), 608–614.

Prentice, C. (2016). Leveraging employee emotional intelligence in casino profitability. *Journal of Retailing and Consumer Services, 33*, 127–134.

Prentice, C., & Thaichon, P. (2019). Revisiting the job performance—Burnout relationship. *Journal of Hospitality Marketing & Management.* https://doi.org/10.1080/19368623.2019.1568340

Prentice, C., Chen, P. J., & King, B. (2013). Employee performance outcomes and burnout following the presentation-of-self in customer-service contexts. *International Journal of Hospitality Management, 35*, 225–236.

Ramaswamy. S. (2017, April 14) How companies are already using AI. *Harvard Business Review.* https://hbr.org/2017/04/how-companies-are-already-using-ai

Robinson, M. (2017, June 13). *This robot-powered restaurant is one step closer to putting fast-food workers out of a job.* https://www.businessinsider.com.au/momentum-machines-funding-robot-burger-restaurant-2017-6

Rozell, E. J., Pettijohn, C. E., & Parker, R. S. (2004). Customer-oriented selling: Exploring the roles of emotional intelligence and organizational commitment. *Psychology & Marketing, 21*(6), 405–424.

Saari, L. M., & Judge, T. A. (2004). Employee attitudes and job satisfaction. *Human Resource Management: Published in Cooperation with the School of Business Administration, the University of Michigan and in Alliance with the Society of Human Resources Management, 43*(4), 395–407.

Serbanescu, L., & Necsulescu, C. (2013). Improving the performance and efficiency of tavel agencies with IT technology. *Lucrări Ştiinţifice, XV*(4), Seria I.

Shi, Y., Prentice, C., & He, W. (2014). Linking service quality, customer satisfaction and loyalty in casinos, does membership matter? *International Journal of Hospitality Management, 40*, 81–91.

Sjöberg, L., Littorin, P., & Engelberg, E. (2005). Personality and emotional intelligence as factors in sales performance. *Scandinavian Journal of Organizational Theory and Practice, 15*(2), 21–37.

Smith, A., & Anderson, M. (2017). *Automation in everyday life*. Pew Research Centre. https://www.pewresearch.org/internet/2017/10/04/automation-in-everyday-life/.

Solomon, M. (2016, March 18). Technology invades hospitality industry: Hilton robot, Domino delivery droid, Ritz-Carlton mystique. *Forbes*. https://www.forbes.com/sites/micahsolomon/2016/03/18/high-tech-hospitality-hilton-robot-concierge-dominos-delivery-droid-ritz-carlton-mystique/#25a0730b120b

Tabachnick, B. G., Fidell, L. S., & Ullman, J. B. (2007). *Using multivariate statistics* (Vol. 5). Pearson.

Vochozka, M., Kliestik, T., Kliestikova, J., & Sion, G. (2018). Participating in a highly automated society: How artificial intelligence disrupts the job market. *Economics, Management, and Financial Markets, 13*(4), 57–62.

Wang, F., Lin, H., Tu, W., Wang, Y., & Huang, Y. (2015). Energy modelling and chillers sizing of HVAC system for a hotel building. *Procedia Engineering, 121*, 1812–1818.

Wirtz, J., Patterson, P. G., Kunz, W. H., Gruber, T., Lu, V. N., Paluch, S., & Martins, A. (2018). Brave new world: Service robots in the frontline. *Journal of Service Management, 29*(5), 907–931.

Wixom, B. H., & Todd, P. A. (2005). A theoretical integration of user satisfaction and technology acceptance. *Information Systems Research, 16*(1), 85–102.

Wu, C. H. J., & Liang, R. D. (2009). Effect of experiential value on customer satisfaction with service encounters in luxury-hotel restaurants. *International Journal of Hospitality Management, 28*(4), 586–593.

Wu, H. C., Cheng, C. C., & Ai, C. H. (2018). A study of experiential quality, experiential value, trust, corporate reputation, experiential satisfaction and behavioral intentions for cruise tourists: The case of Hong Kong. *Tourism Management, 66*, 200–220.

Xiang, Z., Schwartz, Z., Gerdes, J. H., Jr., & Uysal, M. (2015). What can big data and text analytics tell us about hotel guest experience and satisfaction? *International Journal of Hospitality Management, 44*, 120–130.

Xu, X., & Li, Y. (2016). The antecedents of customer satisfaction and dissatisfaction toward various types of hotels: A text mining approach. *International Journal of Hospitality Management, 55*, 57–69.

Yao, S., Wang, X., Yu, H., & Guchait, P. (2019). Effectiveness of error management training in the hospitality industry: Impact on perceived fairness and service recovery performance. *International Journal of Hospitality Management, 79*, 78–88.

Yachin, J. M. (2018). The "customer journey": Learning from customers in tourism experience encounters. *Tourism Management Perspectives, 28*, 201–210.

Yu, G., & Schwartz, Z. (2006). Forecasting short time-series tourism demand with artificial intelligence models. *Journal of Travel Research, 45*(2), 194–203.

Chapter 10
Leveraging Emotional and Artificial Intelligences for Customers

Abstract Customer experience is key to achieving customer engagement and loyalty. Artificial intelligence (AI) permeates in service organisations as a tool to improve customer experience. Reports show that most consumers prefer human interactions with service employees. Drawing on this observation, the current chapter discusses and proposes how customers' service experiences with employees and AI influence customer engagement and loyalty. Researchers in information technology (IT) field have attempted to fuse human and machine intelligence from technological perspective to enhance operation systems. This chapter takes a different angle and investigates how the emotional intelligence possessed by customers affects their experience with AI and employees and their subsequent engagement. This investigation provides a first look into fusion of human and machine intelligences in the business domain and extends emotional intelligence research into the consumer research to understand its influence on customer behaviours.

This chapter examines the relationship between AI, employee service, emotional intelligence, customer engagement, and loyalty by investigating how machine (AI) and human intelligences (emotional intelligence) influence customer experience and relationships with the organisation. In particular, customers' emotional intelligence is proposed as a moderator/facilitator between service experience and customer engagement. A case study was conducted with hotel customers in Australia to confirm the proposed relationships. The results show that whilst both service experience with employees and AI are significantly related to customer engagement and loyalty, only certain dimensions make significant unique variances in these outcomes. The findings indicate that customers prefer employee service. These service experiences also have significant partial mediation effects on customer loyalty. Emotional intelligence has a significant moderation effect on customer engagement. Discussion of these findings and implications derived from this study concludes this paper.

10.1   Understanding Customer Experience

Creating a positive service experience has become a key strategy to achieve competitive advantages for service organisations (Berry, 1995). Service experience involves multiple touchpoints along the customer journey (pre-, during and post-purchase/consumption). These touchpoints include customers' interactions with different service clues (Lemon & Verhoef, 2016). Berry et al. (2006) classify these services into humanic, functional, and mechanic clues. Each clue contributes to customers' service experience with the organisation; hence, is referred to as humanic, functional, and mechanic experience respectively.

Humanic experience is the result of employee behaviours towards customers. In labour intensive industries, humanic experience generally accounts for a major portion of customer response (Liao, 2007; Loveman, 1998; Prentice, 2016; Prentice et al., 2019a). Employee service plays a key role in differentiating customers' perceptions of the organisation's service quality (Prentice, 2016).

Functional clues are pertinent to the technical quality of the service offering, indicating the reliability and competence of the service. AI-powered service can be referred to as functional experience. Recent literature (Wirtz et al., 2018; Xiang et al., 2015) suggests that artificial intelligence (AI) plays an imperative role in influencing customers' service experience. AI-powered service permeates in business operations as a cost-effective means to enhance organisational efficiency and is used to improve service delivery (e.g. providing convenience to customers by using 24 h auto-messaging services).

Mechanic experience is the result of customer interaction with sensory components of the service, such as sights, smells, sounds, and other ambient elements, which have been extensively discussed in the literature as important factors of customer experience. Whilst Berry et al. (2006) indicate that all three categories of experiences play different roles in customers' cognitive and emotional perceptions of the organisation's service quality, this chapter is focused on humanic and functional experiences, aka customer experience with employees and AI. These experiences influence customers' relationship with the organisation (Cronin et al., 2000; Prentice, 2013b, 2016; Zeithaml et al., 1996). Customer relationship manifest with their engagement with the organisation and their loyalty behaviours, namely, customer engagement and loyalty (Lemon & Verhoef, 2016; Prentice et al., 2018).

10.2   Understanding Customer Engagement and Loyalty

Customer engagement is a form of co-creation between service providers and customers and regarded as a marketing strategy to attract customer purchase and loyalty (Brodie et al., 2011; Hoyer et al., 2010; Nambisan & Nambisan, 2008). This concept has been popularised in the marketing literature as the level of engagement with the service organisation and its associated businesses has financial implications for the organisation as well as for customers (van Doorn et al., 2010). As a relatively nascent concept, customer engagement has been conceptualised differently. As such, the literature shows inconsistency in its drivers and outcomes. The relevant literature shows that customer engagement generally captures customers' behavioural, cognitive, and emotional engagement with the business (Hollebeek, 2011; Prentice et al., 2018, 2019b). So et al. (2016) assessed customer engagement from affective, cognitive, and psychological perspectives. This assessment included the dimensions of (1) identification, indicating customers' perceived oneness with, or belongingness to, the brand or organisation; (2) attention, indicating customers' attentiveness, focus, and connection with the brand or organisation; (3) enthusiasm, indicating customers' excitement and interest; (4) absorption, indicating customers' pleasant state; and (5) interaction, indicating customers' participation with the brand or organisation.

Customer engagement can be associated with customer loyalty (Dholakia et al., 2004; Shang et al., 2006; Zheng et al., 2015). As consumers interact with the firm, satisfied customers tend to develop favourable attitudes and subsequent loyalty behaviours; whereas dissatisfied customers may engage in behaviours that have a negative financial impact on the organisation. However, spontaneous engagement often has a positive influence on the brand or the firm. Such engagement may reinforce the relationship between the brand and customer loyalty (e.g. Algesheimer et al., 2010; van Doorn et al., 2010; Wirtz et al., 2013).

The literature has recognised the crucial role of customer engagement as a strategic imperative for attracting customer loyalty. An engaged customer tends to develop more favourable attitudes towards the brand or the organisation, and leads to cognitive complacency, resulting in customer loyalty (Nguyen et al., 2013; So et al., 2014; Vivek et al., 2012). Customer engagement affects customers' perception and attitudes, which also in turn impact customer loyalty (Sprott et al., 2009). So et al. (2016) provided more insights into the relationship between customer engagement and loyalty and indicated that customer engagement generated truly committed and loyal customers.

10.3 AI Experience on Customer Engagement and Loyalty

Bowen and Morosan (2018) provide an overview of how AI and robotics are utilised in the service sector. Their study indicates that AI can extract the true value of the vast quantities of consumer information available, which can be used to improve customer experience through more customised services. For example, auto-cars (a type of AI) can do airport pickup, help customers to check in to a hotel, and set up a customers' smartphone to use a key. The AI-controlled cars can suggest restaurants near the hotels and make a reservation for the customer based on the customer's request. A greeting model in a robot can engage customers due to the maintenance of longer interactions (Rodriguez-Lizundia et al., 2015). Vivek et al. (2012) highlighted the importance of interactive experience as a means to enhance customer engagement in the service organisation. For example, Hayes and MacLeod (2007) demonstrated that if a hotel can offer a memorable, worthwhile, and interactive experience, the customer will be more engageable. By using AI service, a hotel can provide an outstanding experience to enhance customer engagement. When customers receive an engaging experience that has been provided by AI service, they tend to be more engaged with the hotel. A good experience with AI service motivates customers to have more physical, mental, social, and emotional engagement with the firm (Carù & Cova, 2003). A memorable experience created by AI service can also consolidate the link between the customer and the service firm, resulting in a stronger customer engagement and loyalty (Hayes & MacLeod, 2007; Ullah et al., 2018). Hence, the foregoing discussion informs that

Service experience with AI is positively and significantly related to customer engagement and loyalty.

10.4 Humanic Experience and Customer Engagement

Whilst each touchpoint with the organisation constitutes customer experience, in people-intensive industries, the moment of truth is the service encounter with employee service, which is vital to customers' perception of a company's service quality and their willingness to engage with the firm (Prentice, 2016). Employee service is the first and primary contact point for the customer before, during, and after the service process. This contact plays an important role in affecting customers' perceptions of any service encounter and are pivotal in forming a customer's level of perceived service quality (Prentice, 2013a, 2013b, 2019). Customers often base their impression of the organisation largely on the service received from customer contact employees and the communication between employee and customer is a reciprocal interactive process (Prentice, 2019).

The service experience which distinguishes a service organisation is often a result of the unique interaction between customers and employees. Despite spotless facilities, and the service being delivered on time as ordered, a customer may leave with a negative impression based on the attitude of an employee or other efforts that may be overlooked. Employee behaviours and performance over the service encounter constitute the customer experience and form customers' perceptions of service quality, which further leads to their involvement and commitment with the firm and is manifested in their engagement with, and loyalty to, the firm (Delcourt et al., 2013). This discussion informs that.

Service experience with employees is positively and significantly related to customer engagement and loyalty.

10.5 AI and Humanic Experience Are Inadequate

Customer experience with the firm's employees and AI services can be important to attract their engagement with the organisation and subsequent loyalty. However, service experience is an emotional journey (Casidy et al., 2018; Vada et al., 2019). Interacting with the firm's service employees and AI services may not always be a positive experience. Some experiences are pleasant and memorable; whilst others may be negative. For instance, auto-messaging services (a type of AI) used by service firms such as hotels and airlines provide convenience to customers who require assistance out of office hours. This AI tool offers very little scope for customised messages for individual customers which may result in frustration with the service. Numerous reports (e.g., Invoca, date; The Harris Pool, date; see Nanji, 2019) show that most consumers are unsatisfied or frustrated with AI-powered service and prefer personal interactions with service employees.

Nevertheless, experience with employee service may not always be pleasant. Employees may experience moods and emotions which may affect their attitudes and behaviours during interaction with customers (Prentice, 2016, 2019). Situated in the organisation's boundary positions, service employees interact with both internal co-workers/management and external customers. Role conflict and lack of management support can affect employee service performance, hence customer experience and perception (Neves & Eisenberger, 2012; Van Sell et al., 1981). Although these employees are required to perform emotional labour (Ashforth & Humphrey, 1993; Grandey, 2000), such performance may have detrimental effects (job dissatisfaction, emotional dissonance, burnout) on the labourers (Brotheridge & Grandey, 2002; Prentice et al., 2013). Their negative emotions may affect customers' perception and experience with the employee.

When service experience with AI and employees turns to be negative, some customers may complain and switch to competitors, and others may be more empathetic with the employee. From a customer's perspective, the possible switching costs and perceived benefits may compel them to find the means to enhance their experience and engagement with the organisation. Customers' individual abilities such as emotional intelligence may play a role in their relationship with the organisation. Their emotional intelligence may help them expand customers' tolerance zone and empathise with employees to accept a certain level of less desired service. As van Doorn et al. (2010) indicate that customer engagement not only benefits the firm but also themselves. For instance, engaging with the firm's reward-based programs has social and financial benefits for customers. These potential benefits drive customers to actively engage with the firm. As a human intelligence, emotional intelligence in the organisational context has been extensively discussed as a significant factor of individual and organisational outcomes over last three decades (see Prentice, 2019).

10.6 Customer Emotional Intelligence Facilitates Humanic Experience

Emotional intelligence refers to individuals' emotional abilities to recognise, understand, utilise, and manage the emotions of themselves and others (Salovey & Mayer, 1990). Emotional intelligence consists of four hierarchical branches: emotional perception, emotional assimilation, emotional understanding, and emotion management. Each brand represents different emotional abilities (see Prentice, 2019). These abilities enable an emotionally intelligent person to be understanding of, and empathetic with, others. In the case of the service encounter, customers' emotional intelligence may help them connect with employees on an emotional level to enhance their experience with the employee service. This level of connection with employees subsequently affects customers' involvement with the service organisation. Namely,

Customers' emotional intelligence moderates the relationship between service experience with employees and customer engagement.

10.7 Customer Emotional Intelligence Facilitates AI Experience

Although AI has evolved from performing basic tasks such as Siri to artificial super intelligence that is expected to be capable of scientific creativity and social skills like a human (Kaplan & Haenlein, 2019), AI operates through computers. Machines are manoeuvred to standardise tasks and are able to perform low-level jobs (Prentice et al., 2019a). Each customer may demand different services that AI may fail to deliver. However, emotionally intelligent individuals are more empathetic and understanding. Customers with a high level of emotional intelligence may be more tolerant of AI services and appreciate the convenience it offers; whereas customers with a low level of emotional intelligence may prefer to deal with machine-operated AI rather than with employees. In other words, this discussion informs that.

Customers' emotional intelligence moderates the relationship between service experience with AI and customer engagement.

The following empirical study was conducted to verify the proposed relationships above. The following section describes the methods including sampling, data collection procedures and instruments for the study. Findings and discussion are presented subsequently. Implications of these findings are discussed to conclude this chapter.

10.8 The Empirical Study

10.8.1 Sample and Data Collection Procedure

The survey was conducted with consumers who have experienced AI tools and services in Australia. The selected hotels use similar AI tools to provide services to customers. These AI tools facilitate customer service with the intention to enhance customer experience. For the purpose of this research, the prospective respondents must be over 18, understand and have used these AI tools and services, and have stayed, within last three months, at one of the Australian hotels which utilise AI-powered services. Prospective respondents were encouraged by providing incentives (e.g. gift vouchers) to distribute the online survey (the weblinks) through their social media networks (e.g. Facebook) to their friends or relatives who may be suitable for participating in this research.

Among the respondents, about half were female (50.8%). More than 28% of respondents fell in the age group between 18 and 25 (28.2%). About 37% of respondents had university degrees (37.1%) and 43.9% of respondents reported that they travelled for leisure, whereas the percentage of respondents travelled for business and visiting family and friends were 25.3 and 21.1, respectively. The majority of respondents were Australian (84.7%) and mainly lived in Queensland (16.1%), New South Wales (31.1%) and Victoria (26.1%).

10.8.2 Instrument

To understand how humanic service experience affects customer engagement and loyalty, four aspects from Parasuraman et al. (1991) SERVQUAL (namely reliability, assurance, empathy, and responsiveness) that correspond to the service performed by employees were adapted for this study. These dimensions include service promptness, accuracy, consistency, and employee friendliness and caring. Similarly, a measure developed by Wixom and Todd (2005) also includes these aspects of service experience with AI. Four dimensions that are reflective of the reliability, assurance (accuracy and integrity), empathy (comprehensiveness and flexibility), and responsiveness (timeliness) of service experience with AI were selected for this study. The reliability of each dimension was above 0.70 and are reported in the next section.

Emotional intelligence was measured by Law et al. (2004) emotional intelligence scale (WEIS). WEIS was based on four ability dimensions described in the ability EI model (see Brackett & Mayer, 2003) and has been widely used and cited in the literature. The WEIS contains 16 items (statements), and four dimensions. These four dimensions are self-emotion appraisal (SEA), other-emotion appraisal (OEA), use of emotion (UOE), and regulation of emotion (ROE). Each dimension has four items. The reliabilities were 0.90 for SEA, 0.89 for OEA, 0.86 for UOE, and 0.90 for ROE.

Customer engagement was measured by adapting So et al. (2016) multidimensional scale, which was developed in the tourism context and reflects customers' affective, cognitive, and psychological involvement. The scale includes: identification, indicating customers' perceived oneness with or belongingness to the brand or organisation; attention, indicating customers' attentiveness, focus and connection with the brand or organisation; enthusiasm, indicating customers' excitement and interest; absorption, indicating customers' pleasant state; and interaction, indicating customers' participation with the brand or organisation. The reliabilities were 0.91 for identification, 0.96 for attention, 0.96 for enthusiasm, 0.96 for absorption, and 0.96 for interaction. Customer loyalty was measured by adapting Kandampully and Suhartanto's (2003) scale to focus on customers' willingness to provide referrals or positive word-of-mouth communication, or their intention to return and pay a premium price. The reliability in this case was 0.96.

10.8.3   Findings and Discussion

10.8.3.1   Service Experience with Employees and AI

The findings show that overall experience with both employees and AI significantly influence customer engagement and loyalty as shown in Table 10.1. When regressing all sub-dimensions of employee and AI service (Table 10.2), none of the AI dimensions are significantly related to customer engagement. Nevertheless, employee responsiveness, empathy, and assurance exert significant effects on the outcome variable. Responsiveness in the case of employees indicates promptness of service delivery, employees' willingness to help, and availability to respond to customers' requests.

Table 10.1 Results of the proposed relationships

Paths	β	Sig.
Overall model		
Service experience with employees → customer engagement	0.19	*
Service experience with employees → customer loyalty	0.39	**
Service experience with AI → customer engagement	0.71	**
Service experience with AI → customer loyalty	0.28	**
Customer engagement → customer loyalty	0.37	**
R^2		
Customer engagement	0.37	
Customer loyalty	0.71	

Note * $p < 0.05$, ** $p < 0.001$

Table 10.2 Comparison means of all dimensions of service experience with employees and AI

Employee dimensions	Means	AI dimensions	Means
Employee responsiveness	5.15	AI responsiveness	4.84
Employee reliability	5.19	AI reliability	4.80
Employee empathy	5.13	AI empathy	4.89
Employee assurance	5.26	AI assurance	4.65

In the case of AI services, responsiveness indicates the AI tools' timely response. Although AI-powered tools can respond in a timely manner, the responses, operated through machines are standardised in most cases. In comparison, customers prefer to deal with employees and have better experience as a result of employee responses. This is reflected in the post-hoc analysis showing that customers' rating of employee responsiveness is higher (5.15 vs 4.84) (see Table 10.2 and Fig. 10.1).

Assurance indicates error-free services by employees and AI tools. Machines can be manipulated and minimise errors, although human errors, at times, are inevitable. Based on the ratings of both AI and employee assurance, customers rate the later much higher (4.65 vs 5.26). Furthermore, only the employee's assurance service is significantly related to customer engagement. Assurance on the count of employees is not only reflected in error-free service, but also indicative of employee's proactivity

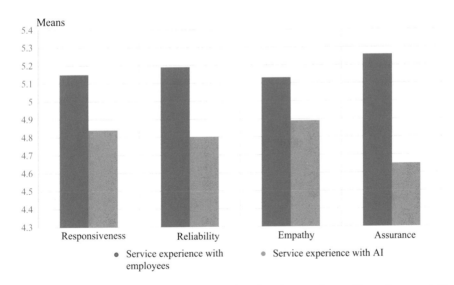

Fig. 10.1 Comparison means between all dimension of service experience with employees and AI

in ensuring customers' safety and comfort. These can hardly be achieved by machine operated AI tools.

Empathy in the case of AI is manifested in a machines' flexibility and versatility in addressing customers' needs. However, employees' empathy is reflective of human's proactive care and empathy for customers. This explains why employees' empathy had a significant effect on customer engagement and was rated higher by customers (4.89 vs 5.16). The importance of empathy manifested in service employees has been widely acknowledged in prior studies (Prentice, 2013a, 2013b, 2014; Wieseke et al., 2012). Although AI tools can be flexible in meeting customers' demands, their applications are rather limited. For instance, auto-messaging is a 24 h service which indicates flexibility, but the responses can be limited and repetitive, and are unlikely to meet customers' diversified demands, whereas employees can customise responses based on customers' requests.

Interestingly, reliability manifested in both AI and employees is not significantly related to customer engagement. Reliability of AI indicates the tools operates and performs reliability and dependably. Employees' reliability is reflected in employees' consistent and dependable service. The insignificant result shows these dimensions are expected by customers. This finding also indicates that reliability cannot be a factor differentiating customer experience with either AI or employees, or one hotel from the other. When regressing all service experience dimensions with employees and AI on customer loyalty, only responsiveness of AI service is significantly related to the outcome variable. This finding confirms the merits of the promptness and timeliness of AI tools.

However, when regressing AI and employee service separately, in the case of employee service when AI is not in the regression equation, it is employees' reliability, empathy, and assurance that engage customers with the hotel. These findings show that customers have different experiences with AI and employees and form different expectations which affect their engagement with the service organisation. Responsiveness and assurance in the case of AI were significantly related to customer engagement. This finding indicates that in the absence of employees, customers expect that AI tools respond to them in timely manner and provide error-free service. The promptness and defect free offerings drive customers to engage with the hotel. Similarly, responsiveness manifested in both service experience with employees and AI is important to attract customer loyalty. These results are shown in Table 10.3.

10.8.4   Emotional Intelligence as a Facilitator

The interaction effect between emotional intelligence and service experience with employees on customer engagement was significant ($\beta = 0.15, p < 0.001$). Figure 10.2 illustrates the moderation effect of emotional intelligence on service experience with employees and customer engagement. Similarly, the moderation effect of emotional intelligence (see Fig. 10.3) on service experience with AI and customer engagement proposed in H6 was also significant ($\beta = 0.15, p < 0.001$).

Table 10.3 Results for the relationships between service experience dimensions and the outcome variables

Service experience with employees and AI	Customer engagement	Customer loyalty
Service experience with employees and AI		
Employee responsiveness	0.04	0.19
Employee reliability	0.65^{**}	0.24
Employee empathy	0.47^{***}	0.06
Employee assurance	0.85^{***}	0.11
AI responsiveness	0.29^{**}	0.23^{**}
AI reliability	0.09	0.14
AI empathy	0.08	0.04
AI assurance	0.21	0.14
R^2	0.49	0.63
Service experience with employees		
Employee responsiveness	0.28	0.38^{*}
Employee reliability	0.73^{***}	0.51^{*}
Employee empathy	0.59^{***}	0.16
Employee assurance	0.88^{***}	0.34
R^2		0.48
Service experience with AI		
AI responsiveness	0.15^{*}	0.33^{***}
AI reliability	0.02	0.18
AI empathy	0.17	0.21^{*}
AI assurance	0.33^{*}	0.10
R^2	0.38	0.55

Note $^{*}p < 0.05$, $^{**}p < 0.01$, $^{***}p < 0.001$

The moderation effect of emotional intelligence was confirmed again with the PROCESS macro (Hayes, 2017) in SPSS with 10,000 bootstrapping samples. The 95% bootstrapping confidence intervals (CI) for the interaction between service experience with employees and emotional intelligence (CI = 0.11, 0.40), and between service experience with AI and emotional intelligence (CI = 0.13, 0.39) do not include 0. Thus, this test confirms the moderation effects of emotional intelligence, supporting H5 and H6 (Table 10.4).

Emotional intelligence has primarily been proposed as a predictor of individual success and organisational outcomes. In the service encounter that involves personal interactions, emotional intelligence exhibited by customers can be used to enhance their service experience. As shown in Fig. 10.2, when customers have more interactions with employees, emotionally intelligent customers tend to engage more with the hotel. Figure 10.3 shows that the moderating effect exerted by emotional intelligence

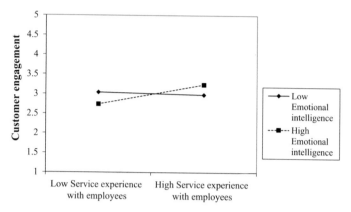

Fig. 10.2 Emotional intelligence and service experience with employees interaction on customer engagement

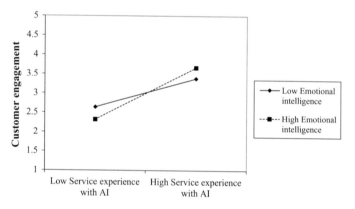

Fig. 10.3 Emotional intelligence and service experience with AI interaction on customer engagement

between AI and customer engagement and indicates that when customers have less interaction with AI services, high emotional intelligence did not improve customer engagement. When the level of interaction increased, customers with a high level of emotional intelligence are more engaged with the hotel.

Previous research has mostly discussed how employees' emotional intelligence improves their performance (Prentice & King, 2011) and customer satisfaction (Prentice, 2019). This study shows that customers' emotional intelligence can also help them to deal with the hotel's employee service and AI applications. Despite the convenience provided by AI tools, the applications can be limited and suffer from a lack of flexibility as AI is computer programmed by humans. For example, the chatbots can provide 24 h services; however, the AI-powered responses are based on algorithms that are not necessarily customised to meet all customers' needs. A report conducted by Invoca (2019) based on a survey on 2048 adults in the USA,

Table 10.4 Results for moderation testing

Path	β	Sig.	β	Sig.
EE → CE	0.12	*	0.11	
EE → CL	0.34	***	0.34	***
AI experience → CE	0.52	***	0.55	***
AI experience → CL	0.24	**	0.41	***
CE → CL	0.51	***	0.17	
EI → CE	−0.01		−0.01	
EE x EI → CE			0.14	***
AI experience x EI → CE	0.15	***		
R^2				
CE	0.39		0.39	
CL	0.79		0.66	

Note * $p < 0.05$; ** $p < 0.01$; *** $p < 0.001$; EI = emotional intelligence, CE = customer engagement, EE = employee experience, CL = customer loyalty

shows more than 50% of respondents were frustrated with automated communications such as chatbots. However, customers with high emotional intelligence are more in control of their own emotions and are more likely to appreciate the positive aspects of AI services (e.g. convenience) and show an understanding of the limitations of AI-powered tools.

Service employees in the service organisation (e.g. hotels) perform emotional labour through acting strategies required by the organisation. Most research has shown that the acting can be emotionally draining hence affecting employees' performance during the service encounter. Their performance has a direct impact on customers' experience with the service organisation which affects customer attitudes and behaviours. However, customers with a high level of EI tend to be more empathetic and this is manifested in their understanding and through the managing of others' emotions. When customers show empathy towards employees, understanding that employees have emotions too, the interaction may be more conductive to their service experience.

10.9 Implications and Conclusion

This study contributes to customer engagement and loyalty research by looking into two major touchpoints during the consumer purchase journey, namely, experience and interaction with AI and employees. Whilst most customer loyalty research is approached from two major marketing approaches: aggressive marketing by competitive marketing promotions and defensive marketing by offering various loyalty programs, this study is focused on customers' experience with employees and AI and provides a fresh perspective on how machines or robots likely contribute to customer experience and organisational performance.

Previous research on AI has primarily focused on the technicality of AI tools. This study extends its application into the domain of customer engagement and loyalty. Hence, AI-powered service are not only tools to facilitate business operational efficiency but can form part of a marketing approach to engage customers and attract customer loyalty. Although employee service has been closely associated with customers' behavioural intentions, this study approached the customer service experience and positioned it in the equation of AI service to understand their respective and unique variances in explaining customer engagement and loyalty. The findings of this study are consistent with those presented in various reports (i.e., Invoca, date; The Harris Poll, date) and show that customers still prefer interactions with employees rather than AI-powered tools.

Emotional intelligence has been extensively discussed in the relevant literature as an individual ability to enhance personal as well as organisational outcomes. In the service context, prior research has primarily approached this from an employee perspective to understand its influence on customers (see Prentice, 2019). This study approached this issue from a customer perspective and reveals how customers' emotional intelligence affects their responses and relationships with the firm. This research extends emotional intelligence research and proposes emotional intelligence as a self-serving means to enhance customer experience and engagement which subsequently affects customer loyalty.

Since this study was conducted in the hotel context, the findings have implications for hotel marketing and management. In particular, the pandemic (i.e. COVID 19) is affecting the hotel industry substantially. To survive and remain competitive, the management and marketers may utilise the findings from this research to develop appropriate and sustainable strategies. This research indicates that hotel management should focus on employee training with regards to their service encounter performance since the findings show that employee service has a significant impact on both customer engagement and loyalty. Although many hotels today incorporate and utilise AI tools to provide cost-effective service and to improve operational efficiency with the intention to provide convenience to customers and enhance their service experience, this study cautions management not to overuse these tools and minimise employee service for the sake of cost savings. Customers prefer human interactions which constitute their service experience, especially in the people-intensive industries such as hotels. The hotel industry is competing with offerings such as Airbnb accommodation, which have become increasingly popular and use less AI tools. Consumers who opt for Airbnb are interested in understanding local culture by interacting with local residents and hosts. Nevertheless, given human interaction restricted during the pandemic, the hotel management should look into the merits of AI tools. Since responsiveness and assurance manifested in these tools are significantly related to customer engagement and loyalty as shown in this study, attention should be attended to reinforce these merits to enhance customer-related outcomes.

Customers' emotional intelligence affects their service experience and engagement, it is important for employees to possess emotional intelligence skills to be able to identify customers with different levels of emotional abilities in order to manage the interactions and customer experience appropriately. Given emotional intelligence is trainable (Prentice, 2013a), staff training programs should include emotional intelligence to enhance employees' emotional competence. Personnel selection should aim to recruit candidates with higher levels of emotional intelligence.

The results also show that not all customer engagement dimensions are related to customer loyalty, it is imperative for management to identify the right factors that influence the dimension that explains the organisational outcome. As this study finds that affective engagement is significantly related to customer loyalty, marketers should seek the means to address customers' emotions (e.g. passion, excitement).

In sum, customer engagement and loyalty are driven by overall experience with both employees and AI, however, these relationships are complex when looking into the specific dimensions of service experience. Overall customers prefer interactions with employees and are more engaged with employees. Emotional intelligence was also found to enhance these relationships.

References

Algesheimer, R., Borle, S., Dholakia, U. M., & Singh, S. S. (2010). The impact of customer community participation on customer behaviours: An empirical investigation. *Marketing Science, 29*(4), 756–769. https://doi.org/10.1287/mksc.1090.0555

Ashforth, B. E., & Humphrey, R. H. (1993). Emotional labor in service roles: The influence of identity. *The Academy of Management Review, 18*(1), 88–115. https://doi.org/10.2307/258824

Berry, L. L. (1995). Relationship marketing of services—Growing interest, emerging perspectives. *Journal of the Academy of Marketing Science: Official Publication of the Academy of Marketing Science, 23*(4), 236–245. https://doi.org/10.1177/009207039502300402

Berry, L. L., Wall, E. A., & Carbone, L. P. (2006). Service clues and customer assessment of the service experience: Lessons from marketing. *Academy of Management Perspectives, 20*(2), 43–57.

Bowen, J., & Morosan, C. (2018). Beware hospitality industry: The robots are coming. *Worldwide Hospitality and Tourism Themes, 10*(6), 726–733. https://doi.org/10.1108/WHATT-07-2018-0045

Brackett, M. A., & Mayer, J. D. (2003). Convergent, discriminant, and incremental validity of competing measures of emotional intelligence. *Personality and Social Psychology Bulletin, 29*(9), 1147–1158. https://doi.org/10.1177/0146167203254596

Brodie, R. J., Hollebeek, L. D., Jurić, B., & Ilić, A. (2011). Customer engagement: Conceptual domain, fundamental propositions, and implications for research. *Journal of Service Research, 14*(3), 252–271. https://doi.org/10.1177/1094670511411703

Brotheridge, C. M., & Grandey, A. A. (2002). Emotional labor and burnout: Comparing two perspectives of "People Work." *Journal of Vocational Behaviour, 60*(1), 17–39. https://doi.org/10.1006/jvbe.2001.1815

Carù, A., & Cova, B. (2003). Revisiting consumption experience: A more humble but complete view of the concept. *Marketing Theory, 3*(2), 267–286. https://doi.org/10.1177/14705931030032004

Casidy, R., Prentice, C., & Wymer, W. (2018). The effects of brand identity on brand performance in the service sector. *Journal of Strategic Marketing*, 1–15. https://doi.org/10.1080/0965254X.2018.1464050

Cronin, J. J., Brady, M. K., & Hult, G. T. M. (2000). Assessing the effects of quality, value, and customer satisfaction on consumer behavioural intentions in service environments. *Journal of Retailing, 76*(2), 193–218. https://doi.org/10.1016/S0022-4359(00)00028-2

Delcourt, C. C., Gremler, D. D., Riel, A. C. R., & Birgelen, M. J. H. (2013). Effects of perceived employee emotional competence on customer satisfaction and loyalty: The mediating role of rapport. *Journal of Service Management, 24*(1), 5–24. https://doi.org/10.1108/09564231311304161

Dholakia, U. M., Bagozzi, R. P., & Pearo, L. K. (2004). A social influence model of consumer participation in network- and small-group-based virtual communities. *International Journal of Research in Marketing, 21*(3), 241–263. https://doi.org/10.1016/j.ijresmar.2003.12.004

Grandey, A. A. (2000). Emotional regulation in the workplace: A new way to conceptualize emotional labor. *Journal of Occupational Health Psychology, 5*(1), 95–110. https://doi.org/10.1037/1076-8998.5.1.95

Hayes, A. F. (2017). *Introduction to mediation, moderation, and conditional process analysis: A regression-based approach. Guilford publications.*

Hayes, D., & MacLeod, N. (2007). Packaging places: Designing heritage trails using an experience economy perspective to maximize visitor engagement. *Journal of Vacation Marketing, 13*(1), 45–58. https://doi.org/10.1177/1356766706071205

Hollebeek, L. (2011). Exploring customer brand engagement: Definition and themes. *Journal of Strategic Marketing, 19*(7), 555–573.

Hoyer, W. D., Chandy, R., Dorotic, M., Krafft, M., & Singh, S. S. (2010). Consumer cocreation in new product development. *Journal of Service Research, 13*(3), 283–296. https://doi.org/10.1177/1094670510375604

Invoca. (2019). *New Invoca research conducted by the Harris Poll.* Retrieved from https://blog.invoca.com/new-research-from-invoca-and-the-harris-poll/

Kandampully, J., & Suhartanto, D. (2003). The role of customer satisfaction and image in gaining customer loyalty in the hotel industry. *Journal of Hospitality & Leisure Marketing, 10*(1–2), 3–25. https://doi.org/10.1300/J150v10n01_02

Kaplan, A., & Haenlein, M. (2019). Siri, Siri, in my hand: Who's the fairest in the land? On the interpretations, illustrations, and implications of artificial intelligence. *Business Horizons, 62*(1), 15–25. https://doi.org/10.1016/j.bushor.2018.08.004

Law, K. S., Wong, C.-S., & Song, L. J. (2004). The construct and criterion validity of emotional intelligence and its potential utility for management studies. *Journal of Applied Psychology, 89*(3), 483–496. https://doi.org/10.1037/0021-9010.89.3.483

Lemon, K. N., & Verhoef, P. C. (2016). Understanding customer experience throughout the customer Journey. *Journal of Marketing, 80*(6), 69–96. https://doi.org/10.1509/jm.15.0420

Liao, H. (2007). Do it right this time: The role of employee service recovery performance in customer-perceived justice and customer loyalty after service failures. *Journal of Applied Psychology, 92*(2), 475–489. https://doi.org/10.1037/0021-9010.92.2.475

Loveman, G. W. (1998). Employee satisfaction, customer loyalty, and financial performance: An empirical examination of the service profit chain in retail banking. *Journal of Service Research, 1*(1), 18–31. https://doi.org/10.1177/109467059800100103

Nambisan, S., & Nambisan, P. (2008). How to profit from a better virtual customer environment. *MIT Sloan Management Review, 49*(3), 53–61.

Nanji, A. (2019). *How consumers feel about brands' use of AI.* Retrieved from https://www.marketingprofs.com/charts/2019/41489/how-consumers-feel-about-brands-use-of-ai?adref=nlt073119. Posted on 31 July 2019

Neves, P., & Eisenberger, R. (2012). Management communication and employee performance: The contribution of perceived organisational support. *Human Performance, 25*(5), 452–464. https://doi.org/10.1080/08959285.2012.721834

Nguyen, T. T. M., Yoshi, T., & Nham, P. T. (2013). Technology acceptance model and the paths to online customer loyalty in an emerging market. *Tržište, 25*(2), 231–248.

Parasuraman, A., Berry, L. L., & Zeithaml, V. A. (1991). Refinement and reassessment of the SERVQUAL scale. *Journal of Retailing, 67*(4), 420–450.

Prentice, C. (2013a). *Emotional labour and its consequences: The moderating effect of emotional intelligence.* Emerald.

Prentice, C. (2013b). Service quality perceptions and customer loyalty in casinos. *International Journal of Contemporary Hospitality Management, 25*(1), 49–64. https://doi.org/10.1108/095 6111311290219

Prentice, C. (2014). Who stays, who walks, and why in high-intensity service contexts. *Journal of Business Research, 67*(4), 608–614.

Prentice, C. (2016). Leveraging employee emotional intelligence in casino profitability. *Journal of Retailing and Consumer Services, 33,* 127–134. https://doi.org/10.1016/j.jretconser.2016. 08.011

Prentice, C. (2019). *Emotional intelligence and marketing.* World Scientific Publishing Co. Pte, Ltd. ISBN 978-981-120-354-1

Prentice, C., & King, B. (2011). The influence of emotional intelligence on the service performance of casino frontline employees. *Tourism and Hospitality Research, 11*(1), 49–66. https://doi.org/ 10.1057/thr.2010.21

Prentice, C., Chen, P.-J., & King, B. (2013). Employee performance outcomes and burnout following the presentation-of-self in customer-service contexts. *International Journal of Hospitality Management, 35,* 225–236.

Prentice, C., Wang, X., & Lin, X. (2018). An organic approach to customer engagement and loyalty. *Journal of Computer Information Systems,* 1–10. https://doi.org/10.1080/08874417.2018.148 5528

Prentice, C., Dominique, S., & Want, X. J. (2019a). Emotional intelligence or artificial intelligence—An employee perspective. *Journal of Hospitality Marketing & Management.*

Prentice, C., Wang, X., & Loureiro, S. M. C. (2019b). The influence of brand experience and service quality on customer engagement. *Journal of Retailing and Consumer Services, 50,* 50–59. https:// doi.org/10.1016/j.jretconser.2019.04.020

Rodriguez-Lizundia, E., Marcos, S., Zalama, E., Gómez-García-Bermejo, J., & Gordaliza, A. (2015). A bellboy robot: Study of the effects of robot behaviour on user engagement and comfort. *International Journal of Human-Computer Studies, 82,* 83–95. https://doi.org/10.1016/j.ijhcs. 2015.06.001

Salovey, P., & Mayer, J. D. (1990). Emotional intelligence. *Imagination, Cognition and Personality, 9*(3), 185–211.

Shang, R.-A., Chen, Y.-C., & Liao, H.-J. (2006). The value of participation in virtual consumer communities on brand loyalty. *Internet Research, 16*(4), 398–418. https://doi.org/10.1108/106 62240610690025

So, K. K. F., King, C., & Sparks, B. (2014). Customer engagement with tourism brands: Scale development and validation. *Journal of Hospitality & Tourism Research, 38*(3), 304–329. https:// doi.org/10.1177/1096348012451456

So, K. K. F., King, C., Sparks, B. A., & Wang, Y. (2016). The role of customer engagement in building consumer loyalty to tourism brands. *Journal of Travel Research, 55*(1), 64–78. https:// doi.org/10.1177/0047287514541008

Sprott, D., Czellar, S., & Spangenberg, E. (2009). The importance of a general measure of brand engagement on market behaviour: Development and validation of a scale. *Journal of Marketing Research, 46*(1), 92–104. https://doi.org/10.1509/jmkr.46.1.92

Ullah, A., Aimin, W., & Ahmed, M. (2018). Smart automation, customer experience and customer engagement in electric vehicles. *Sustainability (switzerland), 10*(5), 1350. https://doi.org/10. 3390/su10051350

Vada, S., Prentice, C., & Hsiao, A. (2019). The influence of tourism experience and well-being on place attachment. *Journal of Retailing and Consumer Services, 47,* 322–330. https://doi.org/10. 1016/j.jretconser.2018.12.007

Van Doorn, J., Lemon, K. N., Mittal, V., Nass, S., Pick, D., Pirner, P., & Verhoef, P. C. (2010). Customer engagement behaviour: Theoretical foundations and research directions. *Journal of Service Research, 13*(3), 253–266. https://doi.org/10.1177/1094670510375599

Van Sell, M., Brief, A. P., & Schuler, R. S. (1981). Role conflict and role ambiguity: Integration of the literature and directions for future research. *Human Relations, 34*(1), 43–71. https://doi.org/10.1177/001872678103400104

Vivek, S. D., Beatty, S. E., & Morgan, R. M. (2012). Customer engagement: Exploring customer relationships beyond purchase. *Journal of Marketing Theory and Practice, 20*(2), 122–146. https://doi.org/10.2753/MTP1069-6679200201

Wieseke, J., Geigenmüller, A., & Kraus, F. (2012). On the role of empathy in customer-employee interactions. *Journal of Service Research, 15*(3), 316–331.

Wirtz, J., den Ambtman, A., Bloemer, J., Horváth, C., Ramaseshan, B., van de Klundert, J., Gurhan Canli, Z., & Kandampully, J. (2013). Managing brands and customer engagement in online brand communities. *Journal of Service Management, 24*(3), 223–244. https://doi.org/10.1108/09564231311326978

Wirtz, J., Patterson, P. G., Kunz, W. H., Gruber, T., Lu, V. N., Paluch, S., & Martins, A. (2018). Brave new world: Service robots in the frontline. *Journal of Service Management, 29*(5), 907–931. https://doi.org/10.1108/JOSM-04-2018-0119

Wixom, B. H., & Todd, P. A. (2005). A theoretical integration of user satisfaction and technology acceptance. *Information Systems Research, 16*(1), 85–102. https://doi.org/10.1287/isre.1050.0042

Xiang, Z., Schwartz, Z., Gerdes, J. H., & Uysal, M. (2015). What can big data and text analytics tell us about hotel guest experience and satisfaction? *International Journal of Hospitality Management, 44*, 120–130. https://doi.org/10.1016/j.ijhm.2014.10.013

Zeithaml, V. A., Berry, L. L., & Parasuraman, A. (1996). The behavioural consequences of service quality. *Journal of Marketing, 60*(2), 31–46. https://doi.org/10.1177/002224299606000203

Zheng, X., Cheung, C. M. K., Lee, M. K. O., & Liang, L. (2015). Building brand loyalty through user engagement in online brand communities in social networking sites. *Information Technology & People, 28*(1), 90–106. https://doi.org/10.1108/ITP-08-2013-0144

Chapter 11
Leveraging Emotional and Artificial Intelligences for Employees and Customers

Abstract On the basis of discussion in the preceding chapters, the current one draws on service profit chain theory and propose an integrated model to examine the influence of artificial and emotional intelligences on employees' and customers' satisfaction, engagement and loyalty. Employees are referred to as internal customers in this chapter. Two studies were undertaken with employees and customers in Australian-based hotels to examine these relationships. The results show that AI service quality is significantly related to internal and external customer satisfaction and engagement. Both internal and external customer engagement have significant effects on customer loyalty and play a significant mediation role in the service quality—customer loyalty relationship. EI has a significant moderation effect on the relationship between AI service quality and customer engagement for internal and external customers. Discussion and implications of the research findings are provided for researchers and practitioners.

11.1 The Service Profit Chain Theory

The service profit chain theory, originally developed by Heskett et al. (1994), links an organisation, employees, and customers as shown in Fig. 11.1, and depicts the chain effect of internal service quality on business profitability through the management of the attitudes and behaviours of employees and customers. The model indicates that business profit and growth are stimulated primarily by customer loyalty; loyalty is a direct result of customer satisfaction; satisfaction is largely influenced by the value of services provided to customers; value is created by happy, loyal, and productive employees; and employee satisfaction, loyalty, and productivity. In other words, Happy and loyal employees tend to be more productive and produce better external service value to satisfy customers and attract loyalty behaviours. Research (e.g., Kurdi et al., 2020; Matzler & Renzl, 2006; Yee et al., 2010) has shown employee satisfaction is not only related to employee loyalty and firm performance, but also customer satisfaction. Employee satisfaction and loyalty primarily result from internal service quality (Prentice et al., 2017).

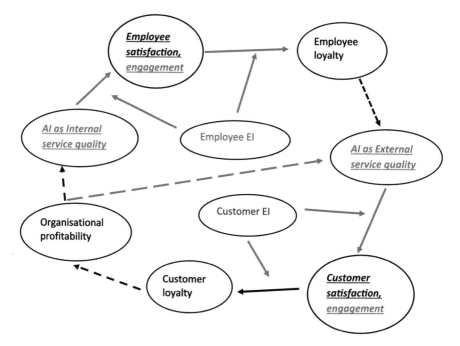

Fig. 11.1 The revised service profit chain model for this study

11.2   Artificial and Emotional Intelligence as Services

The concept of internal service quality was initiated on the rationale that employees should be treated as internal customers (Johnston, 2008). To enhance loyalty and productivity, the organisation should provide the same level of service quality to internal customers as they would for external customers. Internal service quality includes, inter alia, workplace design, job design, employee selection and development, employee rewards and recognition, tools for serving customers. External service quality refers to the physical service environment, employee reliability, assurance, responsive service delivery, and individualised service provision (Prentice, 2013). These quality factors have been extensively discussed in the literature (e.g., Bellou & Andronikidis, 2008; Bowen & Chen, 2001; Helgesen, 2006; Jun & Cai, 2010; Prentice, 2013, 2018; Shi et al., 2014).

   In this technologically dominant era, AI service, derived from AI-powered tools plays an important role in employees' attitudes and behaviours as well as those of customers (e.g., Lu et al., 2020; Odekerken-Schroder et al., 2021; Prentice et al., 2020a, 2020b). EI as a personal trait describes an individual's emotional capacity that can be used to regulate and manage one's behaviour in personal, social, and business contexts, for instance, influencing employees' job attitudes and behaviours (e.g., Prentice, 2016; Prentice & King, 2011; Prentice et al., 2013), and customer satisfaction and loyalty behaviours (e.g., Kernbach & Schutte, 2005; Prentice & Nguyen,

2020). Researchers and practitioners predominantly address customer attitudes and loyalty behaviour from organisational offerings such as loyalty programs, premier memberships, and complimentary services. These programs can be expensive and ineffective (Prentice, 2013, 2014).

This chapter takes a different approach and views AI and EI as internal and external service components to discusses how these intelligences can be integrated into the service profit chain to address internal and external customers satisfaction and loyalty, which are extensively cited as antecedents of business profitability. As satisfaction is an unstable state and often reflective of temporal attitudes towards certain anecdotical incidents. Such attitudes per se may not account for behaviour (Prentice, 2013). Engaged employees and customers tend to be more loyal (Anitha, 2014; Gruman & Saks, 2011; Ou et al., 2020; Prentice & Nguyen, 2020; So et al., 2016). Employee or customer engagement refers to their connection and affiliation with the organisation (Ababneh et al., 2019; So et al., 2014; Swarnalatha & Prasanna, 2013). Hence, engagement is integrated into the service profit chain model in this chapter.

11.3 The Influence of AI on Internal and External Customer Satisfaction and Loyalty

AI-based applications are widely used to facilitate business operations (e.g., Prentice et al., 2020a, 2020b, 2020c, 2020d; Prentice & Nguyen, 2020). From an application perspective, Huang and Rust (2018, 2021) classified AI as mechanical, thinking and feeling AI. Mechanical AI has been designed to undertake automated repetitive and routine tasks, which requires standardisation and consistency, such as packaging, self-service robots (van Doorn et al., 2017). Thinking AI through machine and deep learning was designed for the production and processing of information for users, through the recognition of patterns and themes (e.g. text mining, and facial recognition) for decision making, applied in IBM Watson and recommendation systems (e.g., Netflix movie recommendations, Amazon cross-selling recommendations) (Chung et al., 2016; Huang & Rust, 2018). Feeling AI was designed to analyse human feelings through NLP, text-to-speech technology, and recurrent neural networks (RNN). This type of AI is manifested in chatbots mimicking human speech and service robots sensing affective signals (McDuff & Czerwinski, 2018). Wirth (2018) also classified AI into weak AI, tailored to perform specific tasks, hybrid AI, which blends multiple solutions and adapts to new tasks, and strong AI. More recently, Hoyer et al. (2020) classified AI-powered technologies into the internet of things (IoT), augmented reality (AR), virtual reality (VR), mixed reality (MR), virtual assistants, chatbots, and robots and discussed how these can be applied to transform customer experience.

Prentice et al. (2020a, 2020b) pioneered the classification of AI-powered applications as commercial service to engage customers. Following their approach, the current study conceptualises AI-enabled applications as internal and external services provided to internal (i.e., employees) and external customers to facilitate and enhance their service experience. In the services marketing literature, service quality is defined as a customer's perception or evaluation of a service organisation's overall excellence or superiority (Parasuraman et al., 1985). Consistent with this conceptualisation, AI service quality in this study is determined by internal and external customers' perceptions and evaluations of the relevant AI-powered services.

Service quality has been commonly acknowledged as a key factor explaining customers' attitudes and behaviours towards a provider. Providing premium service quality is intended to generate positive attitudes and loyalty behaviours from employees, as the receivers of internal service quality (e.g., Johnston, 2008; Prentice, 2018), and from customers, as the receivers of external service quality (e.g. Prentice, 2013; Zeithaml et al., 1996). Service quality generally comprises of tangible and intangible components of service offerings, which have been shown to account for customer satisfaction and loyalty (e.g., Shi et al., 2014). The former generally refers to the physical environment and servicescape, whereas the latter primarily refers to employee service (Prentice, 2019). Similarly, AI service quality can manifest in tangible and intangible services. A tangible service can be anything that features in Huang and Rust's mechanical AI and has the physical appearance of humanoid or non-humanoid robots (Connie in Hilton hotels). Intangible services are those that manifest in thinking and feeling AI.

In the case of internal customers, the level of AI service quality indicates an organisation's technological advancement, which allows employees to perform their job tasks. For instance, Cortana can help employees manage their calendar and keep schedules up to date, set reminders and alarms, find facts, definitions, and information. Analytical or thinking AI according to Huang and Rust (2018) performs data mining, modelling for prediction, gathers information about customers, and analyses historical data on purchasing and consumption. This information can be used by employees in sales and marketing departments to predict future sales or to develop or select more appropriate marketing strategies to cater for customers' needs and wants to achieve optimal organisational performance. The 1A-TA robot is used by employees in travel agencies to identify travellers' needs and preferences, creating tailored service provision. From an employees' perspective, whether the organisation is willing to invest in updating the technology is reflective of organisational support for employees. Such support affects employees' job satisfaction (Alias et al., 2014; Jha et al., 2019; Kamalanabhan et al., 2009), which leads to employee loyalty (Matzler & Renzl, 2006; Pandey & Khare, 2012).

In the case of external customers, AI service can be performed by physically humanised or non-humanised robots (e.g. concierge robots such as Connie within the Hilton chain), virtual bots (e.g., chatbots), or simply invisible software programming in the background to facilitate consumers consumption, decision making, and purchasing (e.g., Netflix movie suggestion). In the case of robotic service, AI-powered tools, in hotels for example, can be used to carry out concierge and room services, assist with check-in and check-out, order a taxi, or answer customers' queries. Hilton Worldwide employs a robotic concierge named "Connie" to interact with customers like regular frontline employees. Connie can personalise customers' experience, provide information, and address customers' general needs (Tavakoli & Mura, 2018). In the airline industry, AI-powered "Spencer" adopted by KLM Airlines can answer travellers' queries and enhance their travel experience (West et al., 2018).

AI has also been deployed in contact centres to improve the customer service experience (Kirkpatrick, 2017). Chatbots applying analytical AI can generate automatic responses to customer inquiries (Chung et al., 2018). AI-powered Watson is used by North Face to support customers in choosing the most suitable jackets by providing personalised recommendations based on an analysis of a huge multi-variance dataset. These AI services provide quick and accurate personalised suggestions to enhance customer-brand interaction and saves on labour cost within the organisation (Gursoy et al., 2019). Amazon Echo uses "Alexa" helps customers to place orders. The information AI manifests in movie suggestions on Netflix and travel recommendations from search engines. AI is widely used to improve customer service in a timely manner (Bolton et al, 2013, 2018; Chung et al., 2018) and enhance customer experience (Bowen & Morosan, 2018) which affect customers' attitudes (e.g., satisfaction) and behaviours (e.g., purchase and loyalty) towards the service provider.

Customer satisfaction, regarded a post consumption response, has been defined as an overall feeling of pleasure or disappointment that emerges from comparing perceived performance of a service or product, with pre- service expectations (Antreas et al., 2001; Oliver, 1980). Employee and customer satisfaction are the most discussed outcomes of practicing internal and external service quality in the literature (Back et al., 2011; Bai et al., 2006; Gu & Siu, 2009; Prentice, 2018), and common antecedents of internal and external customer loyalty (e.g., Jun et al., 2006; Matzler & Renzl, 2006; Silverstro, 2002). Equally, customer satisfaction has been cited as a mediator between service quality and customer loyalty for internal customers (Hallowell et al., 1996) and external customers (e.g., Shi et al., 2014).

The foregoing discussion informs the following hypotheses (1) AI service quality is positively related to internal and external customer satisfaction and loyalty; (2) Internal or external customer satisfaction has a positive mediation effect on the relationship between AI service quality with internal and external customer loyalty.

11.4   The Influence of AI on Internal and External Customer Engagement, and Loyalty

Customer satisfaction is an important mediator between service quality and customer loyalty. However, this emotional response can result from discrete elements or events (e.g., friendliness of frontline staff) or from overall service encounter experiences (Cronin et al., 2000; Gustafsson et al., 2005; Ha & Jang, 2010; Veloutsou, 2015). Episodic positive and/negative experiences within a service entity can affect overall satisfaction with the service provider and subsequent loyalty behaviours. As a consequence, customer satisfaction does not always guarantee future patronage. Whereas engagement is more reflective of a connection and relationship with the provider. The concept of engagement has been discussed in social science, management, marketing, and practitioner literature from the perspective of employees and customers.

In the marketing literature, customer engagement refers to customers' emotional, cognitive, and behavioural involvement with the organisation or brand (Hollebeek, 2011; Mollen & Wilson, 2010; Vivek et al., 2020). Customer engagement is driven by various organisational, personal, and social factors, and results in a series of customer and organisational outcomes (Prentice, 2019; Prentice & Nguyen, 2020; van Doorn et al., 2017). Engaged customers remain loyal to the service provider (So et al., 2016; Thakur, 2016). These relationships can function hierarchically, leading from organisational offerings (e.g., AI service quality) to customer engagement and loyalty (van Doorn et al., 2017). Prentice and Nguyen (2020) in their study have detailed how AI-powered services can be used to engage customers and enhance their service experience. Indeed, AI applications in service contexts are novel and convenient for customers. For instance, concierge robots (e.g., Hilton Connie) in hotels can listen to guests' requests, provide them directions and abundant information powered through machine or deep learning that surpasses human brains (Bowen & Whalen, 2017). These services are not only novel but also convenient to customers as robots can function around the clock. Novelty entices engagement. The timeless service production by robots is the process of engaging customers to co-produce with or receive service from these AI-powered robots.

This discussion leads to the following hypotheses (3) AI service quality is positively related to internal and external customer engagement and loyalty; and (4) Internal or external customer engagement has a positive mediation effect on the relationship between AI service quality and internal and external customer loyalty.

11.5 Emotional Intelligence as a Facilitator

EI was introduced into the literature as a valid predictor of individual wellbeing, performance, and success that cannot be accounted for by traditional cognitive intelligence (Austin et al., 2005; Poon, 2004; Schutte et al., 2001, 2007). In the organisational context, employees' EI is shown to affect job satisfaction and performance, commitment, and employee retention (Brown & Yoshioka, 2003; Goleman, 1998; Nikolaou & Tsaousis, 2002; Prentice, 2013; Prentice & King, 2011; Rozell et al., 2004) as well as customer satisfaction (Kernbach & Schutte, 2005). Although EI is mostly modelled as a predictor of job attitudes and behaviours in the literature, studies show that EI can exert moderation effects on employee job-related outcomes. This moderation is reflective of trainability and the variation of EI within individuals (Mattingly & Kraiger, 2019; Nelis et al., 2009).

AI service quality is formed on a users' assessment or evaluation of their experience with AI-powered tools or applications. In the case of employees, AI-powered tools can perform different roles. Some AI-powered tools play a replacing role by performing repetitive employee type tasks, for instance, telemarketing, reception, courier services, market research analysis, and bookkeeping. Some play an assisting role by helping customer-support employees to gather information about customers, filing customer complaints, sorting customers' queries and then passing these queries to relevant employees. Others play an enhancing role by producing accurate information and algorithms about customers or sales forecasts through machine or deep learning. This information allows employees to develop customised services to enhance the customer experience and loyalty behaviour.

Where AI may be perceived as a replacement for human workers, employees may feel threatened by these AI services, and develop a sense of job insecurity. The higher the level of AI service quality, the higher the sense of insecurity. However, employees with a high level of EI are able to regulate and manage negative emotions. Jordan et al. (2002) demonstrated that EI moderated employees' emotional reactions to job insecurity and other job-related stress. In the case of assisting and enhancing the role of AI, employees may find it challenging to work with AI-powered robots or tools. Especially when AI services result in errors and employees with limited IT background may not be able to identify these errors. The errors would affect job effectiveness and efficiency, resulting in negative attitudes and behaviours. Employees with a high level of EI are better at coping with job errors and the relevant stress (Prentice et al., 2020a, 2020b, 2020c, 2020d).

The foregoing discussion indicates that EI may moderate internal customers' perceptions and experiences with AI service quality, subsequently affecting attitudes and behaviours.

This discussion leads to the following hypotheses: (5) EI has a significant moderation effect on the relationship between AI service quality with internal customer satisfaction, engagement, and loyalty.

In the case of customers, AI service quality is assessed through customer experience with AI. Such experience can be an emotional journey (Prentice et al., 2020a, 2020b, 2020c, 2020d). For instance, chatbots provide around the clock service to customers. However, these virtual bots generally provide standardised information which may not suit each customer and result in a negative experience with the service organisation. Emotional intelligent customers may be more patient with these robotic services. Despite rapid AI development and evolution, AI-powered tools are manoeuvred to perform low-level jobs (Prentice et al., 2019). Customers have different needs and demands that AI can be programmed to perform and deliver, which can lead to customer complaints or dissatisfaction, which likely leads to their purchase and loyalty behaviours. Nevertheless, customers with a high level of EI tend to be more empathetic and understanding and have an expanded zone for the tolerance of AI services. Customers with a low level of EI may avoid personal contact with employees and opt for machine-operated AI services. Their emotional abilities can moderate their attitudes and behaviours toward the service provider (Prentice, 2016).

This discussion leads to the following hypothesis: (6) Emotional intelligence has a significant moderation effect on the relationship between AI service quality with external customer satisfaction, engagement, and loyalty.

These proposed relationships are shown in Fig. 11.1.

Two studies were undertaken to understand how EI and AI affect employee satisfaction, engagement, and loyalty. The first tested the influence of AI-powered applications as internal service quality on employee-related outcomes. The second, examined how AI as external service quality affects customers. Australia-based hotels that extensively use AI-powered applications (e.g., chatbots, concierge robots, digital assistance, voice-activated services, and travel experience enhancers) for business operations were opted for the study to ensure the employee and customer sample had similar experiences. The following section outlines the research methods including sampling, data collection procedures and instruments. Results and discussion are presented subsequently. Implications of the research findings are highlighted to conclude this chapter.

11.6   The Empirical Studies

11.6.1   Sample and Data Collection Procedure

Study 1 was undertaken with customer-contact employees working in Australian hotels and were using AI-powered tools on a daily basis. Study 2 targeted customers who had stayed in at least one of these hotels within last 12 months from the time of data collection. To ensure the target sample had adequate knowledge of AI-powered services, a set of screening questions were developed to describe services performed by AI-powered tools that are commonly used by hotels. Only those who indicated they had experience and understanding of these AI tools were encouraged to proceed with the study. The data were collected online through Qualtrics. Virtual snowball sampling was determined to be appropriate for this study. This method can be used for samples that have similar background and knowledge. The general advantage of this sampling method is the ability to increase the sample size in a short period time by accessing a hidden or hard-to-reach population through the virtual network (Baltar & Brunet, 2012).

Prior to data collection, a pilot study was conducted with accessible PhD students who understood AI and had experience with AI service within hotels. This initiative was to ensure appropriate response time and item clarity. As a result, some items were refined or reworded. An online survey was opted, as this method has advantages of being flexible, cost-effective, convenient, and efficient. A leading Australian market research company was approached for data collection. With their assistance, the survey was crafted to ensure timely response and the prevention of skipped questions (Baltar & Brunet, 2012). To distribute the survey, a QR code that directed participants to the survey host was provided to the potential respondents. Respondents were informed that the completion of the questionnaire was taken as implied consent and that their participation was voluntary. Gift vouchers and raffle tickets were provided as incentives to encourage participation and the completion of the survey. The number of responses was determined by the availability of funding for this research. After all endeavours at data collection were exhausted, 219 and 393 usable responses were collected from employee and customer sample cohorts. The confidence level, population size, and margin of error indicate adequacy of the sample size (Tabachnick et al., 2007).

11.6.2 Instruments

To determine the items that represent AI service quality for both internal and external customers, the measure was adapted from several scales that capture internal service quality for employees (internal customers) from Kang et al. (2002) and Jun and Cai (2010). External customer-based online service quality items were taken from Santos (2003), Zeithaml et al. (2002), and technology-based service quality from Wixom and Todd (2005). Although encounter experiences with AI may differ between employees and customers, the literature shows that internal service quality can be measured by adapting external service quality scales such as SERVQUAL for external customers (see Kang et al., 2002; Reynoso & Moores, 1995). Therefore, this study used similar items to assess AI service quality for both employees and customers with wording adjusted to reflect their respective perceptions and experience of AI services. Senior AI researchers and industry practitioners were consulted to ensure that the selected items for measuring AI service quality were reflective of services by AI-powered tools. This process resulted in the rewording or deletion of some items.

Law et al. (2004) self-report emotional intelligence scale (WEIS) was used to measure emotional intelligence for both employee and customer samples. Among the available EI measures in the extant literature, WEIS is an ability-based scale, through self-report. The rationale, merits, drawbacks, and remedies of using a self-report EI scale have been documented in many EI-related publications (see Prentice, 2019). The WEIS consists of four dimensions with four (4) items for each: self-emotion appraisal (SEA), other-emotion appraisal (OEA), use of emotion (UOE), and regulation of emotion (ROE). The items have been adapted with different wording for two cohorts of respondents (employees and customers).

Internal customer satisfaction was measured by adapting the items used in Chi and Gursoy (2009), reflecting employee satisfaction with AI-powered tools and applications within the organisation. External customer satisfaction was measured using four items adopted from Bogicevic et al. (2017) and Cronin et al. (2000). The items addressed overall satisfaction with AI-powered tools and applications from the hotel. Internal customer engagement was measured by adapting employee engagement from Saks and Gruman (2014) and Soane et al., (2012). External customer engagement was measured by adapting So et al. (2016) multidimensional scale including affective, cognitive, and psychological engagement.

Internal customer loyalty was measured with the adaption of Myrden and Kelloway (2015) items. The selected items indicated the respondents' commitment to, and their willingness and intention to stay with, the organisation within foreseeable future. The reliability value for this scale was 0.91. The external customer loyalty scale was adapted from Kandampully and Suhartanto (2003) to focus on customers' willingness to provide referrals and positive word-of-mouth and their intention to return and pay a premium price. The reliability in this case was 0.96.

11.7 Findings and Discussion

11.7.1 Leveraging AI for Internal and External Customer Satisfaction and Loyalty

The research shows that AI service quality had a significant effect on both internal and external customer satisfaction. The finding suggests that, although AI-powered application is reflective of technological service, the quality of such a service affects employee job attitudes and customer experience since AI permeates in service encounters within a service organisation. In this information technology dominant era, AI-powered service has become a key factor for service organisations to improve service offerings and achieve a competitive advantage. These services can be used to enhance employee task efficiency and facilitate business transactions. The level of AI service quality for service employees affects how they perform their job tasks and serve customers. Any technological barrier may result in prolonged job completion or customer dissatisfaction. Service employees are in the boundary spanning position to manage service transactions with customers. Any failure in these interactions may result in dissatisfied employees. Equally, the level of AI service quality affects customers' experience and perceptions of the service provider, hence their attitude towards the provider. Consistent with any service quality research (e.g., Prentice, 2013; Shi et al., 2014), AI service quality has implications for customer (either internal or external) satisfaction. Internal customers need advanced (quality) AI technology to perform their job tasks. External customers need convenient and flexible service offerings that can be supported by service provider AI-powered tools.

The findings suggest the relationships between customer satisfaction and loyalty are consistent with previous research for internal customers (employees) (e.g., Collins et al., 2008; Eskildsen & Nussler, 2000; Matzler & Renzl, 2006; Rust et al., 1996), and external customers (e.g., Bowen & Chen, 2001; Hallowell, 1996; Helgesen, 2006). Satisfaction mediated the relationship between AI service quality and customer loyalty although partially, with significant direct and indirect effects for both internal and external customers. AI service quality, like traditional service quality measures, contributed directly and indirectly to customer loyalty. This finding indicates that customers' attitudes and behaviours are influenced by an organisations' traditional tangible and intangible services such as physical environment and employee service. Services offered by organisation-owned machines and robots operated through AI are also important to attract internal and external customer loyalty behaviour.

11.7.2 *Leveraging AI for Customer Engagement and Loyalty*

The two studies show that AI service quality was significantly related to both internal and external customer engagement, which lead to loyalty. Customer engagement manifests in affective, cognitive, and behavioural involvement with the organisation. The significant effects exerted by AI service quality indicate that the level of technological services powered by AI could draw employees closer to the organisation and encourage customer loyalty. The fast pace of technological disruption and the rise of AI has raised the issue of job security and disengagement within employees. Nevertheless, AI could also enhance employee engagement as shown in this study. For example, training and development have been regarded as an important means to engage employees (Albrecht et al., 2015). AI-powered data analytics can identify appropriate training programs for individual employees. Communication is also important for employee engagement (see Welch, 2011). AI powered social media, messenger apps, and chatbots can facilitate collaboration among employees and help employees engage with co-workers.

AI can also engage customers by enhancing their service experience. For example, AI can pair customers with service employees for support and detect customers' preferences and dislikes. Such information can be used by marketers to create services that would attract customer attention, hence their engagement with the service provider. AI can analyse customers' past purchases, significant life events, and social media participation based on natural language processing and machine learning. These data can be used to engage customers by catering to individual needs. In particular, AI-powered chatbots and virtual assistants are able to engage customers around-the-clock without geographical and time limitations. Engaged customers tend to stay loyal to the brand or organisation. This finding is consistent with that in Prentice et al. (2018) and Prentice and Nguyen (2020).

The study also shows that customer engagement demonstrated a full mediation relationship with AI service quality and internal customer loyalty. Although this relationship is only partial for external customers. Full mediation indicates that the relationship between AI service quality and employee loyalty is dependent upon the inclusion of employee engagement. The quality of AI service determines the level of employee loyalty based on the level of their engagement with the organisation. This finding highlighted the impact of AI applications on employee relationships with the organisation. The partial mediation of external customers indicates that AI service quality can directly affect customer loyalty and customer engagement. Customer engagement provides an additional relationship between AI service quality and customer loyalty (see Prentice & King, 2011). The findings are shown in Tables 11.1 and 11.2.

Table 11.1 The path coefficients for the proposed relationships

Relationship between variables	Internal customers	External customers
AI service quality → customer satisfaction	0.36^{***}	0.58^{***}
AI service quality → customer engagement	0.33^{***}	0.18^{***}
AI service quality → customer loyalty	0.09	0.12^{***}
Customer satisfaction → customer engagement	0.48^{***}	0.61^{***}
Customer satisfaction → customer loyalty	0.30^{***}	0.77^{***}
Customer engagement → customer loyalty	0.22^{*}	0.13^{***}

* Statistically significant ($p < 0.05$); *** Statistically significant ($p < 0.001$)

Table 11.2 Results for mediation testing (biased corrected percentile method)

Path	Direct effects	Indirect effects	Lower bound	Upper bound
$AI \rightarrow customer\ satisfaction \rightarrow customer\ loyalty$				
AI—customer satisfaction	$0.53^{***}/0.66^{***}$		0.37/0.59	0.67/0.72
Customer satisfaction-loyalty	$0.41^{***}/0.84^{***}$		0.18/0.80	0.58/0.89
AI—customer loyalty	$0.20^{*}/0.15^{**}$		0.02/0.09	0.41/0.20
AI—satisfaction-loyalty		$0.22^{**}/0.56^{**}$	0.10/0.50	0.34/0.61
$AI \rightarrow customer\ engagement \rightarrow customer\ loyalty$				
AI—customer engagement	$0.66^{***}/0.58^{**}$		0.55/0.51	0.74/0.65
Customer engagement-loyalty	$0.41^{***}/0.52^{***}$		0.17/0.64	0.29/0.59
AI—customer loyalty	$0.14/0.41^{***}$		−0.08/0.32	0.37/0.50
AI—engagement-loyalty		$0.27^{**}/0.30^{**}$	0.10/0.25	0.45/0.35

Note Values on the left of the dash are for internal customers, the right for external customers
* $p < .05$; ** $p < .01$; *** $p < .0005$

11.7.3 Confirming EI as a Facilitator

The moderation testing demonstrated that, for internal customers, EI had a significant moderation effect on the relationship between AI service quality and employee engagement, but not on job satisfaction. However, EI had a direct and significant effect on job satisfaction. In other words, employee EI can enhance engagement with the organisation by shaping their experience with AI service quality. This is plausible. AI application to the organisation may affect employee job security given that AI could replace some jobs. Emotionally intelligent employees appreciate the technological service provided by AI to facilitate connection and collaboration with co-workers, which may lead to engagement with the organisation.

For external customers, EI had a significant moderation effect on the relationship between AI service quality and customer engagement. The magnitude of the moderation effect was rather substantial at $p < 0.0005$. Although the interaction of AI and EI was not significant for customer satisfaction. EI demonstrated direct and significant

Table 11.3 Results for moderation testing

Path	Internal	External
EI → customer satisfaction	0.34^{***}	0.18^{***}
EI → customer engagement	0.10	−0.04
EI → customer loyalty	0.09	0.46^{***}
AI × EI → customer satisfaction	−0.05	0.03
AI × EI → customer engagement	0.08^{*}	0.14^{***}
AI × EI → customer loyalty	0.09	0.09

Note * $p < 0.05$; ** $p < 0.01$; *** $p < 0.001$; EI = emotional intelligence, AI = AI service quality

relationships with customer satisfaction and loyalty. This finding can be construed by evidence in Homburg and Giering's (2001) study where personal characteristics were found to play a significant moderating role in customer satisfaction and loyalty. These findings indicate that emotional intelligence has a direct influence on individual attitudes and behaviours. Only a few studies in the literature have shown that employee EI affects customer satisfaction (e.g., Delcourt et al., 2013; Prentice, 2016). No research to date has attempted to examine how customers' EI affects their satisfaction and loyalty to a service provider. The findings from the current research are rather refreshing. Customer satisfaction and loyalty are generally driven by the quality offerings of a service provider (external party). However, the study shows that customers with a high level of EI tend to be more satisfied with the service provider and more loyal. Dissatisfaction and switching are often caused by customer frustration with the provider. However, emotionally intelligent individuals are capable of managing negative emotions, and appear more empathetic and agreeable with the service provider. See Table 11.3 for the results.

11.8 Implications and Conclusion

This chapter draws on service profit chain theory and integrates machine and human intelligences to examine their respective influence on the attitudes and behaviours of internal and external customers. Two studies are conducted to reveal the impact of AI -powered services on employees and customers and to understand how technological quality drives organisational outcomes. The findings have implications for researchers as well as for industry practitioners.

First, this research contributes to the service profit chain by incorporating AI and EI into the chain model. The research proposes that AI-powered applications as internal and external services provided to employees and customers may help to understand their attitudes and behaviours towards the service organisation. This initiative also contributes to service quality research by promoting AI as an organisational service quality assessment. Additionally, the current research includes customer engagement in service quality assessment and explores the internal and external customer loyalty relationship to test the respective mediation effects of customer satisfaction and engagement. This inclusion has implications for employee and customer loyalty research. In particular, the inclusion of AI service quality in the model will help to provide insights into the antecedents of customer satisfaction, engagement, and loyalty.

The study provides a fresh perspective on EI research by examining the impact of its interaction with machine intelligence on employees and customers. In particular, the findings that EI affects customer satisfaction and loyalty are rather novel and provide a new venue for EI and consumer behaviour researchers. EI in the extant literature is modelled as a valid predictor of individual wellbeing, success, and an enhancer of interpersonal relationships. Although a few studies have extended the impact of EI on others' attitudes, for instance, employee emotional intelligence on customer satisfaction, no study has attempted to tap into the customer loyalty domain by looking into the influence of their own emotional intelligence.

The research findings also have practical implications for HR practitioners, AI and EI practitioners, as well as service marketers. The significant influence of AI and EI on employee satisfaction, engagement, and loyalty indicates that HR managers can look beyond the traditional means to retain employees. For instance, suggesting the improvement of AI services and by providing EI training, can enhance employee satisfaction, engagement, and retention. The findings should also direct AI experts to develop AI programs and improve AI-powered services to enhance employee relationships within organisations, in addition to enhancing customer experience.

The findings that EI has positive effects on employees and customers indicates that EI consultants and experts should extend training programs to include organisational customers. Most existing training programs relating to EI are directed at employees. EI can be developed and enhanced through training. Whilst training for customers may be unrealistic, such emotional competency may be incorporated into AI programming directly aimed towards emotionally intelligent customers. As AI through data analytics and deep learning can be used to understand customers' likes and dislikes, AI and EI experts could work to develop an integrated program to detect customers' emotional intelligence, not just customers' emotions per se.

For service marketers, this research provides multiple means to satisfy customers and attract customer loyalty. Traditional marketing tends to focus on aggressive marketing promotions to acquire new customers and defensive loyalty programs to build relationships with existing customers. This study shows that improving AI service quality can improve customer attitudes and behaviours. Service marketers should work with AI or IT experts to develop more appropriate AI services to enhance customer satisfaction and loyalty. The significant influence of EI on customer satisfaction and loyalty indicates that customer-contact employees should endeavour to detect customers' emotional abilities during interpersonal encounters. Individuals with a high level of emotional intelligence are more positive and empathetic. Service employees should target these customers in the process of establishing and nurturing relationships during the service encounter. Such efforts could form part of relationship marketing practice and be incorporated into employee training.

The application of AI-powered tools to facilitate employees' task efficiency and to enhance customer experience in service organisations is expanding. This chapter took a novel perspective and positioned these applications as a service/product, like any other commercial service that is provided to customers for value creation. The quality of this service is referred to as AI service quality. Given its relevance to both employees and customers, this research draws on service profit chain theory and refers to employees as internal customers to examine how AI service quality may influence internal and external customer satisfaction and loyalty. In particular, the paper incorporated customer engagement as a mediator and emotional intelligence as a moderator in the commonly acknowledged service quality—customer loyalty relationship. The respective mediation effects of customer satisfaction and engagement of internal and external customers were also assessed. Two studies are included in this research that examines the impacts of AI service quality on employees and customers.

References

Ababneh, O. M., LeFevre, M., & Bentley, T. (2019). Employee engagement: Development of a new measure. *International Journal of Human Resources Development and Management, 19*(2), 105–134.

Albrecht, S. L., Bakker, A. B., Gruman, J. A., Macey, W. H., & Saks, A. M. (2015). Employee engagement, human resource management practices and competitive advantage. *Journal of Organizational Effectiveness: People and Performance., 2*(1), 7–35.

Alias, N. E., Noor, N., & Hassan, R. (2014). Examining the mediating effect of employee engagement on the relationship between talent management practices and employee retention in the Information and Technology (IT) organizations in Malaysia. *Journal of Human Resources Management and Labor Studies, 2*(2), 227–242.

Anitha, J. (2014). Determinants of employee engagement and their impact on employee performance. *International Journal of Productivity and Performance Management., 63*(3), 308–323.

Antreas, A., Spiros, G. & Valssis, S. (2001). Behavioral responses to customer satisfaction: An empirical study. *European Journal of Marketing, 35,* 687–707.

Austin, E. J., Saklofske, D. H., & Egan, V. (2005). Personality, well-being and health correlates of trait emotional intelligence. *Personality and Individual Differences, 38*(3), 547–558.

Back, K. J., Lee, C. K., & Abbott, J. (2011). Internal relationship marketing: Korean casino employees' job satisfaction and organizational commitment. *Cornell Hospitality Quarterly, 52*(2), 111–124.

Bai, B., Brewer, K. P., Sammons, G., & Swerdlow, S. (2006). Job satisfaction, organizational commitment, and internal service quality: A case study of Las Vegas hotel/casino industry. *Journal of Human Resources in Hospitality & Tourism, 5*(2), 37–54.

Baltar, F., & Brunet, I. (2012). Social research 2.0: virtual snowball sampling method using Facebook. *Internet research.*

Bellou, V., & Andronikidis, A. (2008). The impact of internal service quality on customer service behaviour: Evidence from the banking sector. *International Journal of Quality & Reliability Management, 25*(9), 943–954.

Bogicevic, V., Bujisic, M., Bilgihan, A., Yang, W., & Cobanoglu, C. (2017). The impact of traveler-focused airport technology on traveler satisfaction. *Technological Forecasting and Social Change, 123,* 351–361.

Bolton, R. N., McColl-Kennedy, J. R., Cheung, L., Gallan, A., Orsingher, C., Witell, L., & Zaki, M. (2018). Customer experience challenges: Bringing together digital, physical and social realms. *Journal of Service Management*.

Bolton, R. N., Parasuraman, A., Hoefnagels, A., Migchels, N., Kabadayi, S., Gruber, T., Loureiro, Y.K., & Solnet, D. (2013). Understanding Generation Y and their use of social media: a review and research agenda. *Journal of service management*.

Bowen, J. T., & Chen, S. L. (2001). The relationship between customer loyalty and customer satisfaction. *International Journal of Contemporary Hospitality Management., 13*(5), 213–217.

Bowen, J., & Morosan, C. (2018). Beware hospitality industry: The robots are coming. *Worldwide Hospitality and Tourism Themes*.

Bowen, J., & Whalen, E. (2017). Trends that are changing travel and tourism. *Worldwide Hospitality and Tourism Themes., 9*(6), 592–602.

Brown, W. A., & Yoshioka, C. F. (2003). Mission attachment and satisfaction as factors in employee retention. *Nonprofit Management and Leadership, 14*(1), 5–18.

Chi, C. G., & Gursoy, D. (2009). Employee satisfaction, customer satisfaction, and financial performance: An empirical examination. *International Journal of Hospitality Management, 28*(2), 245–253.

Chung, A. W., Schirmer, M. D., Krishnan, M. L., Ball, G., Aljabar, P., Edwards, A. D., & Montana, G. (2016). Characterising brain network topologies: A dynamic analysis approach using heat kernels. *NeuroImage, 141*, 490–501.

Chung, D. Y., Sugimoto, K., Fischer, P., Böhm, M., Takizawa, T., Sadeghian, H., Morais, A., Harriott, A., Oka, F., Qin, T., Henninger, N., Yaseen, M. A., Sakadzic, S., & Ayata, C. (2018). Real-time non-invasive in vivo visible light detection of cortical spreading depolarizations in mice. *Journal of Neuroscience Methods, 309*, 143–146.

Collins, K. S., Collins, S. K., McKinnies, R., & Jensen, S. (2008). Employee satisfaction and employee retention: Catalysts to patient satisfaction. *The Health Care Manager, 27*(3), 245–251.

Cronin, J. J., Jr., Brady, M. K., & Hult, G. T. M. (2000). Assessing the effects of quality, value, and customer satisfaction on consumer behavioral intentions in service environments. *Journal of Retailing, 76*(2), 193–218.

Delcourt, C., Gremler, D. D., Van Riel, A. C., & Van Birgelen, M. (2013). Effects of perceived employee emotional competence on customer satisfaction and loyalty. *Journal of Service Management*.

Eskildsen, J. K., & Nussler, M. L. (2000). The managerial drivers of employee satisfaction and loyalty. *Total Quality Management, 11*(4–6), 581–588.

Goleman, D. (1998). *Working with emotional intelligence*. Bantam Books.

Gruman, J. A., & Saks, A. M. (2011). Performance management and employee engagement. *Human Resource Management Review, 21*(2), 123–136.

Gu, Z., & Siu, R. C. S. (2009). Drivers of job satisfaction as related to work performance in Macao casino hotels. *International Journal of Contemporary Hospitality Management., 21*(5), 561–578.

Gursoy, D., Chi, O. H., Lu, L., & Nunkoo, R. (2019). Consumers acceptance of artificially intelligent (AI) device use in service delivery. *International Journal of Information Management, 49*, 157–169.

Gustafsson, A., Johnson, M. D., & Roos, I. (2005). The effects of customer satisfaction, relationship commitment dimensions, and triggers on customer retention. *Journal of Marketing, 69*(4), 210–218.

Ha, J., & Jang, S. S. (2010). Perceived values, satisfaction, and behavioral intentions: The role of familiarity in Korean restaurants. *International Journal of Hospitality Management, 29*(1), 2–13.

Hallowell, R. (1996). The relationships of customer satisfaction, customer loyalty, and profitability: An empirical study. *International Journal of Service Industry Management, 7*(4), 27–42.

Hallowell, R., Schlesinger, L. A., & Zornitsky, J. (1996). Internal service quality, customer and job satisfaction: Linkages and implications for management. *Human Resource Planning, 19*(2), 20–31.

Helgesen, Ø. (2006). Are loyal customers profitable? Customer satisfaction, customer (action) loyalty and customer profitability at the individual level. *Journal of Marketing Management, 22*(3–4), 245–266.

Heskett, J. L., Jones, T. O., Loveman, G. W., Sasser, W. E., & Schlesinger, L. A. (1994). Putting the service-profit chain to work. *Harvard Business Review, 72*(2), 164–174.

Hollebeek, L. (2011). Exploring customer brand engagement: Definition and themes. *Journal of Strategic Marketing, 19*(7), 555–573.

Homburg, C., & Giering, A. (2001). Personal characteristics as moderators of the relationship between customer satisfaction and loyalty—An empirical analysis. *Psychology & Marketing, 18*(1), 43–66.

Hoyer, C., Ebert, A., Huttner, H. B., Puetz, V., Kallmünzer, B., Barlinn, K., Haverkamp, C., Harloff, A., Brich, J., Platten, M., & Szabo, K. (2020). Acute stroke in times of the COVID-19 pandemic: A multicenter study. *Stroke, 51*(7), 2224–2227.

Huang, M. H., & Rust, R. T. (2018). Artificial intelligence in service. *Journal of Service Research, 21*(2), 155–172.

Huang, M. H., & Rust, R. T. (2021). Engaged to a robot? The role of AI in service. *Journal of Service Research, 24*(1), 30–41.

Jha, N., Sareen, P., & Potnuru, R. K. G. (2019). Employee engagement for millennials: Considering technology as an enabler. *Development and Learning in Organizations: An International Journal., 33*(1), 9–11.

Johnston, R. (2008). Internal service–barriers, flows and assessment. *International Journal of Service Industry Management, 19*(2), 210–231.

Jordan, P. J., Ashkanasy, N. M., & Hartel, C. E. (2002). Emotional intelligence as a moderator of emotional and behavioral reactions to job insecurity. *Academy of Management Review, 27*(3), 361–372.

Jun, M., & Cai, S. (2010). Examining the relationships between internal service quality and its dimensions, and internal customer satisfaction. *Total Quality Management, 21*(2), 205–223.

Jun, M., Cai, S., & Shin, H. (2006). TQM practice in maquiladora: Antecedents of employee satisfaction and loyalty. *Journal of Operations Management, 24*(6), 791–812.

Kamalanabhan, T. J., Sai, L. P., & Mayuri, D. (2009). Employee engagement and job satisfaction in the information technology industry. *Psychological Reports, 105*(3), 759–770.

Kandampully, J., & Suhartanto, D. (2003). The role of customer satisfaction and image in gaining customer loyalty in the hotel industry. *Journal of Hospitality & Leisure Marketing, 10*(1–2), 3–25.

Kang, G. D., Jame, J., & Alexandris, K. (2002). Measurement of internal service quality: Application of the SERVQUAL battery to internal service quality. *Managing Service Quality: An International Journal, 12*(5), 278–291.

Kernbach, S., & Schutte, N. S. (2005). The impact of service provider emotional intelligence on customer satisfaction. *Journal of Services Marketing, 19*(7), 438–444.

Kirkpatrick, G. (2017). *Critical technology: A social theory of personal computing.* Routledge.

Kurdi, B., Alshurideh, M., & Alnaser, A. (2020). The impact of employee satisfaction on customer satisfaction: Theoretical and empirical underpinning. *Management Science Letters, 10*(15), 3561–3570.

Law, K. S., Wong, C. S., & Song, L. J. (2004). The construct and criterion validity of emotional intelligence and its potential utility for management studies. *Journal of Applied Psychology, 89*(3), 483–496.

Lu, V. N., Wirtz, J., Kunz, W. H., Paluch, S., Gruber, T., Martins, A., & Patterson, P. G. (2020). Service robots, customers and service employees: What can we learn from the academic literature and where are the gaps? *Journal of Service Theory and Practice., 30*(3), 361–391.

Mattingly, V., & Kraiger, K. (2019). Can emotional intelligence be trained? A meta-analytical investigation. *Human Resource Management Review, 29*(2), 140–155.

Matzler, K., & Renzl, B. (2006). The relationship between interpersonal trust, employee satisfaction, and employee loyalty. *Total Quality Management and Business Excellence, 17*(10), 1261

McDuff, D., & Czerwinski, M. (2018). Designing emotionally sentient agents. *Communications of the ACM, 61*(12), 74–83.

Mollen, A., & Wilson, H. (2010). Engagement, telepresence and interactivity in online consumer experience: Reconciling scholastic and managerial perspectives. *Journal of Business Research, 63*(9–10), 919–925.

Myrden, S. E., & Kelloway, E. K. (2015). Leading to customer loyalty: a daily test of the service-profit chain. *Journal of Services Marketing. 29*(6/7), 585–598.

Nelis, D., Quoidbach, J., Mikolajczak, M., & Hansenne, M. (2009). Increasing emotional intelligence: (How) is it possible? *Personality and Individual Differences, 47*(1), 36–41.

Nikolaou, I., & Tsaousis, I. (2002). Emotional intelligence in the workplace: Exploring its effects on occupational stress and organizational commitment. *The International Journal of Organizational Analysis., 10*(4), 327–342.

Odekerken-Schröder, G., Mennens, K., Steins, M., & Mahr, D. (2021). The service triad: An empirical study of service robots, customers and frontline employees. *Journal of Service Management., 31*(2), 267–289.

Oliver, R. L. (1980). A cognitive model of the antecedents and consequences of satisfaction decisions. *Journal of Marketing Research, 17*(4), 460–469.

Ou, X., Liu, Y., Lei, X., Li, P., Mi, D., Ren, L., Guo, L., Guo, R., Chen, T., Hu, J., Xiang, Z., Mu, Z., Chen, X., Chen, J., Hu, K., Jin, Q., Wang, J., & Qian, Z. (2020). Characterization of spike glycoprotein of SARS-CoV-2 on virus entry and its immune cross-reactivity with SARS-CoV. *Nature Communications, 11*(1), 1–12.

Pandey, C., & Khare, R. (2012). Impact of job satisfaction and organizational commitment on employee loyalty. *International Journal of Social Science & Interdisciplinary Research, 1*(8), 26–41.

Parasuraman, A., Zeithaml, V. A., & Berry, L. L. (1985). A conceptual model of service quality and its implications for future research. *Journal of Marketing, 49*(Autumn), 41–50.

Poon, J. M. (2004). Career commitment and career success: Moderating role of emotion perception. *Career Development International., 9*(4), 374–390.

Prentice, C. (2013). Service quality perceptions and customer loyalty in casinos. *International Journal of Contemporary Hospitality Management, 25*(1), 49–64.

Prentice, C. (2014). Who stays, who walks, and why in high-intensity service contexts. *Journal of Business Research, 67*(4), 608–614.

Prentice, C. (2016). Leveraging employee emotional intelligence in casino profitability. *Journal of Retailing and Consumer Services, 33*, 127–134.

Prentice, C. (2018). Linking internal service quality and casino dealer performance. *Journal of Hospitality Marketing & Management, 27*(6), 733–753.

Prentice, C. (2019). *Emotional intelligence and marketing.* World Scientific.

Prentice, C., & King, B. (2011). The influence of emotional intelligence on the service performance of casino frontline employees. *Tourism and Hospitality Research, 11*(1), 49–66.

Prentice, C., & Nguyen, M. (2020). Engaging and retaining customers with AI and employee service. *Journal of Retailing and Consumer Services, 56*, 102186.

Prentice, C., Chen, P. J., & King, B. (2013). Employee performance outcomes and burnout following the presentation-of-self in customer-service contexts. *International Journal of Hospitality Management, 35*, 225–236.

Prentice, C., Dominique Lopes, S., & Wang, X. (2020a). Emotional intelligence or artificial intelligence—An employee perspective. *Journal of Hospitality Marketing & Management, 29*(4), 377–403.

Prentice, C., Dominique Lopes, S., & Wang, X. (2020b). The impact of artificial intelligence and employee service quality on customer satisfaction and loyalty. *Journal of Hospitality Marketing & Management, 29*(7), 739–756.

Prentice, C., Han, X. Y., Hua, L. L., & Hu, L. (2019). The influence of identity-driven customer engagement on purchase intention. *Journal of Retailing and Consumer Services, 47*, 339–347.

Prentice, C., Wang, X., & Lin, X. (2020c). An organic approach to customer engagement and loyalty. *Journal of Computer Information Systems., 60*(4), 326–335.

Prentice, C., Weaven, S., & Wong, I. A. (2020d). Linking AI quality performance and customer engagement: The moderating effect of AI preference. *International Journal of Hospitality Management, 90*, 102629.

Prentice, C., Wong, I. A., & Lam, D. (2017). Uncovering the service profit chain in the casino industry. *International Journal of Contemporary Hospitality Management., 29*(11), 2826–2846.

Reynoso, J., & Moores, B. (1995). Towards the measurement of internal service quality. *International Journal of Service Industry Management., 6*(3), 64–83.

Rozell, E. J., Pettijohn, C. E., & Parker, R. S. (2004). Customer-oriented selling: Exploring the roles of emotional intelligence and organizational commitment. *Psychology & Marketing, 21*(6), 405–424.

Rust, R. T., Stewart, G. L., Miller, H., & Pielack, D. (1996). The satisfaction and retention of frontline employees. *International Journal of Service Industry Management., 7*(5), 62–80.

Saks, A. M., & Gruman, J. A. (2014). What do we really know about employee engagement? *Human Resource Development Quarterly, 25*(2), 155–182.

Santos, J. (2003). E-service quality: A model of virtual service quality dimensions. *Managing Service Quality: An International Journal., 13*(3), 233–246.

Schutte, N. S., Malouff, J. M., Bobik, C., Coston, T. D., Greeson, C., Jedlicka, C., Wendorf, G., et al. (2001). Emotional intelligence and interpersonal relations. *The Journal of Social Psychology, 141*(4), 523–536.

Schutte, N. S., Malouff, J. M., Thorsteinsson, E. B., Bhullar, N., & Rooke, S. E. (2007). A meta-analytic investigation of the relationship between emotional intelligence and health. *Personality and Individual Differences, 42*(6), 921–933.

Shi, Y., Prentice, C., & He, W. (2014). Linking service quality, customer satisfaction and loyalty in casinos, does membership matter? *International Journal of Hospitality Management, 40*, 81–91.

Silvestro, R. (2002). Dispelling the modern myth: Employee satisfaction and loyalty drive service profitability. *International Journal of Operations & Production Management., 22*(1), 30–49.

So, K. K. F., King, C., & Sparks, B. (2014). Customer engagement with tourism brands: Scale development and validation. *Journal of Hospitality & Tourism Research, 38*(3), 304–329.

So, K. K. F., King, C., Sparks, B. A., & Wang, Y. (2016). The role of customer engagement in building consumer loyalty to tourism brands. *Journal of Travel Research, 55*(1), 64–78.

Soane, E., Truss, C., Alfes, K., Shantz, A., Rees, C., & Gatenby, M. (2012). Development and application of a new measure of employee engagement: The ISA Engagement Scale. *Human Resource Development International, 15*(5), 529–547.

Swarnalatha, C., & Prasanna, T. S. (2013). Employee engagement: The concept. *International Journal of Management Research and Reviews, 3*(12), 3872.

Tabachnick, B. G., Fidell, L. S., & Ullman, J. B. (2007). *Using multivariate statistics* (Vol. 5, pp. 481–498). Pearson.

Tavakoli, R., & Mura, P. (2018). Netnography in tourism–Beyond web 2.0. *Annals of Tourism Research, 73*(C), 190–192.

Thakur, R. (2016). *The United Nations, peace and security: From collective security to the responsibility to protect.* Cambridge University Press.

Van Doorn, J., Mende, M., Noble, S. M., Hulland, J., Ostrom, A. L., Grewal, D., & Petersen, J. A. (2017). Domo arigato Mr. Roboto: Emergence of automated social presence in organizational frontlines and customers' service experiences. *Journal of service research, 20*(1), 43–58.

Veloutsou, C. (2015). Brand evaluation, satisfaction and trust as predictors of brand loyalty: The mediator-moderator effect of brand relationships. *Journal of Consumer Marketing., 32*(6), 405–421.

Vivek, T. V. S., Rajavarman, V. N., & Madala, S. R. (2020). Advanced graphical-based security approach to handle hard AI problems based on visual security. *International Journal of Intelligent Enterprise, 7*(1–3), 250–266.

Welch, M. (2011). The evolution of the employee engagement concept: Communication implications. *Corporate Communications: An International Journal., 16*(4), 328–346.

West, T. A., Grogan, K. A., Swisher, M. E., Caviglia-Harris, J. L., Sills, E. O., Roberts, D. A., Harris, D., & Putz, F. E. (2018). Impacts of REDD+ payments on a coupled human-natural system in Amazonia. *Ecosystem Services, 33*, 68–76.

Wirth, N. (2018). Hello marketing, what can artificial intelligence help you with? *International Journal of Market Research, 60*(5), 435–438.

Wixom, B. H., & Todd, P. A. (2005). A theoretical integration of user satisfaction and technology acceptance. *Information Systems Research, 16*(1), 85–102.

Yee, R. W., Yeung, A. C., & Cheng, T. E. (2010). An empirical study of employee loyalty, service quality and firm performance in the service industry. *International Journal of Production Economics, 124*(1), 109–120.

Zeithaml, V. A., Berry, L. L., & Parasuraman, A. (1996). The behavioral consequences of service quality. *Journal of Marketing, 60*(2), 31–46.

Zeithaml, V. A., Parasuraman, A., & Malhotra, A. (2002). Service quality delivery through web sites: A critical review of extant knowledge. *Journal of the Academy of Marketing Science, 30*(4), 362–375.